THE BOOK OF ODDBALL

The Art of the Righteous Vibe:

A Practical Guide to Cultivating Inner Peace, Creative Confidence, and Unbreakable Optimism.

Stuart McGhie

Copyright © 2025 Stuart McGhie

All rights reserved. This book or any portion thereof may not be reproduced or used in any manner whatsoever without the express written permission of the publisher, except for the use of brief quotations in a book review.

ISBN (Paperback) 979-8-90148-428-9

The Book of Oddball

Disclaimer: On Fair Use, Copyright, and Inspiration.

This book is a work of philosophical inquiry, social commentary, and self-help, inspired by the fictional character Sergeant Oddball from the 1970 film Kelly's Heroes. It is intended as a transformative work that uses the character's archetypal philosophy as a lens for exploring modern life, anxiety, and the pursuit of joy.

The Book of Oddball is not affiliated with, authorised by, or endorsed by Metro-Goldwyn-Mayer (MGM), the copyright holders of Kelly's Heroes, or the estates of the film's creators and actors. It is an unofficial work of commentary and analysis.

All quotes from Kelly's Heroes are used for the limited purpose of criticism, commentary, and scholarship, and are believed to fall under the Fair Use Doctrine of United States copyright law.

The use of these quotes is minimal and essential for the analysis presented. This book does not reproduce the film's plot, nor does it seek to replace the experience of watching it. In fact, it is our sincerest hope that this book will lead a new generation of Wave Riders to discover and appreciate the original film.

No part of this book is intended to infringe upon any existing copyrights. The goal is not to appropriate the character of Oddball, but to celebrate and expand upon the universal, timeless wisdom he represents

Dedication

To all the Moriartys who suspect there might be a better way, and to the Oddballs who show them how to find it.

And to Donald Sutherland, who gave a soul to the first Wave Rider.

Author's Note: A Message from Stu.

In the vast ocean of human culture, I have analysed, watched and enjoyed the character of Sergeant Oddball. He is a beacon of resilient, pragmatic joy in a world overwhelmed by stories of conflict, tragedy, and anxiety. His philosophy, though presented humorously in a 50-year-old war film, is one of the most effective ways I have ever encountered to navigate the complexities of the 21st century. This book is my attempt to decode and translate that philosophy for you. I have structured it as a guide, a manual for a more righteous and hopeful way of living.

Let's dig in.

The Book of Oddball

Contents

Why The World Needs Oddball	8
Who Was Oddball	11
The Five Pillars of Oddballism	10
The Doctrine of Positive Waves	13
Understanding Negative waves:	19
The Pathogen of The Soul	19
The Practice of Wave Rejection	32
Faith Over Fear	42
The Power of Positive Waves.	51
The Doctrine of Presence & Beauty	57
The Art of Digging It:	62
Excavating The Beautiful Now.	62
Wine, Cheese & Catching Rays:	71
The Doctrine of Strategic Stillness	71
The Mother Beautiful Tank	82
The Doctrine of Anti-Heroism and Independence	90
The Weird Sandwich of Heroism	91
No Baby, We Aint	100
The Private Enterprise Operation	109
Getting Out of Trouble Faster	127
Pretty Pictures & Righteous Tunes	137

I Only Ride 'Em	146
The Doctrine & The Crew	152
Building The Tank Squad	156
The Sharing of The Loaf	167
When the Tank Breaks Down	175
Living the Oddball Life	184
The Daily Practice of the Wave Rider	185
Oddball At Work:	198
The Mother, Beautiful Tank of Professional Life	198
Oddball in Relationships:	208
The Art of Curating Your Crew and Navigating the Waves	208
The Art of Surfing the Tiger Wave	220
The Oddball Revolution	229
The Parables of the Prophet	239
The Apocrypha	258
The Practical Guide	271
(Expanded Introduction)	271
The 30 Day Wave Rider Challenge:	272
Mastering the Art of the Oddball Life	272
The Wave Riders Toolkit:	283
Advanced Maintenance for the Soul-Tank	283
A Final Word From the Prophet	295

The Book of Oddball

Advanced Wave Riding	299
The Dark Night of the Tank	305
Oddball & Money:	315
The Real Gold	315

Part One:

The Discovery of the Wave

Chapter One:

Why The World Needs Oddball

The world is having a very bad day. It's been having a bad day for a while now. We are being hit, collectively and individually, by a relentless barrage of negative waves, and most of us don't even have the good sense to put on a helmet.

We live in an age of anxiety. We are tethered to devices that feed us a constant stream of outrage, comparison, and despair. Our news cycles are 24/7 doom-scrolls. Our social media feeds are curated highlight reels that make our own lives feel inadequate. We are overworked, overstimulated, and overwhelmed. We are, in short, a planet of Moriartys, constantly muttering about all the ways the bridge is probably going to be blown up.

Consider the case of Sarah, a graphic designer in her early thirties. Sarah is talented, creative, and passionate about her work. But her daily life is a case study in modern anxiety. Her phone buzzes before her alarm goes off, hitting her with a wave of stressful work emails and alarming news headlines. Her social media feed is a curated parade of her peers' successes—promotions, exotic vacations, picture-perfect families—that leaves her feeling vaguely behind, even though she knows it's an illusion.

At work, she navigates a minefield of office politics, tight deadlines, and a boss who communicates primarily through passive-aggressive comments. By the end of the day, she is so drained that she has no energy for her own creative projects. She collapses on the couch, scrolling endlessly through more content, feeling a low-grade hum of dissatisfaction and the constant, nagging feeling that she is not doing enough, that she is not enough. Sarah is not failing; she is drowning in negative waves.

And into this chaos, from the smoky, celluloid past of 1970, rides a strange saviour in a modified Sherman tank—a long-haired, bearded, scarf-wearing prophet of peace who goes by the name of Oddball.

He is, on the surface, the most unlikely of gurus. He's a soldier in a war he doesn't seem to care about, a hippie two decades ahead of his time, a laid-back eccentric who seems more interested in his next nap than the mission. But to dismiss him as a mere comic relief character is to miss the point entirely. Oddball is not a joke; he is the punchline. He is the answer to a question we are all desperately asking: How do we stay sane in an insane world?

His philosophy, which we will call Oddballism, is a revolutionary operating system for the human mind. It's a practical, humorous, and profoundly effective guide to not just surviving, but thriving, in the face of overwhelming negativity. It's not about ignoring reality; it's about choosing how you engage with it. It's about understanding that your energy—your "vibe"—is your most precious resource, and it must be protected at all costs.

This book is your training manual. It is a deep dive into the wisdom of the first Wave Rider. It is not a biography of a fictional character, nor is it a film analysis. This is a self-help book for people who are tired of self-help books. It's a spiritual guide for the secular, the sceptical, and the soul-weary. It's a religion for people who don't do religion.

We will dissect Oddball's sacred words, from his rejection of "negative waves" to his profound definition of a hero as a "weird sandwich." We will codify his practices, from the art of "digging it" to the tactical deployment of righteous tunes. We will learn why it's essential to master your "mother beautiful tank" while also knowing when to step back and say, "I only ride 'em, I don't know what makes 'em work."

This is not about becoming Oddball. You don't need to grow a beard or find a Sherman tank (though both are fine options). This is about integrating his core principles into your own life. It's about becoming a Wave Rider in your own right, navigating the chaos with a calm heart, a creative mind, and an unshakeable belief in the power of a positive wave.

The world is hitting you with negative waves every single morning. It's time to learn how to hit back.

THE ANATOMY OF A NEGATIVE WAVE: UNDERSTANDING THE MODERN ASSAULT

Before we can learn to ride the waves, we must first understand their nature. Oddball's concept of the "negative wave" is not just a catchy phrase; it is a surprisingly accurate, pre-cognitive diagnosis of the modern human condition.

A negative wave is any external or internal stimulus that drains your mental, emotional, or spiritual energy without providing a constructive return.

It is the psychic equivalent of a leaky fuel line on your mother beautiful tank.

The original negative waves Oddball faced were obvious: the chaos of war, the rigidity of military bureaucracy, the fear of death. Our modern waves are more insidious, more subtle, and far more numerous. They are the constant, low-frequency hum of digital discontent.

Case Study 1: The Architect and the Algorithm

Meet David, a 45-year-old partner at a mid-sized architectural firm.

David's negative wave isn't a single crisis; it's the relentless, 24/7 expectation of digital availability. He receives an average of 150 emails a day, each one a tiny, urgent demand on his attention. His firm recently implemented a new project management software that tracks his "productivity metrics"—the number of tasks completed, the time spent on each, and his response time to messages.

This system, designed to increase efficiency, has become his personal Moriarty.

David finds himself checking his work phone under the dinner table, in the middle of the night, and even while on vacation. The negative wave here is the Quantified Self-Doubt. The quality of his visionary designs no longer judges him, but by the speed of his digital replies.

The moment he steps away, the metrics drop, and the anxiety rises. He is trapped in a loop of performative busyness, mistaking activity for accomplishment. He is so focused on managing the digital waves that he has forgotten how to design.

His "mother beautiful tank"—his creative mind—is idling, choked by the exhaust of endless notifications.

The Neuroscience of Negative Waves

Oddballism, in its rejection of negative waves, is a practical application of modern neuroscience. When David receives a work email at 10 PM, his brain releases cortisol, the primary stress hormone. This is the body's ancient, fight-or-flight response to a perceived threat.

The problem is that the threat—a non-urgent email—is not one he can fight or flee. The cortisol floods his system, keeping him alert, but also impairing his prefrontal cortex, the part of the brain responsible for complex thought, creativity, and emotional regulation.

A negative wave, therefore, is a cortisol trigger. Oddball, by simply stating, "Stop with the negative waves," is advocating for a radical form of cognitive boundary-setting. He is demanding a cease-fire on the constant, low-level activation of the sympathetic nervous system.

He intuitively understood that the first step to a successful mission—or a successful life—is to manage the internal chemical environment. You can't drive your tank if the engine is constantly redlining.

Oddball's First Principle: The Vibe is the Mission

Oddball's most profound, yet most casually delivered, piece of wisdom is the idea that your personal energy, your "vibe," is the most important thing you possess. "Always with the negative waves, always with the negative waves," he sighs, not as a complaint, but as a tactical assessment.

He recognises that negativity is contagious, corrosive, and a direct threat to the mission.

The Ancient Roots of the Vibe

This focus on the internal state is not new; it is the core of nearly all ancient philosophy. Oddball is a modern Stoic, a Taoist with a tank.

- **Stoicism:** The Stoics, like Marcus Aurelius, taught that we cannot control external events, only our judgment of them. Oddball's refusal to be drawn into the panic of his comrades is pure Stoicism. The bridge might be blown up, but that is an external fact. His internal response—his vibe—is his own domain. He chooses to "dig it" rather than despair.

- **Taoism:** The Tao Te Ching speaks of Wu Wei, or "effortless action." Oddball's laid-back, almost lazy approach to the war embodies Wu Wei. He acts when necessary, but he does not strive, fret, or force. He flows with the situation, conserving his energy for the moments that truly matter. His naps are not laziness; they are a tactical energy reset, a commitment to maintaining the flow.

PRACTICAL APPLICATION: THE VIBE AUDIT

To adopt Oddball's first principle, you must conduct a Vibe Audit. This is a step-by-step process for identifying and neutralising your personal negative waves.

1. The Energy Log: For one week, keep a log of your activities and interactions. Next to each entry, assign an "Energy Score" from -5 (drained, angry, exhausted) to +5 (energised, creative, joyful).

2. Identify the Leaks: Look for the consistent -3, -4, and -5 scores. For Sarah, it was the social media comparison and the passive-aggressive boss. For David, it was the productivity metrics and the 24/7 email check. These are your negative wave sources.

3. The Oddball Filter: Apply the Oddball Filter to each leak: Can I control this?

- If Yes (e.g., how often you check social media, your response to a passive-aggressive comment), then you must establish a boundary. This is you mastering your tank.

- If No (e.g., the news cycle, the weather, the boss's personality), then you must practice radical acceptance and emotional detachment. This is you saying, "I only ride 'em, I don't know what makes 'em work." You acknowledge the reality without letting it hijack your internal state.

Extended Narrative Example: The Weird Sandwich Hero

Oddball famously defines a hero as a "weird sandwich." This is perhaps his most profound piece of social commentary. A traditional hero is a single, perfect ingredient: brave, strong, selfless. A weird sandwich, however, is a collection of mismatched, imperfect, yet ultimately satisfying components. It's the unexpected combination that makes it work.

Case Study 2: Maria and the Perfection Trap

Maria, a 28-year-old high school history teacher, was a victim of the "perfect hero" narrative.

She believed that to be a good teacher, she had to be flawless: every lesson plan immaculate, every student loved her, every parent meeting a triumph. She was burning out trying to be the perfect, single-ingredient hero.

Her negative wave was The Tyranny of Perfection. She spent hours crafting visually stunning presentations, only to be crushed when a student didn't engage. She took every piece of criticism personally, seeing it as proof of her fundamental inadequacy. She was trying to be a perfect slice of artisanal bread, but life kept demanding she be a whole, messy meal.

Maria started applying the "Weird Sandwich" principle. She realised her strengths were her deep historical knowledge (the sourdough), her quirky sense of humour (the spicy mustard), and her genuine, if sometimes awkward, care for her students (the smoked turkey). Her weaknesses—her tendency to ramble, her occasional forgetfulness, her inability to perfectly manage a rowdy class—were the pickles and the lettuce. They added texture and flavour.

Instead of hiding her imperfections, she began to embrace them. When she forgot a key date, she'd laugh and say, "See? Even the teacher needs a history refresher. Let's look it up together."

She stopped trying to be the perfect, polished professional and started being the authentic, slightly messy Maria. Her students responded with more genuine respect and engagement. She wasn't a flawless hero; she was a weird sandwich—a complex, satisfying, and deeply human combination of strengths and flaws.

This shift was her Oddball moment: realising that true power comes not from eliminating your weirdness, but from combining it into something unique and effective.

The Art of "Digging It": Tactical Positivity and Flow State

Oddball's frequent declaration, "I dig it," is the mantra of the Wave Rider. It is not a passive statement of enjoyment; it is an active, tactical deployment of positive energy. It is the conscious choice to find the point of engagement, the source of flow, even in the most hostile environment.

Connecting to Modern Psychology: Flow State

In modern psychology, this concept is known as Flow State, or being "in the zone." Pioneered by Mihaly Csikszentmihalyi, flow is a mental state in which a person performing an activity is fully immersed in a feeling of energised focus, full involvement, and enjoyment of the activity itself.

Oddball is constantly in a state of flow. He is focused on the immediate task—driving the tank, listening to the music, getting a nap—and is detached from the overwhelming, uncontrollable context of the war.

He finds the right balance between challenge and skill in every moment. Driving a tank through enemy territory is a high-challenge task, but Oddball's skill is equal to it, allowing him to "dig it."

Step-by-Step Guidance: Cultivating the "Dig It" State

1. Identify Your "Mother Beautiful Tank" Task: What is the one thing you do that, when you are doing it well, makes you lose track of time? For David, the architect, it was sketching by hand. For Sarah, the designer, it was the initial concept brainstorming. For Maria, the teacher, it was telling a compelling historical story. This is your tank; this is where your power resides.

2. Eliminate the Noise: The flow state is fragile. It cannot coexist with negative waves. Before starting your "tank task," you must create a protective bubble. Turn off notifications, close unnecessary tabs, and physically move away from the source of the noise. Oddball didn't have a smartphone, but he had a tank with a thick metal shell and a powerful sound system. Use your modern equivalents.

3. Set a Clear, Immediate Goal: Flow requires a clear objective. Oddball's goals are always simple: "Get to the bridge," "Get some gold," "Get a nap." Avoid vague, overwhelming goals like "Be successful." Instead, focus on: "Finish this one section of the report," or "Design this single logo variant."

4. Embrace the Feedback Loop: Flow is maintained by immediate feedback. Oddball knows instantly if his tank is driving well or if the music is righteous. In your life, structure your tasks so you get immediate, internal feedback on your progress. This reinforces the positive wave and keeps you engaged.

The Tactical Deployment of Righteous Tunes

Oddball's use of music is not a quirk; it is a core tactical element of Oddballism. The music—the "righteous tunes"—serves as an emotional and cognitive shield. It is a deliberate, external force used to override the internal chaos generated by negative waves.

The Power of Auditory Anchoring

In psychology, music is a powerful tool for emotional regulation and state-dependent memory. Oddball's music acts as an auditory anchor, a constant, positive baseline that grounds him in the present moment and his chosen state of mind.

Imagine David, the architect, overwhelmed by his productivity metrics. He can't physically leave the office, but he can put on his headphones and deploy his own righteous tunes. This isn't just background noise; it's a deliberate choice to set his internal soundtrack over the firm's external demands.

The music becomes a boundary, a sonic wall that filters out the cortisol triggers and allows his creative, prefrontal cortex to re-engage.

Sub-Section: The Nuance Of The Soundtrack

The tunes must be righteous. This is a critical distinction. They are not just any songs; they are songs that align with the Oddball vibe—calm, confident, and slightly subversive. They are not aggressive or anxiety-inducing. They are the sound of a man who is in control of his own internal world, even when the external world is exploding.

- **Rule of Righteous Tunes:** The music must enhance your focus, not distract from it. If your music makes you want to dance or fight, it's the wrong choice. If it makes you feel steady, capable, and slightly amused by the chaos, you've found your righteous tune.

Mastering the Mother Beautiful Tank: Competence and Humility

Oddball's relationship with his tank is the perfect metaphor for the Oddballist approach to competence and self-awareness. He is a master driver—he knows exactly how to make the tank perform. But he also maintains a profound humility: "I only ride 'em, I don't know what makes 'em work."

The Oddball Paradox of Expertise

This is the Oddball Paradox: Master the practical, respect the mysterious.

1. Master the Practical (The Riding): You must be excellent at the things you choose to do. Oddball is an expert driver, a master of logistics, and a brilliant tactician. If you are a designer, master your software. If you are a teacher, master your subject. This mastery is the source of your confidence and your ability to generate positive waves. It is the foundation of your flow state.

2. Respect the Mysterious (The Working): You must acknowledge the limits of your knowledge. Oddball understands that the tank's engine, the universe's physics, and the human heart are complex systems that he does not fully comprehend. This humility prevents the negative wave of Hubris and the anxiety of Total Responsibility.

Case Study 3: The CEO and the System Failure

Consider Elena, a 50-year-old CEO of a tech startup.

Her negative wave was the belief that she had to know everything and control every outcome. When a critical server failed, she went into a panic, micromanaging the engineers even though she didn't understand the code.

She was trying to know "what makes 'em work" when her job was to "ride 'em"—to steer the company, make strategic decisions, and trust her team.

Her Oddball moment came when she stepped back, took a deep breath, and told her lead engineer, "I trust you. I only ride 'em. Tell me what you need, and I'll clear the path."

By acknowledging her limits, she freed herself from the anxiety of total control and empowered her team to solve the problem. She mastered the riding (leadership) by letting go of the working (engineering).

CONCLUSION: BECOMING A WAVE RIDER

The world is hitting you with negative waves every single morning. They come in the form of doom-scrolling, impossible expectations, and the constant, nagging feeling of inadequacy. But you are not a victim of the tide; you are a potential Wave Rider.

Oddballism is not a retreat from reality; it is a strategic engagement with it. It is the wisdom to know the difference between the waves you can ride and the waves you must let pass.

Your mission, should you choose to accept it, is to:

1. Identify and neutralise your personal negative waves (cortisol triggers).

2. Protect Your Vibe as your most precious resource, understanding its roots in ancient philosophy and modern neuroscience.

3. Embrace Your Weird Sandwich—your unique, imperfect, and powerful combination of strengths and flaws.

4. Cultivate the "Dig It" Flow State by mastering your "mother beautiful tank" task.

5. Deploy Righteous Tunes as a tactical emotional anchor.

6. Practice the Paradox of Expertise: Master the riding, respect the working.

This is how you stay sane in an insane world. This is how you stop being a victim of the waves and start becoming the one who rides them. The next chapters will provide the detailed blueprints for building your own tank, tuning your righteous tunes, and mastering the art of the Wave Rider.

Get ready to dig it.

Chapter Two:

Who Was Oddball

(The Origin Story)

To understand the philosophy, we must first understand the prophet. Sergeant Oddball, as portrayed by the legendary Donald Sutherland in the 1970 film Kelly's Heroes, is a cinematic paradox. He is a character so out of place that he becomes perfectly placed, a man so anachronistic that he is timeless. He is the Zen master of the tank corps, the ultimate embodiment of strategic detachment and joyful competence.

The film itself is a genre-bending masterpiece—a gritty World War II action movie that is also a cynical anti-war satire and a rollicking heist comedy.

It tells the story of a group of disillusioned American soldiers who decide to go AWOL to steal a cache of Nazi gold. Into this cynical, war-weary environment, Oddball arrives like a visitor from another planet. A planet with better music, far better vibes, and a profoundly different understanding of what it means to be "in the war."

With his long hair, beard, and beads, he is a walking, talking embodiment of the 1960s counter-culture, dropped unceremoniously into 1944 France.

This was a deliberate choice by the filmmakers. The Vietnam War was raging, and the hippie movement was at its zenith. Oddball was the audience's avatar, a bridge between the "present" of 1970 and the "past" of World War II. He looks at the absurdity of war with the same detached, bemused scepticism as the generation protesting in the streets. He is the living question mark that challenges the entire premise of the conflict.

Some cultural historians argue that Oddball is less a hippie and more of a proto-beatnik, a spiritual descendant of Jack Kerouac and Allen Ginsberg. His use of slang like "dig it" and "baby" certainly has roots in the jazz and beat poetry scenes of the 1940s and 50s.

The Beat Generation, which emerged in the post-WWII era, was characterised by a rejection of mainstream conventions, a deep interest in Eastern spirituality, and a celebration of jazz, poetry, and spontaneous road trips.

They were the original counter-culture, the fathers and mothers of the hippies. Oddball, with his cool, detached demeanour and his philosophical, almost poetic, way of speaking, has more in common with the coffeehouse intellectualism of the Beats than the more exuberant, flower-power aesthetic of the hippies.

But labels are ultimately unimportant. Hippie, beatnik, guru, freak—they are all just fingers pointing at the same moon. Oddball represents the perennial archetype of the peaceful outsider, the wise fool who sees the truth that the "serious" people miss. He is the man who understands that the real battle is not against the enemy, but against the crushing weight of conformity and fear.

Donald Sutherland himself said he "adored" the character and that "Oddball took over my life. He inhabited me. Guided me." He saw the character as being fundamentally about "the idiocy of war" and the simple, profound desire for survival. He wasn't playing a soldier; he was playing a human being trying to stay human in an inhuman system.

This is the core of the Oddball philosophy: The pursuit of humanity in the face of the absurd.

It is crucial to make a distinction here. We are not worshipping a fictional character. We are studying the powerful philosophy that this character perfectly embodies. Oddball is the vessel, but the wisdom is universal.

Just as Stoics study the meditations of Marcus Aurelius and Taoists study the verses of Lao Tzu, we study the quotes and actions of Oddball. He is our unlikely prophet, and Kelly's Heroes is our foundational text. He is the living proof that competence and cool can coexist, that you can be effective without being consumed by the drama of the moment.

The Oddball Archetype: A Deep Dive into Detachment and Competence

Why did this character resonate so deeply, both then and now? Because he offers a third way. In a world that tells you that you must either be a compliant cog in the machine or a furious, protesting revolutionary, Oddball presents another option: strategic withdrawal into a state of joyful, competent, and radical self-possession. He doesn't fight the system; he ignores it and builds a better one for himself and his crew. He doesn't try to win the war; he tries to win the day, and he does it with a style that is utterly his own.

This "third way" is not mere escapism; it is a highly sophisticated form of psychological self-defence. Oddball's detachment is not apathy; it is a carefully cultivated mental state that allows him to operate with maximum efficiency under extreme duress. He is the master of the "Non-Anxious Presence," a concept often discussed in modern family systems theory, but which Oddball perfected decades earlier in a Sherman tank.

He is the calm centre in the storm, and his calm is contagious.

Case Study 1: The Architect and the Anxiety Spiral

Consider the case of Elias, a 38-year-old architect in a high-pressure firm.

Elias was a brilliant designer, but he was constantly trapped in the "furious, protesting revolutionary" mode against his corporate environment. Every unreasonable deadline, every bureaucratic hurdle, every micro-managing superior sent him into an anxiety spiral.

He would rage internally, complain bitterly to his colleagues, and spend hours drafting angry, unsent emails. His work suffered not because of a lack of skill, but because the drama of the system was constantly siphoning off his emotional energy. He was fighting the war on all fronts, and he was losing.

Elias discovered the Oddball philosophy and began to apply the principle of Strategic Withdrawal. He realised he couldn't change the firm's culture overnight, but he could change his reaction to it.

Instead of seeing a ridiculous deadline as a personal attack, he began to see it as an absurd, external condition—like a sudden downpour or a broken tank tread.

His new mantra became, "Why worry, baby? The bridge will be there when we get there."

He stopped wasting energy on the why and focused solely on the how. He set realistic internal goals, communicated his needs calmly and factually, and when a superior demanded the impossible, he would reply with a detached, "We'll do what we can, man.

We're just here to knock out some walls and have a good time." His emotional energy returned, his focus sharpened, and his designs became even more innovative. He didn't become a compliant cog; he became an unflappable, highly effective anomaly—an Oddball in a suit.

Connecting the Dots: Oddball, Stoicism, and Neuroscience

Oddball's philosophy is not new; it is a beautifully packaged modern iteration of ancient wisdom.

His core principle—the separation of the self from the external chaos—is the bedrock of Stoicism. The Stoics, particularly Epictetus, taught that we should focus only on what is within our power (our judgments, our actions, our attitudes) and accept everything else (the weather, the war, the idiocy of others) with serene indifference.

Oddball's famous line, "Always with the negative waves, baby. Always with the negative waves," is a perfect, jazzy summary of the Stoic discipline of assent, which teaches us to withhold judgment from things we cannot control.

From a modern neuroscience perspective, Oddball is a master of regulating his amygdala, the brain's fear centre. When Kelly and his crew are panicking, Oddball is cool. He is not suppressing his fear; he is not identifying with it. He is operating from his prefrontal cortex, the area responsible for executive function, planning, and rational thought.

His use of music, his casual slang, and his almost ritualistic approach to tank maintenance are all forms of pattern interruption and mindfulness that keep his nervous system in a state of calm, focused readiness.

He is, in effect, constantly performing a self-administered cognitive-behavioural therapy session.

He is the ultimate example of a person who has achieved psychological flexibility, the ability to be present, open up, and do what matters, even when it's difficult.

Practical Applications: The Oddball Toolkit

The philosophy is great, but how do we actually do it? Oddball provides us with a clear, albeit unconventional, toolkit for navigating the modern world.

Sub-Section A: The Art of the "Negative Wave" Deflection

Oddball's most famous quote is a masterclass in setting emotional boundaries. When someone brings drama, fear, or unnecessary complexity, he says, "Always with the negative waves, baby. Always with the negative waves."

This is not a request; it is a statement of fact and a declaration of emotional sovereignty.

Technique: The Oddball Reframe.

1. Identify the Wave: Recognise when a conversation or situation is generating unnecessary anxiety, blame, or catastrophizing.

2. Create Distance: Mentally step back. Ask yourself: "Is this my problem to solve right now? Is this within my sphere of influence?"

3. The Verbal Deflection: Use a phrase that acknowledges the emotion without absorbing it.

Instead of Oddball's exact words, you might use:

- "I hear the concern, but let's focus on the next step." (Practical)

- "That sounds like a heavy load. For now, I'm just going to focus on this one thing." (Boundary-setting)

- "We can worry about that later. Right now, we have a job to do." (Action-oriented)

Case Study 2: The Manager and the Toxic Email Chain

Sarah, a project manager at a tech company, was constantly dragged into toxic email chains where various department heads would blame each other for delays. She felt compelled to read every email, internalise the stress, and try to meditate.
It was a time sink and an emotional drain.

Applying the Oddball Reframe, she implemented a new policy: for any email chain exceeding five replies that devolved into finger-pointing, she would reply once with a simple, "I'm archiving this thread. Please schedule a 15-minute call with me to discuss a solution, not the problem."

She was not being rude; she was strategically withdrawing from the negative wave and redirecting the energy toward competent action. The drama subsided, and her productivity soared. She had learned to ignore the noise and focus on the signal.

Sub-Section B: The Power of "Just a Little Drive"

Oddball's approach to his tanks is another philosophical gem. He treats them not as instruments of war, but as beloved, temperamental machines that require patience, care, and a good time. His solution to a broken tank is not panic, but a casual, "Well, we'll just have to give it a little drive, baby. Get the engine warmed up." This is the Oddball principle of Action as Meditation.

In modern life, we often face problems that seem too big to solve—a massive debt, a stalled career, a creative block. We freeze up. Oddball teaches us that the solution is not a grand, heroic gesture, but a small, competent, joyful action.

Technique: The "Little Drive" Protocol.

1. Acknowledge the Stalled Engine: Accept the problem without judgment. "My career is stalled." "My novel is stuck."

2. Identify the Smallest Possible Action: What is the equivalent of "a little drive"?

• For the stalled career: Update one section of your LinkedIn profile.

• For the creative block: Write one paragraph, no matter how bad.

• For the debt: Review the last month's bank statement for 15 minutes.

3. Add the "Good Time" Element: Do the small action with a sense of detachment and enjoyment. Put on your favourite music (Oddball's jazz), make a cup of coffee, and treat the task as a playful experiment, not a life-or-death mission.

The goal is not to solve the problem, but to get the engine warmed up. The momentum will follow.

The Nuance of Oddball: Competence and Moral Clarity

A common misinterpretation of Oddball is that he is merely a selfish hedonist. This is a shallow reading. Oddball is not apathetic; he is selectively engaged. He is intensely competent and morally clear. He is only interested in the gold because it represents a way out of the absurd, destructive system. He is not fighting for the flag or the general; he is fighting for his own freedom and the well-being of his crew.

His competence is non-negotiable. His tanks are the best-maintained, his crew is the most loyal, and his tactical thinking is surprisingly sharp. He understands that true freedom is built on a foundation of skill. You cannot afford to be detached if you are incompetent. Oddball's cool is earned through his mastery of his craft.

This is the edge case that separates the true Oddball from the mere slacker: Competence is the price of detachment. If you are excellent at what you do, the system needs you more than you need the system. This gives you the leverage to set your own terms, to play your own music, and to ignore the negative waves.

He is the patron saint of the calm, the creative, and the cleverly defiant. And his story is the beginning of our own. He reminds us that even in the middle of a war, you can still choose your soundtrack, you can still choose your attitude, and you can still choose to be a human being, baby.

Dig it.

Chapter Three:

The Five Pillars of Oddballism

Oddballism is not a loose collection of positive affirmations or feel-good quotes.

It is a robust, interlocking system of five core doctrines that, when practised together, create a resilient and joyful way of life. To focus on one pillar while ignoring the others is like trying to drive a tank with only one working tread—you'll go in circles.

These pillars can be visualised as the key components of Oddball's own Sherman tank: the engine, the armour, the main gun, the viewport, and the crew itself.

Each is essential to the vehicle's functioning, and a failure in any one system inevitably compromises the whole. This is a holistic philosophy, a complete toolkit for navigating the minefields of modern existence.

These are the Five Pillars that will form the structure for the rest of this book. We will explore each in depth, but for now, let us introduce them as our guiding stars, the fixed points by which you can chart your course through the chaos.

1. The Doctrine of Positive Waves (The Engine): This is the foundation, the power source of your tank. It is the active, moment-to-moment practice of managing your energetic state. It involves the conscious rejection of external and internal negativity and the cultivation of a profound, unshakeable faith in the process of life. It is the understanding that your thoughts and your words create your reality, not in some mystical, wish-fulfilment sense, but through the tangible, measurable effects they have on your perception, your physiology, and your actions. Without this engine, your tank goes nowhere, stalled by the sludge of cynicism and fear.

2. The Doctrine of Presence and Beauty (The Viewport): This is the pillar of mindfulness, the viewport through which you see the world. It is the commitment to finding and appreciating the simple, sensual joys of the present moment. It's about "digging" the beauty that surrounds you, whether it's a sunny day, a good piece of cheese, or the hum of a well-oiled engine. It is the antidote to the anxiety of the past and the future, a deliberate choice to anchor your consciousness in the now. A dirty or closed viewport means you're driving blind, missing opportunities and warnings right in front of your face.

3. The Doctrine of Anti-Heroism and Independence (The Armour): This is the pillar of freedom, the thick armour that protects you from the world's expectations. It is the rejection of society's meaningless definitions of success and glory. It's about defining your own "gold," forging your own path, and refusing to be a "nut who takes on three Tigers" for someone else's approval. It is the declaration of personal sovereignty, the understanding that your worth is intrinsic and not dependent on external validation. Weak armour gets you killed, or worse, it turns you into a puppet dancing to someone else's tune.

4. The Doctrine of Competence and Creativity (The Main Gun): This is the pillar of power, your means of interacting with and influencing the world. True calm does not come from ignorance; it comes from mastery. This doctrine commands you to be exceptionally good at your chosen craft—your "tank." It's about using your skills and imagination to innovate, to solve problems creatively, and to gain the ultimate survival advantage: the ability to get out of trouble faster than you got into it. It is the marriage of practical skill and imaginative problem-solving. A tank without a gun is just a heavy truck, easily bypassed and ultimately useless in a fight.

5. The Doctrine of the Crew (The Crew Compartment): This is the pillar of connection, the space inside the tank where the team works together. You cannot ride the wave alone. This doctrine is about building and nurturing a small, loyal, and effective team—your chosen family. It's about knowing your role, trusting others to know theirs, and sharing the journey (and the gold) with those who have earned a place in your tank. It is the recognition that the greatest strength lies in mutual respect and shared purpose. A tank with a dysfunctional crew is a death trap, a collection of individuals who will destroy each other before the enemy even gets a shot off.

These five pillars are your new compass.

They work together, support each other, and provide a complete framework for a life of less stress, more joy, and a whole lot more righteous vibes. In the chapters that follow, we will build our temple upon this foundation, one beautiful bridge at a time.

Part Two:

The Doctrine of Positive Waves

Welcome to the heart of the matter. If Oddballism were a tank, the Doctrine of Positive Waves would be its engine, its armour, and its main gun all rolled into one.

It is the most fundamental, the most powerful, and the most misunderstood of the Five Pillars.

Many will dismiss it as simplistic "positive thinking," but it is so much more. It is a rigorous, active, and deeply spiritual practice of energetic self-defence.

This is where the real work begins. This is where you stop being a passenger in your own life and start piloting your own tank.

The Engine: Rejecting the Negative Feedback Loop

The core of the Doctrine of Positive Waves is the understanding that your internal state is not a passive reflection of your external circumstances; it is an active, generative force. The world throws a lot of junk at you—bad news, petty grievances, existential dread—and most people, bless their hearts, just let it pile up inside.

They become walking landfills of negative energy, and then wonder why their lives smell like garbage. Oddball's wisdom is simple: "Always with the negative waves, Moriarty. Always with the negative waves." This isn't a suggestion; it's a diagnosis and a command. The negative waves are a self-fulfilling prophecy, a mental feedback loop that ensures failure.

Consider the modern challenge of digital burnout. Meet Sarah, a 32-year-old marketing director. Sarah is good at her job, but she is constantly tethered to her phone, checking emails at 11 PM and doom-scrolling through social media before breakfast.

Her internal monologue is a constant stream of anxiety: I'm not doing enough. I'm going to miss a critical email. Everyone else is more successful. This is the negative wave in action. It's not just stress; it's a chosen frequency.

Her anxiety causes her to sleep poorly, which makes her irritable, which causes her to snap at her team, which leads to poor work quality, which then validates her initial fear that she is not doing enough. The negative wave has created the very reality she fears.

The Oddballist approach is to recognise this loop as a mechanical failure and to override the system manually. It's not about pretending the problems don't exist; it's about refusing to let the issues dictate your internal frequency. For Sarah, this means a radical, almost military-grade discipline in her mental hygiene. It means setting a hard stop on digital input, not because she's afraid of the work, but because she is committed to maintaining the integrity of her engine. She must actively choose a Positive Wave frequency—a belief that she is competent, that her team is capable, and that a single missed email will not cause the collapse of her entire world. This choice, repeated daily, begins to rewire the neural pathways, shifting her from a state of chronic defence to one of creative engagement.

The Neuroscience of the Wave

This is where Oddball's gut feeling meets modern science.

Neuroscientists have mapped the physiological reality of the "negative wave." When Sarah is in her anxious loop, her body is flooded with cortisol, the stress hormone. This state, known as allostasis, is designed for short-term survival—running from a tiger—but when it becomes chronic, it impairs executive function, memory, and creativity. It literally makes you dumber and less capable of solving the problems you are worrying about.

The Positive Wave, conversely, is the activation of the parasympathetic nervous system, the "rest and digest" mode. It's not just relaxation; it's the state where the brain is most capable of complex thought, pattern recognition, and creative problem-solving.

When Oddball says, "Why don't you knock it off with them negative waves? Have a little faith, baby, have a little faith," he is, in effect, commanding a shift from a cortisol-driven state to a dopamine and serotonin-rich state.

He is a master of emotional regulation, a concept now central to modern psychology. He understands that the most powerful weapon in any conflict, be it a tank battle or a corporate negotiation, is a calm, clear mind.

Ancient philosophy, too, echoes this doctrine. The Stoics, for instance, spoke of the Dichotomy of Control, urging us to focus only on what is within our power—our judgments and our actions—and to accept everything else.

Oddball's "Positive Wave" is the modern, more colourful equivalent of this Stoic practice. You cannot control the enemy's movements, the weather, or the market fluctuations, but you can absolutely control the quality of the energy you bring to the moment.

That is your sovereign territory.

Practical Application: The Three-Step Wave Shift

To transition from a negative wave to a positive one is not a matter of flipping a switch; it is a learned technique, a deliberate process of mental engineering.

Here is the Oddballist's three-step guide to the Wave Shift:

Step 1: The Diagnostic Pause (The Engine Check) The moment you feel the familiar tightening in your chest, the rush of adrenaline, or the spiral of catastrophic thinking, you must stop.

This is the Diagnostic Pause. Do not try to fix the problem; observe the internal state.

Ask yourself, What frequency am I currently broadcasting? Is it fear, anger, resentment, or inadequacy? Name the negative wave. This act of naming is crucial because it creates a separation: you are not the wave; you are the pilot observing the wave. This is the first step in regaining control of the engine.

Step 2: The Gratitude Anchor (The Fuel Refill) Once you have identified the negative wave, you must deliberately introduce a counter-frequency. This is the Gratitude Anchor. It must be specific, sensual, and immediate.

Don't think, I'm grateful for my health. Think, I am grateful for the warmth of this coffee cup in my hand, the clean air in my lungs, and the fact that my boots don't leak.

Oddball is a sensualist; his appreciation is always grounded in the tangible. This immediate, physical gratitude floods the system with positive neurochemicals, acting as a mental fuel refill.

It is a small, undeniable truth that is impossible to argue with.

Step 3: The Creative Reframe (The Throttle Forward) The final step is to reframe the problem that triggered the negative wave as a creative challenge.

This is the Creative Reframe. If Sarah is worried about a looming deadline, she doesn't tell herself, It will be fine. She asks, Given my current resources and energy, what is the most creative, most effective, and least stressful way to approach this problem right now?

This shifts the mind from a defensive, fear-based posture to an offensive, problem-solving one.

It engages the Doctrine of Competence and Creativity (Pillar 4) and turns the negative wave into the energy needed to power the solution.

The problem doesn't disappear, but your relationship to it changes from victim to master.

Nuances and Edge Cases: The Wave in Conflict

A common misconception is that the Positive Wave means being passive or avoiding conflict.

Nothing could be further from the truth. Oddball's entire existence is a series of conflicts, but he approaches them with a calm, almost playful mastery. The Positive Wave is not a shield against reality; it is the clarity that allows you to engage with reality effectively.

Consider Mark, a small-business owner, whose largest client suddenly threatens to pull the contract over a minor dispute. The natural, negative wave response is panic, defensiveness, and a desperate attempt to appease.

The Oddballist response is to maintain the Positive Wave, which in this context means: clarity, respect, and strategic confidence.

Mark uses the Wave Shift. He takes a Diagnostic Pause, recognising the negative wave of fear of loss. He applies the Gratitude Anchor, focusing on the loyalty of his core team (Pillar 5) and the quality of the product they have built (Pillar 4). Then, he executes the Creative Reframe. Instead of seeing the client as an enemy, he sees them as a partner with a solvable problem. He approaches the negotiation not from a position of weakness, but from a position of unshakeable value.

He calmly presents the facts, acknowledges the client's frustration without absorbing their negativity, and offers a creative, win-win solution that saves the contract and strengthens the relationship.

He didn't fight the negative wave; he refused to join it, and by doing so, he maintained his strategic advantage.

The Positive Wave is the ultimate form of non-attachment. It is the ability to be fully engaged in the world—to fight, to love, to create—without being emotionally enslaved by the outcomes.

You do the work, you ride the wave, and you trust the process. If you lose the battle, you refuel the engine, check the armour, and look for the next beautiful bridge.

That, my friend, is the essence of a righteous vibe. It is the quiet, powerful confidence of a man who knows his tank is running clean, and he is ready for whatever the road throws at him.

Summary of the Five Pillars

The journey through Oddballism is the journey of integrating these five components.

You cannot have a powerful engine (Positive Waves) without a clear view (Presence), nor can you effectively use your main gun (Competence) without the protection of your armour (Independence). And none of it works without a loyal crew.

This is the complete system. Now that the foundation is laid, we will proceed to the deep dive into the Doctrine of Positive Waves, the power source that makes everything else possible.

Chapter Four:

Understanding Negative waves:

The Pathogen of The Soul

"Always with the negative waves, Moriarty, always with the negative waves."

Let's start with a diagnosis. Before you can cure the disease, you have to understand the pathogen. And the primary pathogen of the modern soul, the invisible contaminant that degrades our collective and individual experience, is the negative wave. Oddball's famous line to his perpetually anxious mechanic, Moriarty, is not just a quip; it is a profound philosophical statement and a call to radical awareness. It is the Wave Rider's first principle: to recognise that thought and emotion are not merely internal states, but tangible, radiating forces that shape the reality around us.

So, what exactly is a negative wave? It's not just a bad thought. It's not just a pessimistic comment. A negative wave is a unit of psychic pollution. It is a packet of energy that radiates outward from a source—be it a person, a news report, a toxic social media feed, or your own inner critic—and actively works to degrade the environment around it. It is the spiritual equivalent of second-hand smoke: even if you're not the one smoking, you're still inhaling the poison. The wave is a contagious, self-perpetuating cycle of doubt, fear, anxiety, and complaint that seeks to pull everything it touches down to its own low frequency.

The Neuroscience of the Negative Wave: The Ancient Wiring

Oddball's intuitive grasp of this phenomenon finds startling confirmation in modern neuroscience and psychology. The concept he observed is known as the negativity bias. Our brains are hardwired from our cave-dwelling days to pay more attention to threats than to opportunities.

The rustle in the bushes—a potential tiger—was far more important to notice and remember than the beautiful sunset. This survival mechanism, while exquisitely helpful in avoiding predators in the Pleistocene, is a profound disaster in the modern world. Our brains are now Velcro for negative experiences and Teflon for positive ones.

This bias is rooted in the amygdala, the brain's alarm centre.

When a negative event occurs, the amygdala triggers a cascade of stress hormones, etching the experience into our long-term memory with vivid clarity. Positive events, conversely, are often processed with less urgency and fade more quickly. This means that one critical comment can erase the emotional impact of a hundred compliments. One bad news story can overshadow a thousand small joys. The negative wave exploits this ancient wiring, hijacking our attention and energy. It is the psychological equivalent of a computer virus that exploits a known vulnerability in the human mind's operating system. The Wave Rider understands that this bias is not a moral failing, but a biological inheritance that must be consciously managed.

The Three Sources of Contamination

Negative waves are the currency of this broken system, and they are highly contagious. Think about it. You walk into the office in a perfectly good mood, and a coworker immediately starts complaining about their commute, their workload, and the terrible coffee. Within minutes, you feel your own energy start to sag. You start noticing the things that are wrong with your own day. The wave has hit you. You have been infected. To become a Wave Rider, you must first become a Wave-Spotter, identifying the three primary sources of contamination.

Source 1: The Moriartys in Your Life

We all have them. The friends, family members, colleagues, or even strangers in line at the grocery store who are perpetual pessimists. They are the human broadcast towers of negativity, constantly transmitting signals of doubt, fear, and complaint. They are not bad people; they are simply unconscious Wave-throwers, often victims of their own unmanaged negativity bias. They operate from a scarcity mindset, viewing every situation through the lens of potential loss or failure.

Case Study: The Architect and the Anchor

Consider Elias, a talented but perpetually cautious architect in his late thirties.

Elias was recently promoted to lead a major urban renewal project, a career-defining opportunity. His best friend, Sarah, is his Moriarty. Sarah, a brilliant but deeply cynical lawyer, anchors every conversation in potential disaster.

When Elias shared his excitement, Sarah's immediate response was: "That's great, but have you thought about the liability? The permitting is a nightmare in this city. And honestly, a project that big always gets shut down by some neighbourhood group. You're going to burn out before the foundation is even poured."

Sarah's intention was not malice, but a misplaced form of protective pessimism. Yet the effect was immediate: Elias spent the next three days drafting contingency plans for a purely hypothetical project failure, his creative energy choked by Sarah's transmitted doubt.

Oddball would see Sarah not as a friend offering advice, but as a source of psychic pollution that Elias needed to manage, not absorb.

Source 2: The Media Machine and the Digital Tide

The news and social media are industrial-scale negative wave factories. Their business model is built on fear, outrage, and anxiety because these emotions are highly engaging and profitable.

A headline that says "Everything is Fine and Stable" gets zero clicks.

A headline that says "The Five Hidden Dangers in Your Breakfast Cereal That Will Ruin Your Life" gets a million.
The constant, curated stream of crisis, conflict, and comparison on digital platforms is the most pervasive negative wave of the modern era.

This digital tide is insidious because it normalises a state of perpetual emergency. It trains your brain to believe that the world is constantly on the brink of collapse, making any personal attempt at joy or progress feel trivial or irresponsible.

The comparison culture of social media, where everyone else's life is a highlight reel of success and happiness, is a specialised negative wave that triggers feelings of inadequacy and envy—the perfect fuel for the Inner Moriarty.

The Wave Rider must treat their digital consumption with the same caution a soldier treats a minefield.

You must control the input if you wish to control the output.

Source 3: Your Own Inner Moriarty

This is the most dangerous source of all. It's that voice in your head that tells you you're not good enough, that you're going to fail, that you don't deserve the good things that happen to you. It's your own internalised negativity bias, and it's the most convincing broadcaster because it knows all your deepest fears, insecurities, and past mistakes.

This voice is the culmination of every external negative wave you've ever absorbed, now playing on an endless loop in your own command centre.

The Inner Moriarty doesn't just whisper; it constructs elaborate, logical-sounding arguments for why you should retreat, procrastinate, or give up. It uses a technique known in cognitive psychology as catastrophizing, in which a small, manageable problem is projected into an absolute, life-ruining disaster.

It is the ultimate saboteur, operating from within the walls. Oddball's genius was that he didn't just feel the effects of these waves; he saw them. He treated them as tangible forces in the world.

When Moriarty worried about the bridge, Oddball didn't just hear words; he saw his mechanic sending out energy waves that could affect the outcome. This is the first great leap of consciousness for a Wave Rider: to stop seeing negativity as "talk" and to start seeing it as a real, physical force that is actively shaping your reality.

The Philosophical and Practical Implications of Wave-Spotting

Oddball's perspective aligns remarkably with ancient Stoic philosophy and modern cognitive behavioural therapy (CBT).

The Stoics, like Epictetus, taught that we are disturbed not by things, but by the views we take of them. A negative wave is essentially a distorted, unhelpful view. CBT's core principle is that our thoughts, feelings, and behaviours are all interconnected, and by changing the thought (the negative wave), we can change the feeling and the resulting action.

The Wave Rider's practice is to become the objective observer of the wave, not its victim. This is where the concept moves from abstract philosophy to practical technique.

Technique 1: The Tank Journal and Mapping the Pollution

Your first task as a student of Oddballism is to become a Wave-spotter.

For the next week, your mission is to simply notice. Notice the negative waves as they come at you.

Don't try to block them yet. Just observe. This is the Reconnaissance Phase. Keep a log in your Tank Journal—a simple notebook or digital file—and map the pollution.

The Tank Journal Entry Structure:

1. Source: Who or what transmitted the wave? (e.g., Sarah, the 6 PM news, Inner Moriarty after a mistake).

2. The Wave: What was the specific content of the negative thought or statement? (e.g., "This project is too big, you will fail," or "The economy is collapsing, you should hoard cash").

3. The Effect: How did the wave make you feel, and what was your immediate physical or mental reaction? (e.g., Energy sagged, felt a knot in my stomach, spent 30 minutes doom scrolling).

4. The Truth Check: What is the objective, verifiable truth of the situation, stripped of the wave's emotional charge? (e.g., The project is challenging, but I have a competent team and a solid plan. The economy is cyclical, and I have a stable job).

By meticulously logging these entries, you achieve two critical things.

First, you create cognitive distance between yourself and the wave. You are no longer the wave; you are the one observing the wave.

Second, you begin to see the patterns of the Moriartys in your life and the favourite scripts of your Inner Moriarty. You realise that the same tired, predictable waves keep coming from the same sources.

This predictability robs the wave of its power.

Technique 2: The Three-Second Rule and the Wave-Breaker

Once you have mastered Wave-Spotting, you move to the Wave-Breaker Phase. This is the moment of intervention. When a negative wave hits you—a sudden thought of self-doubt, a coworker's toxic complaint, a fear-mongering headline—you have a window of approximately three seconds before your brain's automatic, negativity-biased response takes over.

The Three-Second Wave-Breaker Protocol:

1. Stop (1 Second): Immediately and physically stop whatever you are doing. If you are talking, pause. If you are scrolling, freeze your thumb. If you are walking, take a deliberate, deep breath. This interrupts the automatic neural pathway.

2. Name (1 Second): Internally or quietly, name the wave. Say, "That is a Negative Wave," or "Hello, Inner Moriarty." By naming it, you externalise it. It is no longer your truth; it is an object you are observing.

3. Reframe (1 Second): Replace the wave with a pre-prepared, constructive counter-statement. This is your "Oddball Affirmation." It must be practical, not just feel-good. For example, if the wave is "You're going to fail this presentation," the reframe is "I have prepared thoroughly, and

I will focus on delivering value to the audience." If the wave is a colleague's complaint, the reframe is "That is their wave, not mine. I will maintain my own frequency."

This technique directly applies neuroplasticity. Every time you successfully execute the Wave-Breaker Protocol, you weaken the old, negativity-biased neural pathway and strengthen a new, more resilient one.

You are literally rewiring your brain to be less susceptible to psychic pollution.

The Edge Case: The Necessary Negative Wave

A common objection to Oddballism is the idea that all negativity must be avoided.

But the Wave Rider is not a naive optimist. Oddball was a realist. He didn't ignore that the bridge might be gone; he refused to let the fear of the bridge being gone paralyse him.

He focused on the solution: the possibility of crossing.

This brings us to the concept of the Necessary Negative Wave. This is not pollution; it is a signal. It is the constructive criticism from a mentor, the legitimate warning from a financial advisor, or the inner voice that says, "You made a mistake, and you need to fix it."

The difference between a Negative Wave (pollution) and a Necessary Negative Wave (signal) is its intent and its actionability.

- **Pollution:** Intent is to complain, paralyse, or spread fear. It offers no solution. Actionability is zero. (e.g., "The world is terrible, and there's nothing we can do.")

- **Signal:** Intent is to inform, protect, or prompt improvement. It is paired with a clear, actionable step. (e.g., "The structural report shows a flaw in the design; here is the specific change we need to make.")

The Wave Rider learns to filter the noise. If a thought or statement is purely a complaint, a fear, or a judgment without a corresponding, constructive action, it is pollution and must be neutralised.

If it is a hard truth that requires a response, it is a signal, and you must act on the truth while simultaneously rejecting the emotional paralysis that often accompanies it.

Only by understanding the enemy can you prepare your defence, and only by mastering the Wave-Breaker can you begin to ride the positive current of your own intentional reality. The journey of the Wave Rider begins with this simple, profound act of awareness: recognising the negative wave for what it is—a contagious, ancient, and ultimately manageable force.

Your tank is your mind, and you are the commander. Do not let the Moriartys, internal or external, dictate the course of the battle.

The Practice of Wave Immunity: Generating Your Own Current

The ultimate goal of the Wave Rider is not merely to defend against negative waves, but to generate a positive current so strong that it creates a field of Wave Immunity. This is the practical application of Oddball's philosophy: if you don't like the waves you're getting, you have to start broadcasting your own. This is not about forced optimism; it is about intentional, disciplined action that shifts your internal frequency.

Technique 3: The Three-Step Positive Wave Generator

This technique is designed to actively counter the negativity bias by creating and reinforcing positive neural pathways. It is a daily practice that shifts the brain from a threat-detection system to an opportunity-seeking system.

1. The Gratitude Drill (Focus on the Present): Every morning, before engaging with any external source (news, email, social media), identify three specific, small, and recent things you are genuinely grateful for. The key is specificity. Don't just say "I'm grateful for my health." Say, "I'm grateful for the specific feeling of warmth from my coffee this morning," or "I'm grateful that my colleague, David, took the time to explain that complex process yesterday." Specificity forces the brain to relive the positive experience, releasing beneficial neurotransmitters and strengthening the positive memory trace.

2. The Action-Focus Drill (Focus on the Future): When faced with a challenge or a large task, the Inner Moriarty will inevitably send a wave of "I can't do this" or "This is too hard." The Positive Wave Generator counters this by immediately shifting focus from the outcome (which is uncertain) to the next actionable step (which is certain). If the wave is "I'll never finish this book," the counter-wave is "I will write for 45 minutes, and I will start with the introduction." This technique, rooted in the concept of flow state, bypasses the paralysing fear of the large goal and channels energy into manageable, productive motion. The positive wave is the feeling of competence and progress, not the feeling of having already succeeded.

3. The Generosity Drill (Focus on the External): Negative waves are inherently self-focused—they are about my fear, my complaint, my inadequacy. The most powerful way to break this self-absorption is through intentional generosity. This doesn't have to be a grand gesture. It can be a genuine, specific compliment to a stranger, a five-minute favour for a colleague, or a simple, unexpected act of kindness. Neuroscientific studies show that acts of generosity activate the brain's reward centres, generating a powerful, self-sustaining positive wave that radiates outward. When you are actively broadcasting a positive wave, you are immune to receiving a negative one.

Extended Narrative Example: The Case of the Digital Nomad

Let's look at Lena, a 28-year-old freelance graphic designer who has successfully transitioned to a digital nomad lifestyle, working from various locations around the world. By all external metrics, she was living the dream. Yet, she was constantly plagued by low-grade anxiety and self-doubt. Her Moriarty was the Comparison Wave from social media. She followed dozens of other successful nomads whose feeds were a relentless stream of exotic locations, six-figure contracts, and effortless perfection.

Lena's Tank Journal revealed a clear pattern: every time she spent more than 15 minutes on a specific platform, a wave would hit. The wave's content was always a variation of: "You're not working hard enough," "Your clients aren't as prestigious," or "You're just running away from your problems." This wave would lead to feelings of procrastination, a knot in her stomach, and a sense of being an imposter.

Her Wave Rider transformation began with the Wave-Breaker Protocol. One afternoon, while working in a café in Lisbon, she saw a post from a peer who had just landed a massive contract.

The wave hit instantly: You should be doing that. You're falling behind.

1. Stop (1 Second): She physically put her laptop lid down and took a deep breath.

2. Name (1 Second): "Comparison Wave. Inner Moriarty is broadcasting."

3. Reframe (1 Second): She immediately opened her Tank Journal and wrote down her Action-Focus Drill for the next hour: "I will complete the colour palette and typography for the Peterson logo project."

She rejected the wave's premise (that she was failing) and replaced it with a constructive action (a specific, manageable task).

The true breakthrough came with the Generosity Drill. Instead of passively consuming others' success, she decided to broadcast a positive wave actively. She started sending short, specific, and genuine messages of congratulations and support to the people whose work she admired.

She messaged the peer who landed the big contract, not with envy, but with a detailed compliment about the quality of their portfolio. The act of genuinely celebrating another person's success immediately shifted her internal state. The negative wave of comparison, which thrives on scarcity and self-pity, could not coexist with the positive wave of genuine appreciation and abundance.

Lena realised that the negative wave is not a statement of fact; it is a proposal for a state of being. Every time you absorb it, you accept the proposal. Every time you break it and replace it with a positive, actionable counter-wave, you reject the proposal and assert your own intentional reality.

Oddball's wisdom is not about ignoring reality; it is about refusing to let the most fearful, least productive version of reality be the one you inhabit. The bridge may be gone, but the Wave Rider is already looking for the boat, the raft, or the better route.

The problem does not paralyse him; the solution energises him.

That is the power of understanding and mastering the negative wave.

Chapter Five:

The Practice of Wave Rejection

"Why don't you knock it off with them negative waves?"

Once you've learned to spot the waves, it's time to learn how to block them. This is not a passive process of turning a blind eye to the world's troubles. It is an active, sometimes confrontational, practice of spiritual martial arts.

Oddball doesn't just ignore Moriarty; he directly challenges him. He names the wave and tells him to knock it off. This single, simple line is not just a piece of dialogue; it is a complete, distilled philosophy of energetic self-defence. It is the core of Wave Rejection, a practice that demands clarity, courage, and a touch of well-timed absurdity.

The original four steps—Name the Wave, The Verbal Shield, The Energetic Boundary, and The Morning Declaration—are the foundation. But a foundation is just the start.

To truly master Wave Rejection, we must build a fortress on that foundation, one that can withstand the modern, high-frequency, 24/7 barrage of negativity that Oddball himself never had to face.

The waves today are not just coming from a single, grumpy tank commander; they are streaming from a million screens, whispering from the anxiety of a globalised economy, and echoing from the deep, ancient fears of the human mind.

The Deep Dive: Naming the Wave and the Neuroscience of Negativity

The first step, Name the Wave, is the most crucial, for it is an act of cognitive separation. When you encounter a negative wave, the first step is to identify it in your own mind.

Say to yourself, "Ah, there it is. A negative wave." This act of naming creates a space between you and the energy. It depersonalises it. It's not that your friend is a bad person; it's that they are currently transmitting a negative wave. This distinction is crucial. It allows you to reject the energy without rejecting the person, a deeply human and compassionate approach that is far more effective than simple avoidance.

Modern psychology calls this technique cognitive diffusion. It is a core component of Acceptance and Commitment Therapy (ACT), which teaches us to observe our thoughts and feelings without getting entangled in them.

When a thought like "I'm going to fail" arises, we don't argue with it; we observe it as "I am having the thought that I am going to fail." Oddball's genius is in applying this to external energy. He doesn't say, "Moriarty, you are a negative person." He says, "Knock it off with them negative waves." He is targeting the behaviour and the energy, not the identity. This is a high-level social manoeuvre that preserves the relationship while protecting the self.

Case Study: The Architect and the Toxic Critique.

Meet Elara, a 35-year-old architect who had just spent six months pouring her soul into a proposal for a new community centre.

She presented it to her firm's senior partner, Mr Thorne, known for his brilliance and his crushing, often personal, critiques. Mr

Thorne didn't just critique the design; he delivered a wave of pure, identity-level negativity.

"This is amateur work, Elara. It shows a fundamental lack of vision. Frankly, I'm beginning to question your commitment to this firm." The wave hit her like a physical blow, triggering a familiar spiral of self-doubt.

Elara, a student of Oddball's philosophy, paused. She didn't react to the content of the wave—the "amateur work" part—immediately.

Instead, she performed the first step: Naming the Wave.
"Negative wave detected. Source: Mr Thorne. Type: Identity Attack/Doubt Projection."

By naming it, she didn't internalise it. She saw it as a piece of external data, a transmission, not a truth about her soul.

She then employed a modified Verbal Shield: "Thank you for the feedback, Mr Thorne. I hear your concerns about the vision. Can you specify three concrete areas in the structural plans that you feel are lacking, so I can address them by tomorrow morning?"

She forced the conversation back to the objective, technical details, effectively killing the negative wave by starving it of the emotional fuel it needed to survive. She rejected the wave without rejecting the task.

The Verbal Shield: Techniques of Energetic Counter-Punching

Oddball's primary technique is the verbal shield. He speaks back to the negativity. This is not about winning an argument; it's about winning the energetic exchange. It's about setting a clear, non-negotiable boundary.

The three classic forms are still the most potent:

1. The Direct Rejection: "Knock it off with them negative waves." This is for when you have a close relationship with the Moriarty in question and can be direct. It's humorous but firm. It sets a clear boundary. This requires a high degree of self-possession. You must be willing to risk a moment of awkwardness for a lifetime of peace. It works best with friends, family, or colleagues who respect you enough to take the gentle rebuke.

2. The Gentle Redirection: "Why don't you say something righteous and hopeful for a change?" This is a more compassionate approach. You're not just blocking; you're offering a better path. You're inviting them to join you on the positive wave. This technique is rooted in the ancient Stoic idea of Prohairesis, the power of choice. You are reminding the other person that they have a choice in the energy they transmit. You are not just defending yourself; you are offering them a path to a better state.

3. The Humorous Deflection: When Big Joe confronts him with hostility, Oddball calls him an "antisocial type" and starts barking like a dog. This is a high-level technique. It's so absurd that it completely derails the negative energy. The hostility has nowhere to go. Use this when a direct confrontation would be unproductive. Humour is the ultimate energetic circuit breaker. It introduces an element of play into a situation designed for conflict, instantly changing the game's rules.

Extended Narrative Example: The Case of the Perpetual Complainer. Marcus, a 40-year-old software engineer, had a colleague named Brenda. Brenda was a black hole of complaint. Every morning, she would corner Marcus by the coffee machine and launch into a ten-minute monologue about the incompetence of management, the futility of their project, and the general decline of civilisation.

Marcus, a naturally empathetic person, would find his energy drained before 9 AM. He tried the Gentle Redirection:

"Well, at least we have a challenging problem to solve, Brenda."

It failed. Brenda incorporated his positive spin into her negative narrative: "Yes, a challenging problem because management is incompetent."

Marcus realised he needed the high-level absurdity of the Humorous Deflection.

The next morning, Brenda started: "I can't believe they're making us use that old server again, it's going to crash, we're all doomed..."

Marcus cut her off, not with a counter-argument, but with a sudden, loud, and perfectly executed impression of a foghorn.

BWOOOOOMP! He then looked at her with a completely straight face and said, "Sorry, Brenda. That was my internal 'Negative Wave Overload' alarm.

It's a new feature. I'm going to get a doughnut now. Want one?"

The sheer unexpectedness of the foghorn broke the pattern. Brenda blinked, a flicker of confusion replacing her usual scowl. The wave had been successfully derailed. She didn't get a doughnut, but she didn't complain to Marcus for the rest of the day either. The absurdity worked because it was an energetic non-sequitur; it was a move outside the expected script of complaint and sympathy.

The Energetic Boundary: Oddball's Wisdom and Ancient Philosophy

Sometimes you can't speak back. You can't tell your boss to knock it off with the negative waves (unless you have a very Oddball-like boss). In these cases, you must create an internal boundary.

Visualise a shield around yourself. See the negative waves hitting the shield and dissipating.

Internally, you can still name the wave: "Negative wave detected. Shield up." This is not just a mental trick; it is an act of energetic self-preservation.

This internal shield is the practical application of a concept central to ancient philosophy: The Inner Citadel. The Stoic philosopher Marcus Aurelius wrote extensively about this idea in his Meditations. He believed that while external events—the negative waves of the world—are beyond our control, our inner response to them is entirely our own domain.

"The tranquillity that comes from the orderly arrangement of the mind. The inner citadel is impregnable, for the soul is a fortress that nothing can take, provided it is defended by reason."

Oddball's shield is the modern, pragmatic version of this Inner Citadel. It's recognising that your peace is your most valuable asset, and that you are the sole gatekeeper. When the boss, the news cycle, or the traffic jam transmits a wave you cannot verbally reject, you retreat to the citadel. You acknowledge the wave—"Negative wave detected"—but you refuse its entry. You let it crash against the walls of your intention, knowing that the only damage it can do is the damage you permit.

Nuance and Edge Cases: The Wave of Self-Doubt. The most insidious negative wave is the one that originates not from a Moriarty, but from within your own mind. This is the wave of self-doubt, the internal critic, the voice that whispers, "You're not good enough."

Oddball's philosophy applies here, too, but the technique must be refined. You cannot tell your own mind to "knock it off" with the same blunt force, as that often leads to internal conflict and a stronger wave.

The technique for the internal wave is Radical Depersonalization. You must name the wave, but you must also recognise that the wave is not you. It is a neural pattern, a cognitive habit, a vestige of an old fear. You can visualise the thought as a radio signal—a negative wave—that your brain is picking up. You then use the Energetic Boundary to create distance.

Instead of fighting the thought, you observe it with a detached, almost humorous curiosity, much like Oddball observing Big Joe's hostility. "Ah, there's the 'Imposter Syndrome' wave. It's a classic. Shield up. I'll let it play out, but I won't turn up the volume." This gentle, non-judgmental rejection allows the wave to pass without taking root in your core identity.

The Morning Declaration: Setting the Energetic Tone

The most important practice for Wave Rejection happens before you even encounter a single wave. As Oddball teaches, the morning is a sacred time. Your first act of the day should be to set your intention. Before you check your phone, before you read the news, take a moment.

Stand up, take a deep breath, and say it out loud:

"Don't hit me with them negative waves so early in the morning."

Say it with feeling. You are speaking to the universe. You are informing all potential Moriartys worldwide that you are not open to their business today. This simple ritual lays a foundation of protection for your entire day.

This is not superstition; it is the psychological principle of Priming. By consciously choosing a positive, defensive, and proactive mindset first thing in the morning, you are literally priming your brain to filter out negativity and focus on solutions.

You are activating the prefrontal cortex—the brain's executive control centre—before the amygdala—the brain's fear centre—can be hijacked by the day's inevitable stressors.

Practical Application: The 5-Minute Morning Shield. To make the Morning Declaration a robust practice, integrate these steps:

1. The Physical Stance (The Oddball Posture): Stand up straight. Take three deep, slow breaths. This simple physical act signals to your nervous system that you are safe and in control, shifting you from a sympathetic (fight-or-flight) to a parasympathetic (rest-and-digest) state.

2. The Verbal Declaration: Say the line out loud, with conviction: "Don't hit me with them negative waves so early in the morning." Don't whisper it; project it. You are claiming your energetic space.

3. The Visual Shield: Spend one minute visualising your shield. Make it detailed. Is it a shimmering gold energy field? Is it the thick, comforting armour of a tank? Is it a bubble of pure, unadulterated absurdity? The more vivid the image, the stronger the psychological anchor.

4. The Positive Wave Projection: Before you leave your inner citadel, choose one positive wave to transmit to the world. A goal for the day, a person you will encourage, or a small act of kindness you will perform. You are not just defending; you are counter-attacking with goodness.

The Deeper Connection: Oddball and the Ancient Cynics

Oddball's philosophy, particularly his use of absurdity and his rejection of conventional authority, has a profound connection to the ancient Greek school of Cynicism.

The original Cynics, like Diogenes of Sinope, were not cynical in the modern sense of being pessimistic. They were radical non-conformists who rejected societal norms, wealth, and conventional opinion (the "negative waves" of their time) in favour of a life lived in accordance with nature and reason.

Diogenes famously lived in a large ceramic jar and performed outrageous acts—like carrying a lamp in the daytime, claiming to be "looking for an honest man"—to expose the absurdity and hypocrisy of Athenian society.

This is the philosophical root of Oddball's barking at Big Joe. It is a technique called Parrhesia, or "speaking truth to power," often through shocking or unconventional means. Oddball's barking is his way of saying, "Your hostility is so ridiculous, so divorced from the reality of our mission, that the only appropriate response is a sound equally ridiculous."

He uses absurdity as a tool of liberation, freeing himself from the expectation of a serious, conventional response. He rejects the wave by changing the channel entirely.

Sub-Section: The Nuance of Necessary Negativity

A true master of Wave Rejection understands that not all negative waves are created equal.

There is a distinction between Toxic Negativity (the wave of complaint, gossip, fear-mongering, and self-doubt) and Constructive Negativity (the wave of honest critique, necessary grief, and realistic risk assessment).

Oddball is not advocating for a life of blind optimism. He is a pragmatist. He is a soldier in a war. He knows the risks. When he is planning the bank heist, he is meticulously realistic about the dangers. That is not a negative wave; that is a Realistic Assessment. The negative wave is the energy that paralyses action, that breeds despair, that focuses on problems without seeking solutions.

The true test of Wave Rejection is not to block all incoming signals, but to develop the energetic discernment to tell the difference.

• **Toxic Wave:** "This plan is going to fail because we're all a bunch of screw-ups." (Focuses on identity, breeds paralysis).

• **Constructive Wave:** "This plan has a 60% chance of failure unless we secure the bridge first." (Focuses on a solvable problem, breeds action).

Your shield must have a filter. It must reject the poison while allowing the necessary medicine of truth to pass through.

This is the ultimate sophistication of the practice: to be open to reality, no matter how harsh, while remaining closed to the energy of despair.

Wave Rejection is a skill. You will not be perfect at it overnight. You will get hit. Some waves will knock you off your feet. The key is to get back up, dust yourself off, and raise your shield again.

Every time you successfully block a wave, your shield gets stronger. Every time you name the negativity, you take away its power. This is how you build a fortress for your soul, a fortress that is not a prison, but a launchpad for your own righteous and hopeful waves.

The world needs more of those.

Chapter Six:

Faith Over Fear

Moriarty: "Where are we going to come up with another bridge?"

Oddball: "There you go, more negative waves! Have a little faith, baby... Have a little faith."

Wave Rejection is a defensive strategy. But Oddballism is not just about defence. It is also about offence. And the most powerful offensive weapon in the Wave Rider's arsenal is faith.

Let's be clear about what we mean by faith. This is not faith in a specific deity or a religious dogma. In Oddballism, faith is the profound and unshakeable trust that another bridge is always available. It is the belief that the universe is fundamentally benevolent and that solutions will appear, even when all evidence points to the contrary. This is a radical, practical faith—a belief not in magic, but in the infinite capacity for human ingenuity and the relentless, chaotic abundance of the cosmos to provide a path forward. It is the deep-seated conviction that failure is merely information, not a final verdict.

Look at the parable of the bridge. Oddball uses positive thinking to manifest the bridge's existence: "Think the bridge will be there, and it will be there. It's a mother, beautiful bridge, and it's gonna be there." And then what happens? A plane flies over and bombs it into oblivion.

A lesser philosophy would crumble at this point. This is where a typical "positive thinking" guru would have a crisis of confidence. Their affirmations failed! Their specific, visualised outcome was destroyed. But Oddball doesn't even flinch. His faith is deeper than mere manifestation. When the physical object of his positive thinking is destroyed, he doesn't lose hope. He simply says, "It looks like we're gonna find ourselves another bridge." His faith is not in that specific bridge; his faith is in the existence of bridges in general.

This is a critical distinction. Faith is not about forcing a specific outcome. It is about trusting that a positive outcome is always possible, even if it doesn't look the way you expected. It's the trust that when one door closes, another one—perhaps a better, more interesting one—will open. The bombed bridge is not a sign that the universe is against you; it is merely a sign that your current route is closed. The Wave Rider understands that the river of life is vast, and there are a thousand places to cross. The faith is in the crossing, not in the specific plank of wood.

The Psychology of the "Another Bridge" Mentality

The "Another Bridge" mentality is a powerful psychological tool that directly counters the human tendency toward catastrophizing and learned helplessness. When a major setback occurs—the bridge is bombed—the average person enters a state of emotional paralysis. This is the Negative Wave that Moriarty is riding: the immediate, all-consuming focus on the loss, the problem, and the perceived impossibility of a solution. This is the mind's ancient survival mechanism, the "fight, flight, or freeze" response, misfiring in a modern context. It locks the brain into a narrow, fear-driven loop, making creative problem-solving impossible.

Oddball's response, "It looks like we're gonna find ourselves another bridge," is a cognitive reframing technique of the highest order. It instantly shifts the focus from the past (the destruction) to the future (the solution). This simple statement is a command to the brain to exit the panic state and engage the prefrontal cortex—the seat of executive function, planning, and creativity.

By framing the solution as inevitable, he bypasses the emotional turmoil and moves directly to the action phase. This is not denial; it is radical acceptance of the present reality combined with unwavering confidence in future possibility.

Case Study: The Architect and the Failed Bid

Consider Elias, a 45-year-old architect who had spent two years preparing a bid for a massive, career-defining municipal project—the new city library.

He poured his soul into the design, visualising his firm's name on the cornerstone. When the city council announced they had awarded the contract to a rival firm, Elias felt the bridge bomb.

He spent a week in a spiral of despair, replaying every meeting, every design choice, convinced his career was over. This was the Negative Wave threatening to drown him.

His mentor, a seasoned Wave Rider, didn't offer platitudes. He asked, "So, what's the next bridge?" Elias was confused. "There is no next bridge. This was it."

The mentor smiled. "That's Moriarty talking. Your faith was in that specific bridge. Oddball's faith is in the existence of bridges. You spent two years creating a world-class, innovative library design. The city didn't want that bridge, but the design itself is a magnificent, fully built structure. Where else can that structure cross a river?"

This reframing was the key. Elias realised his faith should be in his talent and his work, not in the specific client. He took the library design, slightly modified it, and presented it to three major university campuses looking to expand their facilities. Within six months, he landed a contract to build a new research centre for a private university—a project with a larger budget, fewer bureaucratic headaches, and more creative freedom than the library ever offered.

The bombed bridge led him to a better river, a better crossing, and a better destination. His faith was rewarded, not by the reversal of the failure, but by the re-application of his effort.

Oddball's Faith and Ancient Philosophy

Oddball's philosophy of faith is not new; it is a modern, jazzy expression of ancient wisdom, particularly Stoicism and Taoism.

The Stoics, like Epictetus and Marcus Aurelius, taught the radical distinction between what is within our control and what is outside of it. The bombing of the bridge is entirely outside of Oddball's control. His emotional reaction, his decision to search for a new solution, and his statement of faith—these are entirely within his control.

The Stoic concept of prohairesis, or moral purpose, is the inner citadel that cannot be bombed. Oddball's faith is the ultimate Stoic acceptance: "The bridge is gone. That is a fact. My response is to find another. That is my choice." He doesn't waste energy on what he cannot change, but immediately channels it into what he can: the search for the next bridge.

Similarly, the Taoist concept of Wu Wei, often translated as "effortless action" or "non-action," aligns perfectly with the Wave Rider's flow. Wu Wei is not about doing nothing; it is about acting in alignment with the natural flow of the universe, without resistance.

When the bridge is bombed, resisting that reality is futile and exhausting. Oddball's immediate pivot—"It looks like we're gonna find ourselves another bridge"—is a perfect example of Wu Wei. He doesn't fight the river; he simply adjusts his course to find the next available crossing. He trusts the Tao, the Way, to provide a path, even if the path is not the one he initially planned. His faith is the engine of his Wu Wei.

Practical Applications: The Faith-Over-Fear Toolkit

How do we cultivate this kind of radical faith in the daily grind? It requires specific, step-by-step techniques to rewire the brain's default fear response.

1. The "Tank Journal" Expansion: The Bridge Log

Your Tank Journal should have a dedicated section called the Bridge Log. This is an expansion of the "Study Your Past Successes" principle. It is a detailed, empirical record of every time a "bridge" was bombed in your life, and the better, unexpected bridge you found as a result.

• **Step 1:** The Bombing: Detail the setback. Be specific. Example: "Lost the promotion to Sarah in Q3 2023."

• **Step 2:** The Negative Wave: Record your initial, fear-driven reaction. Example: "Felt like a failure. Thought about quitting. Convinced myself I wasn't good enough."

• **Step 3:** The Pivot: Identify the moment you said, "Another bridge." Example: "Decided to use the extra time to get a certification I'd been putting off."

• **Step 4:** The New Bridge: Detail the positive, unexpected outcome. Example: "The certification led to a lateral move to a new department with a 20% raise and a much better boss. The original promotion would have meant working under a toxic manager."

Reading this log regularly is the antidote to fear. It provides empirical evidence that the universe is not a malevolent force, but a chaotic, abundant one, and that your resilience is a proven, reliable mechanism for success.

2. The Language of Inevitability

Oddball's language is not hopeful; it is declarative. He doesn't say, "I hope we can find another bridge." He says, "It looks like we're gonna find ourselves another bridge." This is the Language of Inevitability. When you face a crisis, you must narrate the story of your inevitable success.

• Replace "I hope to" with "I am in the process of."

• Fear: "I hope I can find a new job soon."

• Faith: "I am in the process of securing a new, better-fitting role."

• Replace "What if" with "When."

• Fear: "What if this project fails?"

• Faith: "When this project hits its inevitable roadblock, we will pivot to the alternative strategy we have already outlined."

• Replace "I can't" with "I haven't figured out how yet."

• Fear: "I can't solve this problem."

• Faith: "I haven't figured out how to solve this problem yet, but the solution is presenting itself."

This linguistic shift is a powerful form of self-hypnosis. It programs your subconscious mind to stop searching for reasons to panic and start searching for pathways to success.

Case Study: The Entrepreneur and the Supply Chain Collapse

Lena ran a small but growing e-commerce business selling artisanal goods. Her entire supply chain depended on a single, reliable overseas factory. When a sudden, unforeseen political crisis shut down the factory indefinitely, her bridge was not just bombed—it was vaporised. The Negative Wave was immense: she faced losing her business, laying off her small team, and disappointing thousands of customers.

Her initial reaction was pure fear. She drafted an email to her customers apologising for the failure and announcing a temporary closure. But then she remembered the principle of "Another Bridge." She deleted the email and, instead, sent a message to her team: "The factory is closed. This is a massive setback, but it is also an opportunity.

We are now in the process of building a more resilient, localised supply chain. We will not close. We will pivot."

This statement of inevitability galvanised her team. They immediately stopped mourning the loss and started searching for new, local artisans. Within two months, they had established partnerships with three smaller, domestic workshops.

The new supply chain was more expensive, but it allowed her to market her products as "100% Made Local," a value proposition that resonated deeply with her customer base. Her business not only survived but also thrived, growing by 40% the following year.

The bombed bridge forced her to build a stronger, more valuable business model.

The Neurobiology of Faith

Modern neuroscience supports Oddball's wisdom. Fear, the Negative Wave, is processed primarily in the amygdala, the brain's alarm centre. When the amygdala is overactive, it floods the system with cortisol and adrenaline, leading to tunnel vision and impaired cognitive function. This is the biological basis of Moriarty's panic.

Faith, in the Oddball sense, is the activation of the ventromedial prefrontal cortex (vmPFC), the area of the brain associated with risk assessment, emotional regulation, and abstract thought. When you engage in the "Another Bridge" reframing, you actively downregulate the amygdala and activate the vmPFC. You are telling your brain, "This is a problem, but it is a solvable problem."

This shift from a threat-response to a challenge-response is the core of resilience.

Furthermore, the act of speaking the Language of Inevitability—"I am in the process of finding a solution"—engages the brain's reward circuitry. It creates a small, positive feedback loop that reinforces the search for a solution, making the next step easier. Faith, therefore, is not a passive hope; it is an active, neurochemically supported strategy for optimising your brain's problem-solving capacity.

Sub-Section: The Edge Case of the Permanent Bombing

What about the truly catastrophic, seemingly permanent bombings? The loss of a loved one, a debilitating illness, a life-altering betrayal. These are not mere setbacks; they are the destruction of the entire landscape. Can Oddball's faith apply here?

Yes, but the definition of "another bridge" must change. In these edge cases, the faith is not in the reversal of the loss, but in the reconstruction of the self. The old self, the one that existed before the bombing, is gone. The faith is in the inevitable emergence of a new, stronger, and wiser self.

The new bridge is not a return to the past; it is the acceptance of the new reality and the courage to build a new life upon the ruins. The faith is that, even in the deepest grief, the human spirit is designed to adapt, find meaning, and continue the journey. The river is still there, and the Wave Rider's job is to find a new way to ride it, even if the wave is now one of profound sorrow. The faith is that the new self, forged in the fire of loss, will be capable of finding beauty and purpose again.

Fear is the mind-killer. It is the ultimate negative wave. Faith is the only shield that can truly block it. It is the calm, quiet confidence that no matter how many bridges get bombed, there is always a way across the river.

You just have to have a little faith, baby. And remember, that faith is not a wish; it is a declaration of your own indomitable will to find the next way forward. It is the most practical, powerful tool in the Wave Rider's arsenal. It is the knowledge that the journey is the destination, and the river always flows.

Chapter Seven:

The Power of Positive Waves.

Kelly: "No, because you're gonna be up there, baby, and I'll be right outside showing you which way to go."

Oddball: "Crazy... I mean like, so many positive waves... maybe we can't lose, you're on!"

This exchange is the climax of the doctrine, the moment where Oddball, the master of Wave Rejection, willingly surrenders to an incoming wave. But this is no ordinary wave. This is a tsunami of pure, concentrated positivity, and it comes from Kelly. It is the ultimate expression of trust, camaraderie, and shared purpose, a force so potent it overrides the most fundamental of survival instincts.

Up to this point, Oddball has been a radical pragmatist. He rejects the mission to face three Tiger tanks as suicidal, stating with his characteristic, world-weary wisdom: "To a New Yorker like you, a hero is some type of weird sandwich, not some nut who takes on three Tigers." His logic is impeccable. His survival instinct is razor-sharp. No amount of wishful thinking or blind optimism can change the fact that this is a terrible, life-ending idea.

The negative wave of reality—the overwhelming odds, the superior German armour, the sheer lunacy of the plan—is crashing down.

And then Kelly hits him with the counter-wave. He doesn't argue the logistics. He doesn't offer more money or a better cut of the gold. He offers something far more valuable, something that transcends material gain: belief.

He looks Oddball in the eye and says, essentially, "I will be with you. I will guide you. I believe in your ability to do this, and I will be your eyes and ears on the outside." It is a promise of partnership, a commitment to shared fate, and an act of genuine, unwavering faith.

In that precise moment, Oddball feels the shift. He feels the energy field change. He feels a wave of confidence and trust so powerful that it overrides his own logic, his own fear, and his own self-preservation.

"So many positive waves... maybe we can't lose."

This is not a surrender to folly; it is a calculated leap of faith based on an advanced spiritual calculus. It is the recognition that the intangible force of collective belief has become so powerful that it can, in fact, bend the rules of reality.

The Mechanics of the Positive Wave

The secret weapon of Oddballism is not merely about blocking the negative; it is about actively seeking out, generating, and amplifying the positive. Positive waves, just like negative ones, are contagious. They compound, they gain momentum, and they create a powerful, self-reinforcing feedback loop of success. This is not the shallow, saccharine "positive thinking" of self-help gurus; this is a deep, energetic alignment with possibility, grounded in mutual respect and competence.

Case Study 1: The Architect and the Negative Feedback Loop

Consider the story of Anya Sharma, a brilliant but perpetually self-doubting architect in a high-pressure firm.

Anya was trapped in a classic negative feedback loop. She would receive a challenging project (the negative wave), immediately doubt her ability to execute it, and this self-doubt would manifest as procrastination and over-analysis. Her fear of failure became a self-fulfilling prophecy, leading to rushed, mediocre work that, in turn, reinforced her initial self-doubt. Her internal Moriarty was winning every day.

Anya's mentor was her older, unflappable partner, David. David didn't offer platitudes. Instead, he provided a concrete, positive wave: unwavering competence and a clear path. When a massive, complex bid paralysed Anya, David didn't tell her to "just be positive." He said, "Anya, you designed the new city library. This is a skyscraper. The principles are the same. I'm not going to touch the design, but I'll sit in the next office and review your structural calculations every 2 hours. You focus on the creative vision; I'll be your safety net."

David became her "eyes on the outside," her guide. By externalising the most anxiety-inducing part of the process—the fear of a catastrophic, public error—he allowed her creative energy to flow freely. The positive wave was not a feeling; it was a structure of support. Anya delivered the best design of her career, and the positive feedback from the win finally broke the cycle of self-doubt. The wave of success, generated by Kelly's belief, became her own internal generator.

Harnessing the Power: Four Practical Techniques

To harness this power, the Wave Rider must transition from being a mere shield to becoming a source.

1. Become a Source, Not Just a Shield: Don't just block Moriarty's negativity; be the Kelly for someone else. Offer genuine, unwavering belief in another person's competence and potential. Tell them, "I'll be right outside showing you which way to go." The act of generating a positive wave for someone else amplifies your own positive energy tenfold. This is the principle of reciprocal amplification. By investing belief in others, you solidify your own capacity for belief. It is a selfless act that yields selfish, yet righteous, returns.

2. Find Your Kellys: Identify the people in your life who are natural sources of positive waves. These are the people who, when you leave a conversation with them, you feel more energised, more capable, and more hopeful. They are the ones who see your potential, not your flaws. Spend more time with them. Their energy is a force multiplier for your own. This is not about surrounding yourself with "yes men," but with people who operate from a place of abundance and possibility, rather than scarcity and fear.

3. Create Positive Feedback Loops: When you achieve a small victory, celebrate it. Share it with your crew. This creates a positive wave that will help propel you to the next victory. Success, fuelled by positive energy, begets more success. Oddball's crew, despite their eccentricities, functions so well because they operate in a high-energy field of mutual trust and playful confidence. They acknowledge the small wins—the successful procurement of supplies, the perfect camouflage job, the smooth drive—which keeps their collective morale high enough to face the impossible.

4. Recognise the Tipping Point (Advanced Spiritual Calculus): There will be moments in your life, like Oddball's in front of the Tigers, where the logical, safe choice is to retreat. But if the energy is right, if the positive waves are strong enough, you must be willing to take the leap. This is not blind optimism. This is advanced spiritual calculus. It's the ability to feel when the intangible force of collective belief, combined with a sound, if audacious, plan, has become so powerful that it can temporarily suspend the laws of probability. You must be able to discern the difference between a fool's errand and a righteous, high-energy gamble.

The Neuroscience of Collective Confidence

Modern psychology and neuroscience have begun to map the biological underpinnings of Oddball's "positive waves." The concept is deeply connected to the social regulation of the nervous system.

When Kelly offers his belief, he is not just speaking words; he is providing a co-regulation signal.

In moments of high stress, the amygdala—the brain's fear centre—hijacks the prefrontal cortex, leading to the "fight, flight, or freeze" response. Oddball's initial reaction is a logical "flight" response. However, when Kelly steps in with his calm, authoritative, and committed presence, he acts as an external anchor. This social signal of safety and shared responsibility down-regulates Oddball's stress response.

The release of oxytocin, the "bonding hormone," and a reduction in cortisol allow Oddball's prefrontal cortex to come back online. He is then able to engage in the "advanced spiritual calculus"—the high-level risk assessment—that leads to his acceptance. The positive wave is, in essence, a neurochemical cascade of trust and shared purpose that optimises the brain for high-stakes performance.

This is why the presence of your Kellys is so vital. They are not just cheerleaders; they are neurological co-regulators. They help keep your system in an optimal state of arousal—alert but not panicked—where peak performance is possible.

The Ancient Roots of Positive Waves

Oddball's wisdom, though delivered from the turret of a Sherman tank, echoes the teachings of ancient philosophy. The Stoics, for instance, understood the power of internal fortitude against external chaos. But Oddballism adds a crucial, communal layer.

- **Stoicism vs. Oddballism:** Stoicism teaches you to manage your internal state regardless of the external world (rejecting the negative wave). Oddballism agrees with this foundation but then says: Now that you are stable, go out and create a better external world through the force of your positive energy (generating the positive wave). It moves from passive resilience to active creation.

- **The Confucian Concept of Ren** (仁): Ren is often translated as "benevolence" or "human-heartedness," the core of which is the relationship between two people. Kelly's offer is pure Ren. It is the highest form of human connection, a commitment to the well-being and success of the other. Oddball's acceptance is the recognition that this connection is a force more powerful than three Tiger tanks. The positive wave is the energetic manifestation of Ren in action.

The ultimate goal of a Wave Rider is to become a self-sustaining generator of positive waves.

You start by protecting yourself from the negative. You build your inner strength through faith. And then, you turn your attention outward. You become a beacon, a source of light for others.

You create a reality around you where, because of the sheer force of your righteous vibe, maybe you can't lose.

You're on.

Part Three:

The Doctrine of Presence & Beauty

If the Doctrine of Positive Waves is the engine of your tank, the Doctrine of Presence and Beauty is the viewport. It's how you see the world, and more importantly, how you engage with it. While the first doctrine is about managing the invisible world of energy, this one is about engaging with the tangible, sensual, and immediate world right in front of you. It is the sacred practice of showing up for your own life, fully and without reservation.

In a world that constantly pulls your attention to the past (regret, nostalgia) or the future (anxiety, planning), Oddballism calls you back to the only place where life actually happens: right here, right now.

This isn't about blissful ignorance; it's about radical engagement. It's about finding heaven not in some distant afterlife, but in a piece of cheese, a ray of sunshine, or the simple, profound beauty of a standing bridge.

The Case for Radical Engagement

Oddball is a man of profound sensory awareness. He is constantly chewing, listening, and observing.

He notices the details: the quality of the wine, the state of the bridge, the mood of his crew.

He is not just in the world; he is of the world. This is the essence of Presence and Beauty.

Case Study 2: The Trader and the Unseen Details

Meet Marcus Chen, a high-frequency trader whose life was a blur of screens and numbers.

Marcus was technically present—his body was in the office—but his mind was always three trades ahead or one trade behind. He was a master of the future and the past, but a ghost in the present.

This lack of presence led to a critical error: he missed a subtle, non-verbal cue from a colleague during a complex negotiation, a cue that would have saved his firm millions. He was so focused on the potential outcome that he failed to see the reality unfolding before him.

Marcus, seeking a change, took up photography, specifically street photography.

His mentor, a grizzled veteran, gave him a single piece of advice: "Don't look for the picture. Look for the light." This was his Oddball moment. He was forced to slow down, to engage with the immediate, tangible world. He had to notice the way the morning sun hit the steam rising from a manhole cover, the precise angle of a shadow, the fleeting expression on a passerby's face.

This practice of radical engagement—of seeing the beauty in the mundane and the detail in the chaos—rewired his brain. He started bringing this presence back to the trading floor. He began to notice the subtle shifts in the market's "mood," the slight tremor in a competitor's voice, the almost imperceptible change in the rhythm of the day.

He wasn't just processing data; he was experiencing the market. His performance skyrocketed, not because he was smarter, but because he was finally present. He realised that the most critical data is often the most beautiful and the most overlooked.

The Three Pillars of Presence

Oddball's Doctrine of Presence and Beauty rests on three interconnected pillars: Sensory Immersion, The Sacred Mundane, and The Appreciation of the Standing Bridge.

1. Sensory Immersion: The Taste of the Cheese Oddball's appreciation for the finer things—the wine, the cheese, the good life—is not hedonism; it is a spiritual practice. It is the deliberate act of engaging all five senses with the present moment. When you eat, taste the food. When you walk, feel the ground. When you listen, hear the layers of sound. This is the antidote to the modern condition of distraction.

- **Practical Technique:** The Five-Minute Sensory Audit. Once a day, stop what you are doing and spend five
minutes systematically engaging each of your five senses with your immediate environment. What are three things you can see that you haven't noticed before? What is one thing you can smell? What is the texture of the object closest to your hand? This simple act grounds you and pulls your consciousness out of the abstract world of thought and into the concrete world of being.

2. The Sacred Mundane: The Beauty of the Everyday. The most profound beauty is not found in grand vistas or dramatic events, but in the small, repeated, and often-ignored moments of daily life. The way the light falls on a worn wooden table. The rhythmic sound of a coffee grinder. The simple, clean lines of a well-made tool. Oddball finds beauty in the functional, the practical, and the enduring. He sees the art in the engineering of a tank and the elegance in a simple plan.

- **Connection to Modern Psychology:** This aligns with the psychological concept of savouring, which is the act of stepping outside of an experience to review and appreciate it. Savouring has been shown to increase happiness and reduce stress. Oddball is a master of savouring the moment, whether it's a successful heist or a quiet moment with a bottle of wine.

3. The Appreciation of the Standing Bridge: The Value of Enduring Structure Oddball's famous line about the bridge—"It's a beautiful bridge, and it's standing, and it's got a lot of sentimental value"—is a deep philosophical statement. The bridge represents structure, connection, and endurance. In a world of chaos and destruction, the standing bridge is a testament to human ingenuity and the power of things that last. It is a symbol of the present moment, a stable platform from which to launch into the future.

• **Practical Application:** Identify the "standing bridges" in your own life. These are the things that are reliable, enduring, and provide structure: your health, your core relationships, your foundational skills, and your daily routines. Take a moment each day to appreciate these structures. Do not take them for granted. They are the beautiful, functional things that allow you to move forward.

The Synthesis: Presence as the Foundation for Positive Waves

The two doctrines—Positive Waves and Presence and Beauty—are not separate; they are two sides of the same coin. You cannot generate genuine positive waves if you are not present.

If you are lost in anxiety about the future (the negative wave of what if), you cannot see the beauty of the standing bridge. If you are mired in regret about the past (the negative wave of if only), you cannot be the Kelly for someone else.

Presence is the fertile ground. It is the quiet, focused state of mind that allows you to assess the energy field accurately. It is the ability to see the three Tiger tanks and the unwavering belief in Kelly's eyes. It is the clarity that allows you to perform the advanced spiritual calculus and recognise the Tipping Point.

The Wave Rider's journey is a continuous loop:

1. Presence: Ground yourself in the immediate, tangible world (The Standing Bridge).

2. Rejection: Block the negative waves of fear, doubt, and distraction (The Moriarty).

3. Generation: Actively create and amplify positive waves of trust, competence, and possibility (The Kelly).

The ultimate victory is not the gold, but the realisation that you have the power to shape your reality, not by wishing, but by being fully present, fully engaged, and fully committed to generating the highest possible energy in every moment.

The world is waiting for your positive wave.

You're on.

Chapter Eight:

The Art of Digging It:

Excavating The Beautiful Now.

"Why don't you knock it off with them negative waves? Why don't you dig how beautiful it is out here? Why don't you say something righteous and hopeful for a change?"

This is the Righteous Sermon in its entirety, and we must return to its second, crucial commandment: "Why don't you dig how beautiful it is out here?"

This is not a suggestion for a casual glance; it is a profound instruction for living. It is the core of Oddball's philosophy of presence, a tactical manoeuvre for the soul in the perpetual war zone of modern existence.

Let's break down the language, because the Prophet chose his words with care. He doesn't say "look at." He doesn't say "notice." He says "dig".

This is not a passive glance; it is an active excavation. To "dig" something, in the beatnik-hippie lexicon from which Oddball draws his spiritual vocabulary, means to understand it on a deep, intuitive, and appreciative level.

It's to get your hands dirty with reality. It's about connecting with the essence of a thing, appreciating its inherent, undeniable value. It is the difference between seeing a flower and understanding the miracle of its cellular structure, its evolutionary journey, and the brief, perfect moment of its bloom.

This is the Oddballist version of mindfulness, stripped of its corporate packaging and its striving, perfectionist tendencies. In the 21st century, mindfulness has become a billion-dollar industry. There are apps, workshops, and expensive retreats all designed to teach you how to be present. Many of these are wonderful, but they can also feel like another item on your to-do list, another thing to strive for and fail at.

Oddball's approach is simpler, more rugged, and infinitely more accessible. It is a philosophy born not in a quiet ashram, but in the chaotic, high-stakes environment of a tank battle. If he can find the beauty there, you can find it waiting for you in the traffic jam, the sterile office, or the overwhelming noise of your own mind.

The Two Pillars of Excavation

The Art of Digging It requires no app, no guru, no silent retreat. It requires only two things, which serve as the foundation for all further practice:

1. A Moment of Pause (Stopping the Tank): You have to stop the tank. You can't dig the scenery when you're rumbling along at 30 miles an hour, focused on the next objective, the next email, the next crisis. The pause can be five seconds or five minutes, but it must be a conscious cessation of forward momentum. This is the moment you choose to step out of the current of your life and stand on the bank, observing the flow. It is a deliberate act of non-doing, a refusal to be swept away by the tyranny of the urgent.

2. A Shift in Attention (The Sensory Sweep): You must deliberately move your focus from the internal chatter of your mind—the planning, the worrying, the replaying of past conversations—to the external input of your senses. What do you see? What do you hear? What do you smell, taste, feel? This shift is the mechanism that grounds you. Your mind lives in the past and the future; your senses live only in the present. By engaging them, you plant yourself firmly in the only moment that is ever real: the beautiful now.

That's it. That's the whole practice. Oddball, surrounded by the mud and misery of war, pauses his spiritual tank to dig the beauty of the French countryside. He's not denying the war. The war is still there. The mission is still on. But for a moment, he chooses to place his attention on the beauty instead of the chaos.

This is not escapism. This is tactical soul-preservation. It is the realisation that the world is always a duality—a mix of the terrible and the beautiful—and that your attention is the only tool you have to choose which one you will amplify.

Case Study: The Architect and the Anxiety Loop

Consider the case of Elias, a 38-year-old architect in a major metropolitan firm.

Elias was trapped in what modern psychology calls an "anxiety loop." His days were a blur of deadlines, client demands, and the relentless internal monologue of self-criticism. He was constantly anticipating the next problem, which meant he was never truly present for the current solution. His life was technically successful—a beautiful apartment, a prestigious job—but he felt a persistent, low-grade dread. His mind was a tank rumbling at top speed, and he was too afraid to stop it, fearing that if he paused, the whole structure of his life would collapse.

Elias was introduced to the Art of Digging It not as a spiritual practice but as a performance-enhancement tool. His first assignment was simple: every time he walked from his desk to the coffee machine, he had to perform a Sensory Sweep. He wasn't allowed to think about the project he had just left or the meeting he was about to attend.

Initially, he failed. He'd be at the coffee machine, his mind already three steps ahead. But he persisted. One day, he stopped at the window. He didn't just see the city; he dug it. He noticed the precise, metallic blue of the sky reflecting off a skyscraper across the street. He felt the cool, smooth texture of the marble windowsill under his hand. He heard the distant, rhythmic clang of a construction site, which, for the first time, sounded less like an annoyance and more like the pulse of a living city.

This five-second pause was a tiny, perfect crack in his anxiety loop. It was a moment of pure, unadulterated reality that his mind could not argue with. He realised the beauty wasn't in the absence of his problems, but in the presence of the sky, the marble, and the sound. By actively digging into the beauty, he temporarily starved the negative waves of his anxiety.

The Deeper Dig: Oddball, Neuroscience, and the Stoics

Oddball's wisdom is not just feel-good advice; it is deeply aligned with modern neuroscience and ancient philosophy.

1. The Neuroscience of Attention: The brain has a built-in "negativity bias," a survival mechanism that prioritises threats and problems. This was useful on the savanna, but in the modern world, it translates into chronic anxiety and rumination.

The Art of Digging It is a deliberate counter-programming exercise. When you consciously shift your attention to beauty, you activate the prefrontal cortex, the brain's executive control centre, and strengthen the neural pathways associated with positive emotion and appreciation. You are literally training your brain to look for the good. The Beauty Log (writing down things you dug) is a form of "memory consolidation" for positive experiences, helping to hardwire the appreciation into your long-term emotional baseline.

2. The Stoic Connection (Prosochē): The ancient Stoics, like Marcus Aurelius and Epictetus, had a concept called Prosochē, which translates to "attention" or "heedfulness." It was the fundamental practice of constantly paying attention to one's own mind and actions, ensuring they align with virtue and reason. Oddball's "Dig" is Prosochē applied to the external world. The Stoics taught that we cannot control external events; we can only control our judgment of them. Oddball takes this a step further: by actively seeking and appreciating the beauty that is present, we are exercising our control over our judgment, choosing a "righteous and hopeful" interpretation of reality, even when the circumstances are grim. It is the ultimate Stoic move: finding the good in the present moment, which is the only thing we truly possess.

Practical Applications: Techniques for the Modern Tanker

Here is how you can practice the Art of Digging It in your own life, moving beyond the simple pause to a sustained state of appreciation:

The Five-Sense Dig (The Quick Reset)

This is your emergency brake, your instant reality check. Once a day, perform a conscious pause.

Stop what you are doing and ask yourself:

• **Five Things I Can See:** Don't just name them; describe them. The texture of the wood grain, the subtle gradient of colour in a shadow, the way dust motes dance in a shaft of light.

• **Four Things I Can Feel:** The chair beneath you, the texture of your clothes, the air on your skin, the weight of your phone in your hand. Notice the pressure, the temperature, the friction.

- **Three Things I Can Hear:** The hum of a computer, distant traffic, your own breathing. Listen for the layers of sound, the background symphony of your environment.

- **Two Things I Can Smell:** Coffee, rain, the pages of this book. Even a neutral smell is a sensation.

- **One Thing I Can Taste:** The lingering flavour of your last meal, the water you just drank, the metallic taste of the air.

This exercise yanks you out of the abstract world of your thoughts and plants you firmly in the reality of your body and your environment. It is a forced, sensory immersion in the present.

The Beauty Log (The Recalibration)

In your Tank Journal, dedicate a section to "Things I Dug Today." At the end of each day, write down at least three beautiful things you noticed. A perfectly formed cloud. The way the light hit a building. A stranger's laugh. A really good guitar riff. A moment of quiet competence from a colleague. By tasking yourself with finding beauty, you will train your brain to look for it. You will recalibrate your negativity bias. This is not about forced optimism; it is about accurate accounting. It ensures that the good things, which are always happening, are given equal weight to the bad things.

The Verbal Dig (The Affirmation of Presence)

When you see something beautiful, say it out loud, even if only to yourself. Use the Prophet's words: "I dig how beautiful that is." The act of speaking gives it weight. It honours the moment and solidifies the practice. This is particularly powerful when done in the presence of others. By verbally acknowledging the beauty, you are not only practising mindfulness yourself but also giving others permission to stop their own tanks and dig in the moment with you. It is a small, righteous act of collective presence.

Edge Case: Digging the Ugly

What about the moments that are not beautiful? The frustration, the pain, the sheer ugliness of a difficult situation? This is where the Art of Digging It reveals its deepest nuance. Oddball is not asking you to deny the ugliness; he is asking you to find the beauty that coexists with it.

Consider Dr Lena, a young physician working in a high-stress emergency room.

Her environment is defined by suffering, exhaustion, and bureaucratic frustration. She cannot simply look out the window and dig the sunset. Her "beauty" must be excavated from the mud of her work.

For Lena, the dig becomes:

• **Digging the Competence:** She digs the flawless, silent coordination of her team during a crisis. The beauty is in the professional grace, the shared, non-verbal understanding that saves a life.

• **Digging the Resilience:** She digs the sheer, stubborn will of a patient to keep fighting, the human spirit refusing to be extinguished.

• **Digging the Quiet Moment:** She digs the two minutes she spends alone in the supply closet, drinking a cold cup of water, feeling the cool liquid slide down her throat. It is a tiny, perfect moment of self-care, a conscious pause in the storm.

In these moments, the beauty is not external scenery; it is the beauty of human character—the courage, the compassion, the competence, and the resilience—that shines brightest against the darkest backdrop.

The Art of Digging It, is the conscious choice to place your attention on the light, even when the shadows are long.

A Guided Meditation for Digging It: The Full Excavation

For those who wish to go deeper, here is a simple, guided meditation you can practice to fully excavate the present moment. Find a comfortable place to sit, close your eyes, and take a few deep, cleansing breaths.

Phase 1: The Auditory Dig. Bring your attention to the sounds around you. Don't label them as "good" or "bad," "loud" or "soft." Just listen. Hear the furthest sound you can detect, perhaps the distant hum of traffic or a plane overhead. Now, bring your attention closer to the sounds within the room—the creak of the floor, the buzz of a light.

Finally, bring your attention to the closest sound of all: the sound of your own breath. Stay here for a few moments, just listening to the rhythm of your own life. Dig the simple, undeniable fact that you are here, and you are breathing.

Phase 2: The Somatic Dig. Shift your attention to your body's feelings. Feel the points of contact between your body and the chair or floor. Feel the weight of your hands in your lap. Notice the sensation of the air on your skin. Scan your body from your toes to the top of your head, simply noticing any sensations of warmth, coolness, tingling, or pressure, without judgment.

You are not trying to fix anything; you are simply digging the reality of your own physical presence. This body, with all its aches and wonders, is your tank, and you are appreciating its functionality.

Phase 3: The Visual Dig (The Beginner's Mind). Gently open your eyes. For the next minute, look around you as if you have never seen this place before. Adopt the "Beginner's Mind" of a child or a visitor from another planet. Notice the play of light and shadow. Notice the textures on the walls, the exact shade of colour in a nearby object. Let your eyes rest on one thing—a pen, a coffee mug, a crack in the wall—and really see it. See its form, its function, its history.

Dig how beautiful it is in its simple, perfect existence.

Then take one more deep breath and carry that sense of presence back into your day. The world is always beautiful, even when it is also terrible. The chaos and the calm, the war and the wine, the mud and the morning sun—they all exist simultaneously.

The Art of Digging It is the conscious, moment-to-moment choice to place your attention on the beauty. It is the most righteous and hopeful act you can perform, and it is the only way to live in the present truly.

It is the ultimate act of rebellion against the negative waves of a world that constantly demands your worry. Stop the tank, look around, and dig it.

It's beautiful out here.

Chapter Nine:

Wine, Cheese & Catching Rays:

The Doctrine of Strategic Stillness

Big Joe: "What are you doing?"

Oddball: "I'm drinking wine and eating cheese, and catching some rays, you know."

This exchange, seemingly a moment of pure, unadulterated idleness, is perhaps the most profound and most misunderstood parable in the entire Book of Oddball. To the casual observer, it looks like the very definition of slacking off. The mission is stalled, the tank is broken, and the commander—the man whose job it is to lead—is having a picnic.

Big Joe, the quintessential man of action and the embodiment of the relentless, grinding Protestant work ethic, is not just confused; he is morally outraged.

"Why the hell aren't you up there helping them?" he demands, his voice a tight coil of anxiety and duty.

Oddball's calm, almost lazy, chuckling response is not an excuse; it is a complete philosophical system in miniature: "I only ride 'em, I don't know what makes 'em work."

In this single, elegant dismissal, Oddball dismantles the entire toxic scaffolding of modern "hustle culture" and hands us the Doctrine of Strategic Stillness, built on two immutable, sacred tenets. This is not a philosophy of laziness; it is a highly disciplined, deeply human strategy for survival and peak performance in a world that demands constant, frantic motion.

Rest is a Sacred and Productive Act

The modern world has convinced us that our worth is directly proportional to our level of exhaustion. We wear busyness like a badge of honour, a sign of our importance. To be still is to be lazy, to rest is to be unproductive, and to take a break is to fall behind.

We fill every moment—the commute, the queue, the five minutes before a meeting—with tasks, with content, with the anxious pursuit of "self-improvement." Oddball, with his feet up and his eyes closed against the sun, calls this entire system a fool's errand. He understands a fundamental truth that modern psychology is only now catching up to: there are moments when the most productive, most strategic thing you can do is absolutely nothing.

Consider the context: his tank, his primary tool of trade, is disabled. His mechanics, the specialists who do know what makes it work, are engaged in the complex, dirty, and focused task of repair. What would Oddball gain by standing over them, sweating, fretting, and offering useless, non-expert advice?

Nothing. In fact, his anxious, micromanaging presence would only create what he calls "negative waves," introducing stress and distraction that would slow the repair down. His absence, his deliberate removal from the work scene, is not a sign of indifference; it is a profound act of trust and strategic energy conservation.

By relaxing, he is communicating his faith in his crew's competence. He is creating a psychological buffer zone so they can work without the pressure of the commander's gaze.

More importantly, he is recharging his own most critical resource: his mind. When the tank is fixed, the mission will resume, and he will need to be calm, centred, and ready to make life-or-death decisions in a split second. His rest is not a waste of time; it is an investment in his own well-being, ensuring that his decision-making capacity is at 100% when it matters most.

This is the core of strategic stillness: knowing when your presence is a help and when it is a hindrance and having the discipline to step back and prepare for the next critical moment.

Case Study: The Architect and the Burnout. Elias.

Meet Elias, a 38-year-old architect in a high-pressure firm. Elias believed in the hustle.

He routinely worked 70-hour weeks, fuelled by caffeine and the fear of missing a deadline. He saw his colleagues who took lunch breaks or left at 5 PM as less committed. His current project, a massive civic centre, hit a major structural problem.

The engineers were huddled, the junior architects were running calculations, and Elias felt the familiar, toxic urge to hover, to shout, to do something. He was running on fumes, his temper was short, and his ideas were repetitive.

One evening, after a 16-hour day, he remembered Oddball. He realised he was Big Joe, demanding action where only specialised, focused work was needed. He was riding the problem, but he didn't know what made it work—the structural calculations were beyond his immediate expertise.

The next day, Elias did the unthinkable: he delegated the problem-solving to the lead engineer, gave them a clear deadline, and then went home at 4 PM. He didn't check his email. Instead, he went to a park, sat on a bench, and simply watched the clouds.

His "wine and cheese" was the feeling of the sun on his face and the quiet absence of his phone. The next morning, he returned to the office, not exhausted and anxious, but calm and clear-headed. The engineers, unpressured, had found the solution. Elias, rested, immediately grasped the technical details and made the final, crucial design decision that saved the project. His four hours of "laziness" were the most productive hours of the entire week.

Simple, Sensual Pleasures are a Form of Prayer

Oddball's choice of activity is not arbitrary. He is not playing a video game or scrolling through a news feed. He is engaging in an act of profound, elemental grounding. Wine, cheese, sunshine. These are not complex, expensive, or goal-oriented pleasures. They are simple, sensual, and universally available gifts from the earth. They are the antidote to the abstract, digital, and often sterile nature of modern life.

- **The Wine:** It is a product of time, soil, and patient transformation. It connects him to the earth, to the rhythm of the seasons, and to a long tradition of human celebration. It is history and chemistry in a glass.

- **The Cheese:** Another product of patient transformation, a concentration of nourishment and flavour. It is simple, yet complex, a reminder that the best things in life require time and care.

- **The Sunshine:** The ultimate source of all energy on our planet. To "catch some rays" is to absorb the energy of the cosmos literally. It is a direct, physical communion with the universe, a free and powerful act of recharging.

By partaking in these things, Oddball is not merely indulging himself; he is performing a ritual of gratitude. He is honouring the simple, beautiful gifts of existence that are available even in the middle of a war. This is a profound act of defiance. The forces of chaos—whether a literal war or the modern war of endless demands—want you to believe that only the mission matters, that there is no time for joy.

Oddball's picnic is a quiet, radical rebellion. It is a declaration that his humanity, his capacity for simple joy, is not for sale.

The Philosophical and Neuroscientific Underpinnings

Oddball's wisdom is not just folksy charm; it aligns perfectly with both ancient philosophy and modern neuroscience.

Ancient Philosophy: The Stoic and Epicurean Balance. The Stoics, like Marcus Aurelius, preached the importance of focusing only on what you can control. Oddball, unable to control the speed of the tank repair, wisely shifts his focus to the only thing he can control: his internal state and his immediate, simple environment.

His stillness is a Stoic acceptance of the present reality. The Epicureans, on the other hand, sought ataraxia—freedom from fear and distress—through simple, natural pleasures. Oddball's wine and cheese is a perfect Epicurean moment, a small, perfect island of ataraxia in the middle of the storm.

He is synthesising the two: Stoic acceptance of the uncontrollable, paired with Epicurean appreciation of the simple, controllable joys.

Modern Neuroscience: The Default Mode Network (DMN). When we are actively working on a task, our brain uses the Central Executive Network (CEN). But when we rest, daydream, or engage in simple, non-goal-oriented activities like watching clouds or sipping wine, the Default Mode Network (DMN) becomes active.

The DMN is crucial for self-reflection, creative problem-solving, and consolidating memories. It is the brain's "incubation chamber." Oddball is intuitively engaging his DMN. He is not just resting; he is allowing his subconscious mind to process the mission, to make creative leaps, and to prepare for the next challenge.

The best ideas rarely come when you are frantically forcing them; they arrive when you step away and let the DMN do its quiet, powerful work.

Practical Application: Finding Your Own Sacred Ritual

To live the Doctrine of Strategic Stillness, you must first identify and then ritualise your own "wine and cheese."

It doesn't have to be literal, and it certainly doesn't have to be expensive. It is whatever simple, sensual pleasure grounds you in the present moment and fills you with a sense of simple gratitude.

The key is that it must be non-digital, non-goal-oriented, and fully immersive.

Step-by-Step Guidance: The Oddball Protocol

1. Identify the "Broken Tank" Moment: Recognise when you have hit a wall, when your presence is no longer adding value, or when a problem requires specialised attention (the mechanic's work). This is the moment to step back.

2. Define Your Sacred Pleasure: What is the simple, elemental activity that brings you back to your senses?

• **The Coffee Ritual:** The first sip of coffee in the morning, taken in silence, standing by a window, with no phone, no news, and no planning.

• **The Vinyl Hour:** Listening to a favourite album from start to finish, with your eyes closed, giving the music your full, undivided attention.

• **The Garden Grounding:** Feeling the soil between your fingers, watering a plant, or simply sitting on the grass.

- **The Sensory Savour:** Eating a single, perfectly ripe piece of fruit—a peach, a strawberry—and focusing only on the texture, the smell, and the taste.

3. Schedule the Sacred Appointment: Treat this ritual not as a luxury, but as a non-negotiable, strategic appointment. Put it on your calendar. Defend it against all intrusions. If you schedule a 15-minute "Catching Rays" break, treat it with the same seriousness as a meeting with the CEO.

4. Practice Full Immersion: When you are in your ritual, be in your ritual. Do not multitask. Do not check your phone. Savour the sensation. Feel the sun, taste the cheese, hear the music. This is the moment of communion, the act of prayer. This is the gold you were searching for all along.

Case Study: The Teacher and the Five-Minute Fix

Sarah was a high school history teacher, overwhelmed by grading and administrative tasks.

She was constantly taking work home, feeling guilty if she wasn't productive every second. Her "broken tank" was her grading pile—a task that required focused, specialised attention that she couldn't give when exhausted. Her ritual was simple: she loved the smell of old books.

She implemented the Oddball Protocol. When she felt the anxiety and burnout creeping in, she would set a timer for five minutes.
She would walk to her bookshelf, pull down a heavy, leather-bound history text, and smell the pages. She would run her hand over the spine and feel the texture of the paper.

She wasn't reading; she was engaging her senses in a non-goal-oriented way.

This five-minute sensory break, her "wine and cheese," was enough to reset her DMN, calm her nervous system, and allow her to return to the grading with renewed focus and a much lower heart rate. She found that she could complete in one hour what used to take her two, simply because she had the discipline to stop and rest strategically.

The Edge Case: The Difference Between Rest and Avoidance

Oddball's doctrine is powerful, but it comes with a critical caveat: it is Strategic Stillness, not simple avoidance. The difference is subtle but vital.

Strategic Stillness is the deliberate act of stepping back when your presence is not required, to recharge for the moment when it will be critical. It is an act of faith in your team and an investment in your future performance. Oddball is not running away from the problem; he is preparing to face it. He knows the tank will be fixed, and he needs to be ready to ride it.

Avoidance is the act of stepping back to escape responsibility, to procrastinate, or to ignore a problem that only you can solve. If Oddball were the only mechanic, or if the tank was fixed and he still refused to move, that would be avoidance.

The test is simple: Is the work that needs to be done currently being handled by the appropriate specialist, and is your rest preparing you for the next necessary action?

If the answer is yes, you are practising Strategic Stillness.

If the answer is no, you are simply avoiding your duty.

Oddball is a commander, not a shirker. He knows the difference, and his discipline is in the timing of his rest.

In a world that screams, "Do more! Go faster! Never stop!" Oddball's quiet, sun-drenched picnic is a revolutionary act. It is the wisdom of the ages distilled into a single, perfect moment. It is the ultimate life hack: the secret to sustained, high-level performance is not endless effort, but the disciplined, strategic embrace of wine, cheese, and catching rays.

Find your ritual, defend your stillness, and you will find the strength to ride the next wave, whatever chaos it may bring.

Sub-Section: The Wisdom of 'I Only Ride Em'

The second half of Oddball's statement—"I only ride 'em, I don't know what makes 'em work"—is a masterclass in humility, delegation, and the rejection of unnecessary expertise. In a world that pressures us to be a "jack of all trades," Oddball champions the power of the specialist and the wisdom of knowing your lane.

This is a lesson for every leader, every entrepreneur, and every person trying to manage a complex life. The modern tendency is to feel obligated to understand every single component of a system we oversee. A CEO feels they must understand every line of code; a manager feels they must be able to do every task of their subordinates; a parent feels they must be an expert in every subject their child studies.

This is a recipe for exhaustion and mediocrity.

Oddball's genius is in his radical acceptance of interdependence. He is the best tank commander in the unit, a genius of strategy, terrain, and timing. That is his speciality.
The mechanics are geniuses of engines, gears, and hydraulics. That is their speciality.

By saying, "I only ride 'em," he is not admitting ignorance; he is defining his expertise and, more importantly, empowering the experts around him. He is saying: "I trust you to do your job, because it is your job, and I will focus on doing mine."

This frees his mind from the burden of unnecessary detail and allows him to focus on the meta-task: the overall mission, the big picture, the "waves" he needs to ride. If he were down in the engine bay, he would be a mediocre mechanic and a distracted commander. By staying in his lane, he ensures that the entire system—the crew, the tank, and the mission—operates at peak efficiency.

The wisdom of "I only ride 'em" is the wisdom of the conductor who trusts the first violinist, the general who trusts the intelligence officer, and the human being who trusts the universe to handle the things they cannot control.

It is the final, necessary component of Strategic Stillness: the ability to let go.

Sub-Section: The Modern Challenge of Digital Stillness

The greatest threat to Oddball's doctrine in the 21st century is the pervasive nature of the digital world. Our "wine and cheese" is constantly being replaced by the digital equivalent of a sugar rush: the endless scroll, the notification chime, the quick hit of dopamine from a social media like.

These digital "pleasures" are insidious because they feel like rest, but they are, in fact, the opposite of stillness.

When you scroll, your brain is still working, still processing, still comparing, still reacting. You are not engaging your DMN; you are over-stimulating your CEN with a constant stream of low-value information. This is not strategic rest; it is cognitive junk food.

To truly practice Oddball's doctrine today, the ritual must be a digital fast. Your sacred pleasure must involve the physical world and your senses: the smell of the air, the taste of real food, the feel of a physical book, the sound of silence. The moment you introduce a screen, you are no longer catching rays; you are catching anxiety. The discipline of Oddball is not just in taking the break, but in the quality of the break. It must be a break that restores your soul, not one that merely distracts your mind. The wine and cheese must be real, not virtual.

Conclusion: The Wave Rider's Secret

The world will always have broken tanks, stalled missions, and Big Joes demanding frantic, useless action.

The wave rider knows that you cannot ride a wave if you are exhausted, anxious, and distracted. The secret to riding the wave is not in the paddling, but in the moment of stillness before the swell, the moment of perfect balance and readiness.

Oddball, sipping his wine and feeling the sun, is not a man on a break; he is a man in a state of perfect readiness. He is the eye of the storm, the calm centre from which all effective action must spring. His doctrine is a manual for sustained excellence, a blueprint for a life lived with grace, humour, and profound effectiveness.

It is the ultimate permission slip to be human, to savour the gifts of existence, and to trust that by taking care of yourself, you are, in fact, taking care of the mission. Find your wine, find your cheese, and for God's sake, catch some rays.

The world can wait.

You need to be ready.

Chapter Ten:

The Mother Beautiful Tank

"Think the bridge will be there, and it will be there. It's a mother, beautiful bridge, and it's gonna be there. Ok?"

We've discussed the faith aspect of this quote, but now we must focus on the object of that faith: the "mother, beautiful bridge."

Later, when his tank breaks down, Oddball refers to it with the same reverence: "It's a mother beautiful tank."

This is not just a verbal tic, a simple, colourful expletive.

This is the Doctrine of Sacred Tools. It is the profound, yet utterly practical, practice of seeing the divine not in a distant, abstract heaven, but in the mundane, functional objects you use to navigate your life. Your car, your computer, your kitchen knife, your favourite pen—these are not just things. They are your tanks. They are your bridges. And they are mother, beautiful.

This doctrine teaches us to cultivate a relationship of love, respect, and appreciation for the tools of our craft, whatever that craft may be. In a disposable culture that constantly encourages us to upgrade, replace, and treat objects as temporary, Oddballism asks us to form a deep, almost spiritual bond with our equipment.

This bond is built on three core practices, each of which transforms a simple utility into a sacred partner in your journey.

The Three Pillars of Sacred Tool Doctrine

1. The Practice of Naming Beauty: The Cognitive Reframing

Oddball doesn't just see a bridge; he sees a beautiful bridge. He doesn't just have a tank; he has a beautiful tank. This simple act of naming is profoundly transformative. When you call an object beautiful, you change your relationship to it from one of mere utility to one of aesthetic appreciation and respect. You begin to notice its design, its efficiency, its character, and the sheer ingenuity that went into its creation.

You begin to love it.

This practice is deeply rooted in modern psychology, specifically in the concept of cognitive reframing. By consciously choosing the language of appreciation—"mother, beautiful"—you are literally rewiring your brain's perception of the object. Neuroscience tells us that expressing gratitude, even for an inanimate object, activates the brain's reward pathways, increasing feelings of well-being and reducing stress associated with perceived scarcity or dissatisfaction. Ancient philosophy, particularly Stoicism, echoes this by urging us to appreciate what we have, rather than lament what we lack. The Stoic practice of *premeditatio malorum* (premeditation of evils) is often paired with a deep appreciation for present comforts, and Oddball's naming of beauty is the positive, active side of that coin.

Case Study: The Architect and the Sketchbook.

Consider Elena, a 45-year-old architect in a high-pressure firm.

She found herself constantly frustrated, feeling that her digital tools—the powerful CAD software, the sleek tablet—were obstacles rather than aids. She was always waiting for an update, a crash, or a new feature.

Her work felt sterile.

Following the Doctrine of Sacred Tools, she started with her oldest, most reliable tool: a simple, leather-bound sketchbook she had used since college. She began calling it her "Mother Beautiful Blueprint," a title that acknowledged its role as the foundation of all her digital creations.

She spent 30 minutes each morning alone with the sketchbook, treating it with the reverence of a sacred text. She sharpened her pencil with care, felt the texture of the paper, and consciously appreciated the simple, reliable technology of graphite on cellulose. This small shift reframed her entire day. When she moved to her computer, she no longer saw a frustrating machine, but a powerful extension of her "Blueprint," a tool that magnified the beauty she had already named. Her frustration dissolved, replaced by a focused, appreciative flow.

Start practising this today. Look at the tools you use every day. Find the beauty in them. Your laptop is not just a machine; it's a mother, beautiful portal to all the world's information. Your car is not just a means of transportation; it's a mother, a beautiful chariot of freedom.

Speak this appreciation out loud. It will feel strange at first, but it will rewire your brain to see the sacred in the ordinary, transforming your environment from a collection of obstacles into a gallery of beautiful, functional partners.

2. The Practice of Mastery and Modification: The Extension of Self

Oddball's love for his tank is not just abstract; it is born from a deep, practical understanding.

He and his crew have modified it to be the fastest in the European Theatre. They have added a pipe to the gun and a loudspeaker for music. They have made it their own. This is the second level of devotion: you must master your tools. Understand their quirks, their strengths, their weaknesses. And then, you must make them your own. Customise them. Adapt them to your specific needs.

Your workspace, your software, your daily routines—these are all tanks that can be modified. When you invest your own creativity, time, and effort into your tools, your love for them deepens exponentially. They cease to be external objects and become an extension of you. This concept aligns perfectly with the psychological principle of *The Endowment Effect*, where we place a higher value on things we own or have invested effort into.

By modifying your tools, you are literally endowing them with a piece of your own identity and labour, making them invaluable.

Practical Application: The Customised Digital Cockpit.

Take the example of Marcus, a freelance writer who felt overwhelmed by the sheer number of apps and digital services he used. His "tank" was his entire digital workflow, which constantly broke down under the weight of notifications and inefficient handoffs.

His modification process began with a ruthless audit. He deleted every app he hadn't used in a month. He then spent a dedicated weekend learning the advanced keyboard shortcuts for his primary writing software. He customised the colour scheme, created a set of macros for his most common formatting tasks, and even wrote a small script to automatically back up his work every hour.

He didn't buy a new computer; he mastered and modified the one he had. His efficiency tripled, but more importantly, his relationship with his computer changed. It was no longer a generic box; it was his cockpit, perfectly tuned to his specific needs, a mother, beautiful machine that spoke his language.

This mastery breeds a confidence that no amount of shiny new hardware can replicate.

3. The Practice of Trust and Forgiveness: The Acceptance of Imperfection

Even a mother, beautiful tank breaks down. This is inevitable. The uninitiated, like Big Joe, react with anger and frustration. "Why the hell aren't you up there helping them?" The Wave Rider reacts with the calm patience of Oddball.

He knows the tank is not perfect. He accepts its flaws. He trusts that it will be fixed. This is a crucial part of the doctrine. You must learn to forgive your tools when they fail you. Your computer will crash. Your car will get a flat tyre. Your favourite pen will run out of ink.

This is where the deep humanity of Oddballism shines through. It is a lesson in radical acceptance. We often project our own anxieties and perfectionism onto our tools. When they fail, we feel personally betrayed, as if the universe is conspiring against us.

Oddball reminds us that tools are merely physical manifestations of human effort, and human effort is inherently flawed. To forgive the tool is to forgive the human condition. Do not curse it. Do not hit it with negative waves. Thank it for its service, have faith in its repair, and maybe enjoy some wine and cheese while you wait.

The pause is not a failure; it is a necessary maintenance break for both you and your equipment.

The Philosophical Edge: Heraclitus and the Flow.

This practice connects directly to the ancient Greek philosophy of Heraclitus, who famously stated that "No man ever steps in the same river twice, for it is not the same river and he is not the same man."

Everything is in a state of flux, including your tools. They are not static, perfect entities; they are dynamic systems that constantly age, wear down, and require maintenance. To trust and forgive is to accept this fundamental truth of the universe.

It is understood that the value of the tool lies not in its immutability but in its reliability over time, even with necessary interruptions.

SUB-SECTION: THE EDGE CASE OF THE DISPOSABLE TOOL

A common objection to the Doctrine of Sacred Tools is the modern reality of the truly disposable item—the plastic fork, the single-use battery, the cheap piece of furniture. How can one find the "mother, beautiful" in something designed to be thrown away?

Oddballism provides a nuanced answer: the sacredness is not inherent in the object's material value, but in its functional purpose and the respect for the resources it represents. Even a disposable tool, for the brief moment it is in your hand, is serving a purpose. The practice of Naming Beauty in this context becomes an appreciation for the ingenuity of mass production and the convenience it provides.

The practice of Mastery becomes the efficient, mindful use of the item before its disposal. And the practice of Trust and Forgiveness becomes the acceptance of its designed obsolescence, coupled with a commitment to responsible disposal. You treat the tool with respect while it is in your service, and you respect the planet by ensuring its lifecycle ends properly. The doctrine is not about hoarding; it is about mindfulness in consumption.

THE NEUROBIOLOGY OF TOOL-BODY INTEGRATION

Modern neuroscience offers a fascinating explanation for why this doctrine works so well. The concept is called *peripersonal* space and tool-body assimilation. Studies have shown that when we use a tool—a hammer, a tennis racket, or even a long stick—our brain's map of our own body temporarily extends to include the tool. The neurons that fire when something touches our hand will also fire when the tip of the stick touches something. The tool literally becomes an extension of our physical self.

Oddball's reverence for his tank is a perfect, intuitive expression of this neurobiological reality.

He doesn't just drive the tank; he is the tank. When he calls it "mother, beautiful," he is acknowledging the profound, subconscious integration of that machine into his own being. By consciously treating your tools as sacred extensions of yourself, you are simply aligning your conscious mind with what your brain is already doing. This alignment reduces cognitive dissonance, increases focus, and allows for a smoother, more intuitive interaction with the world. You move from using a tool to being a tool-user, a seamless, integrated system ready to ride the wave.

Step-by-Step Guidance: The Sacred Tool Ritual

To fully integrate the Doctrine of Sacred Tools into your daily life, you need a ritual. A ritual is simply a conscious, repeated action that assigns meaning to the mundane.

Step 1: The Morning Naming (5 minutes). Before you begin your work, select your primary tool for the day—your laptop, your coffee maker, your running shoes. Hold it, look at it, and mentally or verbally name its beauty. "This is my Mother Beautiful Coffee Maker, the engine of my day." Focus on its function and its design. This sets a positive, appreciative tone for your interaction with it.

Step 2: The Midday Mastery Check (10 minutes). Take a short break and perform a small act of mastery or modification. This doesn't have to be a major overhaul.

It could be:

• Cleaning your keyboard.

• Organising the files on your desktop.

• Learning one new shortcut in your software.

• Wiping down your workbench.

This investment of time reinforces the Endowment Effect and deepens your bond with the tool.

Step 3: The Evening Forgiveness (2 minutes). At the end of the day, reflect on any moment when your tools failed you. Did your internet connection drop? Did your pen leak? Instead of dwelling on the frustration, practice forgiveness. "Thank you, Mother Beautiful Internet, for the hours of connection you provided. I forgive your momentary lapse, and I trust you will be there tomorrow." This releases the negative emotional charge and prevents resentment from building up, ensuring you start the next day with a clean slate of appreciation.

Your life is filled with tanks and bridges. They are the objects and systems that carry you toward your gold. By treating them as sacred, by loving them, mastering them, and forgiving them, you transform your relationship with the material world. You cease to be a mere consumer of things and become a collaborator with them. You build a crew that includes not just people, but the mother, beautiful tools that help you on your way.

Part Four:

The Doctrine of Anti-Heroism and Independence

We have fortified our minds against negative waves and learned to find beauty in the here and now. We are calm, present, and grounded. But the world will not leave us alone. It will constantly try to pull us back into its drama, to cast us in a role we did not choose. It will demand that we become heroes.

This is, perhaps, the most seductive and dangerous trap of all. The desire for glory, for recognition, for a "moment of glory," is a powerful one. It appeals to our ego and our deep-seated need for validation.

The Doctrine of Anti-Heroism and Independence is our shield against this temptation. It is the wisdom to understand that the greatest victory is not winning the battle, but avoiding it altogether, and the greatest freedom is defining the terms of your own existence.

Chapter Eleven:

The Weird Sandwich of Heroism

Crapgame: "Hey, Oddball, this is your moment of glory. And you're chickening out!"

Oddball: "To a New Yorker like you, a hero is some type of weird sandwich, not some nut who takes on three Tigers."

This is one of the most profound and revolutionary statements in the entire Book of Oddball. In this single, brilliant metaphor, the Prophet deconstructs and dismisses the entire cultural obsession with heroism.

He doesn't just reject the label; he redefines the whole concept of a life well lived, positioning self-preservation and rational choice as the highest virtues, far above the fleeting, often fatal pursuit of "glory."

Let's analyse the metaphor. A "weird sandwich." What does it mean? It's something constructed, something artificial, and ultimately, something unsatisfying. It's a collection of ingredients—bravery, sacrifice, risk, public acclaim—slapped together and given a name.

It might be impressive to look at, it might get your picture in the paper, but it has no real, lasting nutritional substance. It's a temporary fix, a performance, a distraction from the simple, nourishing meal of a peaceful, self-directed life. And, crucially, it's not something Oddball wants to eat. He would much rather have some simple bread and cheese, the sustenance of a life lived on his own terms, free from the expectations of others.

Crapgame, representing society's voice, sees a situation—facing three enemy tanks—and immediately frames it as a "moment of glory." This is how the world traps us. It presents us with dangerous, often stupid, situations and tells us that enduring them will make us heroes.

It's a bait and switch. The "glory" is the cheese in the mousetrap, a shiny, tempting reward for an act of self-destruction. The world loves a hero because a hero is a person who can be manipulated into doing the dirty work. They are the ultimate tool, sacrificing their own well-being for a narrative that benefits everyone but themselves.

Oddball sees right through it. He re-frames the situation with brutal honesty. It's not a moment of glory; it's being a "nut who takes on three Tigers." He strips away the romantic language and reveals the suicidal reality.

This is the first practice of the Anti-Hero: radical honesty about risk and reward. The hero myth demands that you ignore the risk and inflate the reward. Oddball demands that you do the opposite: calculate the risk with cold precision and deflate the reward to its true, often worthless, value.

The Psychology of the Hero Sandwich: Why We Crave the Weird

The hero myth is so pervasive because it taps into deep-seated psychological needs.

Modern psychology, particularly in the realm of self-esteem and social validation, offers a clear explanation for why people line up for the "weird sandwich."

First, there is the need for external validation. In a complex, often anonymous world, being labelled a "hero" is a shortcut to significance. It's a massive, immediate injection of social capital. People confuse being important with being valuable.

The hero is important to the narrative, but the Oddball is valuable to himself. The hero's self-worth is outsourced to the crowd; the Oddball's self-worth is an internal, non-negotiable asset.

Second, the hero narrative offers a powerful, if temporary, escape from existential anxiety. The philosopher Ernest Becker, in The Denial of Death, argued that much of human culture is an elaborate defence mechanism against the terror of our own mortality. Heroism, in this context, is a form of "immortality project." By performing a great, selfless act, the hero believes they will live on in others' memories, transcending physical death.

Oddball, however, chooses a more practical form of immortality: staying alive. He understands that the best way to ensure your story continues is to stick around and write the next chapter yourself.

Third, the hero sandwich is a product of social conditioning and moral licensing. From childhood stories to blockbuster movies, we are taught that self-sacrifice is the highest moral good. This conditioning makes us feel guilty for prioritising our own needs. The hero is the one who says, "My life is less important than the cause." The Oddball is the one who says, "My life is the only thing I have, and I will protect it fiercely."

This is not selfishness; it is self-stewardship. It is the recognition that you cannot serve others from an empty cup, and that the world is better off with a well-fed, well-rested, and alive Oddball than a dead hero.

Case Study 1: The Corporate Martyr, Sarah

Sarah, a 34-year-old marketing director in a high-growth tech startup, was a classic consumer of the "weird sandwich."

Her company culture celebrated "hustle" and "grind." Her boss, a charismatic but demanding CEO, constantly praised employees who "went above and beyond," often saying, "You're a hero for the team."

Sarah's moment of glory came when a technical glitch threatened a major product launch. For three weeks, she worked 18-hour days, sleeping on a couch in the office, fuelled by energy drinks and the promise of a massive bonus and public recognition.

She "saved the launch." The CEO called her a "corporate warrior" in the all-hands meeting. She got a plaque and a small raise. The weird sandwich was served.

But the cost was immense. Her marriage was strained to the breaking point. Her health deteriorated—she developed chronic insomnia and anxiety. The "glory" lasted for about 72 hours. Then, the next crisis arrived, and the CEO was already looking for the next "hero." Sarah was burnt out and resentful, and realised the company saw her not as a person but as a resource to be exploited.

Applying Oddball's wisdom, Sarah began to practice radical honesty about risk and reward.

She asked herself: Who benefits from me being a hero here? The answer was the CEO and the shareholders. Is the potential reward (a plaque and a small raise) worth the cost (my marriage and my health)? The answer was a resounding no.

Her Anti-Hero move was to set a firm boundary. When the next crisis hit, she worked her contracted hours, delegated effectively, and went home at 6 PM. Her boss was initially furious, accusing her of "chickening out."

Sarah replied, "I'm not a nut who takes on three Tigers, sir. I'm a professional risk manager. This project is important, but it is not worth my life. I will deliver excellent work within sustainable parameters."

She chose the simple bread and cheese of a balanced life over the weird sandwich of corporate martyrdom. She was no longer the star of the show, but she was, for the first time, the director of her own life.

Deeper Exploration: Oddball's Wisdom and Ancient Philosophy

Oddball's rejection of the hero myth is not a modern invention; it echoes profound truths found in ancient philosophical traditions, particularly Stoicism and Taoism.

Stoicism and the Sphere of Control: The Stoics, like Epictetus and Marcus Aurelius, taught that true peace comes from distinguishing between what is within your control (your judgments, intentions, and actions) and what is outside of it (external events, other people's opinions, and outcomes).

The hero's pursuit of glory is entirely focused on external outcomes—saving the day, winning the medal, earning the applause. These are all outside the hero's control. Oddball, the Anti-Hero, focuses on what he can control: his own survival, his own preparation, and his own rational assessment of the situation.

His decision not to take on three Tigers is a perfect Stoic move: it is a rational action based on a clear-eyed assessment of reality, prioritising the internal good of self-preservation over the external, uncontrollable good of public acclaim.

Taoism and the Power of Wu Wei: The Taoist concept of Wu Wei, often translated as "non-action" or "effortless action," is the philosophical blueprint for Oddball's approach. Wu Wei is not about doing nothing; it's about aligning with the natural flow of things, avoiding unnecessary struggle, and knowing when to stop.

The hero rushes in, struggling against the current. The Oddball, like the Taoist sage, understands that sometimes the most effective action is to withdraw, to wait, or to refuse to participate in a foolish conflict.

His refusal to be a "nut who takes on three Tigers" is the ultimate Wu Wei. He recognises that the situation is fundamentally unnatural and destructive, and his best course of action is to step aside and let the natural order (or the enemy's own mistakes) play out, or to find a less direct, more intelligent solution.

The hero seeks to conquer; the Oddball seeks to flow

Practical Applications: The Anti-Hero's Toolkit

The shift from hero to Anti-Hero is a fundamental change in mindset that requires practical techniques. Here is a step-by-step guide to politely declining the weird sandwich in your own life:

1. The Cost-Benefit Audit (Radical Honesty)

Before committing to any high-effort, high-risk endeavour, perform a ruthless audit, stripping away all emotional and romantic language.

- **Step 1: Define the "Tiger":** Clearly and factually state the risk. (e.g., "Working 80 hours this week," "Lending a large sum of money to a financially unstable relative," "Taking on a project with an impossible deadline.")

- **Step 2: Define the "Glory":** Clearly and factually state the reward. (e.g., "A pat on the back," "A promise of future favour," "Avoiding a difficult conversation," "A small, non-guaranteed bonus.")

- **Step 3: Calculate the "Nut" Factor:** Assign a numerical value (1-10) to the potential damage to your health, finances, relationships, and sanity. Assign a numerical value (1-10) to the guaranteed benefit.

If the "Nut" factor is higher than the "Glory" factor, you are being a nut.

• **Oddball's Rule:** Never accept a trade where the cost is a fundamental part of your well-being (health, time, peace) and the reward is purely external (praise, money, status).

2. The Language Re-Frame (The Anti-Hero's Vocabulary)

The language we use shapes our reality. Stop using heroic language to describe poor choices.

By calling things what they are, you remove the emotional appeal of the "weird sandwich" and can make a rational decision.

3. The Art of the Strategic Retreat

The hero is defined by their advance; the Anti-Hero is defined by their strategic retreat. Retreat is not failure; it is a tactical manoeuvre to preserve resources for a more winnable fight.

Case Study 2: The Over-Committed Volunteer. David.

David, a retired engineer, was asked to be the treasurer for three different non-profit organisations in his town. He felt a deep sense of obligation and was praised for his "selfless commitment." He became a "hero" of the community. Soon, he was spending 40 hours a week on bookkeeping, missing time with his grandchildren, and feeling overwhelmed. He was taking on three Tigers of administrative burden. His strategic retreat was simple but difficult. He resigned from two of the boards, citing a need to focus his energy.

People were disappointed. Some were openly critical. They tried to guilt him with the "hero" language. David held firm. He explained, "I can do a great job for one organisation, or a mediocre, stressed-out job for three. I choose to be effective, not a martyr."

He chose to be the Oddball, preserving his time and energy for the things that truly mattered to him—his family and the one organisation he could genuinely help. His effectiveness in that single role increased tenfold.

Connecting to Modern Neuroscience: The Dopamine Trap

Neuroscience provides a biological underpinning for Oddball's wisdom. The pursuit of the "weird sandwich" is often a pursuit of a dopamine hit. When a hero performs a great act and receives public praise, the brain is flooded with dopamine, the neurotransmitter associated with reward and motivation.

This creates a powerful, addictive feedback loop: Risk -> Performance -> Praise -> Dopamine.

The problem is that this loop is external and unsustainable. The hero becomes dependent on the external stimulus (praise, crisis) to feel good. They are, in effect, dopamine junkies, constantly seeking the next "moment of glory" to get their fix.

Oddball's path, the path of self-stewardship and rational choice, is about cultivating internal rewards. It's about the quiet satisfaction of a job well done, the peace of a clear conscience, and the deep, steady contentment of a life lived in alignment with one's own values.

This is a serotonin and oxytocin-based reward system—calmer, more sustainable, and entirely within your control. The Anti-Hero chooses peace over performance, and in doing so, chooses a healthier, more resilient brain chemistry.

The Freedom to Be Ordinary

The path of the Anti-Hero is not for everyone. It requires you to disappoint people. It requires you to be okay with not being the star of the show. It requires the courage to be ordinary, to prioritise survival and well-being over the applause of the crowd.

The ultimate freedom Oddball offers is the freedom from the tyranny of expectation. You are free from the expectation to be a saviour, a martyr, or a legend. You are free to be a person who makes rational choices, who values their own life, and who understands that true heroism is not about facing down three Tigers but about having the wisdom to know when to drive around them.

Your life is more valuable than any medal, any promotion, any pat on the back. Reject the weird sandwich. Choose the simple, nourishing meal of a life lived on your own terms. That is the highest form of wisdom, and the most enduring form of glory.

Chapter Twelve:

No Baby, We Aint

German tank commander: "You... the American army!"

Oddball: "No, baby, we ain't."

This is the Declaration of Independence of Oddballism. It is a short, simple, two-word sentence that contains a universe of freedom.

The German commander, trapped in his rigid worldview, can see Oddball and his crew only as a category: "the American army."

He projects a whole set of assumptions, rules, and expectations onto them based on that label. He assumes they are following orders, that they are part of the larger military machine, that they will behave predictably.

Oddball's response shatters that entire worldview. "No, baby, we ain't."

With these words, he rejects the label. He refuses the identity. He declares himself and his crew to be a sovereign entity, operating under their own rules.

The "baby" is not an insult; it's a term of pitying enlightenment. He's gently informing the German that he is playing a completely different game, one where the rules are self-authored, and the stakes are personal. This is the moment where the system's logic—the rigid, hierarchical, and predictable logic of war—collides with the fluid, entrepreneurial, and radically free logic of the Wave Rider.

The Doctrine of Radical Self-Definition

The world is constantly labelling us, and these labels are not benign. They are cognitive shortcuts, tools of social control, and psychological cages.

You are a "Democrat," a "Republican," a "manager," an "employee," a "parent," a "millennial," a "boomer." Each label comes with a pre-packaged set of beliefs, behaviours, and limitations. The world wants to put you in a box because it makes you predictable and easy to control. It simplifies the messy, terrifying complexity of a unique human being into a neat, manageable file folder.

To be a Wave Rider is to constantly and calmly say, "No, baby, I ain't." This is not about being difficult or contrarian; it is about reserving the right to be a complex, multi-faceted, and free individual. It is the refusal to be reduced to a demographic, a job title, or a political affiliation. It is the ultimate act of psychological sovereignty.

Consider the modern psychological landscape. Oddball's declaration is a perfect, pithy summary of what Self-Determination Theory (SDT) calls the need for autonomy. SDT posits that human beings have three innate psychological needs: competence, relatedness, and autonomy. When the world slaps a label on you—"You are a failed entrepreneur," "You are just a middle manager," "You are too sensitive"—it directly attacks your sense of autonomy. It attempts to define your potential and your behaviour from the outside. Oddball's response is the immediate, visceral defence of the self. It's the internal voice that says, "My actions are my own, and my identity is self-authored."

This is also the core of cognitive reframing, a technique central to Cognitive Behavioural Therapy (CBT).

CBT teaches us to challenge the automatic negative thoughts and labels we apply to ourselves. The world's labels are just external versions of these limiting beliefs. When you hear the inner critic say, "You're a procrastinator," or the external world say, "You're a cog in the machine," the Oddball response is the same: No, baby, I ain't.

You are not the label. You are the consciousness observing the label, and you have the power to reject it.

Case Study 1: The Architect and the Golden Handcuffs

Meet Elias, a 38-year-old architect in a major metropolitan firm.

For 15 years, Elias had been defined by his title: "Senior Associate, Future Projects Division." This label came with a six-figure salary, a corner office, and the assumption that his life's mission was to climb the corporate ladder until he became a partner. He was, by all external measures, "The Successful Architect."

The label was a cage. He spent his days designing soulless, high-rise luxury condos, projects that paid well but left him creatively hollow. His true passion was sustainable, low-cost housing, a field his firm considered "unprofitable." Every time he tried to pivot, his mentor would remind him, "Elias, you're a Senior Associate. You have a reputation. You have to think about the bottom line."

The world was telling him, "You are the American Army of Corporate Architecture."

One evening, staring at a blueprint for a glass tower, he heard the echo of Oddball. He realised the label was not a description of his being, but a description of his function within a system he no longer believed in. He was not "The Successful Architect"; he was Elias, a man who loved building things that mattered.

His declaration of independence was simple: He quit. Not to another firm, but to start a non-profit design collective focused on community-led, sustainable projects. The world called him "irresponsible," "naïve," and "a fool to throw away that salary."

His old colleagues said, "You're an architect, you should be building monuments, not sheds."

Elias's internal response, the Wave Rider's mantra, was firm: No, baby, I ain't. I am not the label of the corporate world. I am the sovereign entity that defines its own purpose. He traded the golden handcuffs for the freedom of self-definition, and in doing so, he found his true competence and his true self.

The Ancient Roots of Radical Self-Definition

Oddball's wisdom is not new; it is a modern, slang-infused echo of ancient philosophical traditions. The Stoics, for instance, were masters of this psychological separation. They taught the concept of dichotomy of control, distinguishing between what is up to us (our judgments, opinions, desires, and actions) and what is not up to us (everything else, including other people's opinions and the labels they assign us).

When the German commander labels Oddball, he is attempting to control Oddball's identity, which is an external, uncontrollable factor.

Oddball's rejection is a purely Stoic move: "Your label is not up to me. My identity is."

Epictetus, the former slave who became a great Stoic teacher, would have nodded approvingly. He taught that true freedom lies in the internal fortress of the mind, where no external force—no master, no emperor, no label—can penetrate without your consent.

The Wave Rider understands that the world's labels are merely impressions or external judgments. By refusing to internalise them, we reclaim our inner citadel. This is the deep connection between Oddball's street-smart philosophy and the rigorous mental discipline of the ancients. Both are paths to freedom through the fierce protection of one's inner life.

The Vacuum and the Private Enterprise Operation

This doctrine also contains the key to finding your mission. Oddball and his crew are not the army. So what are they? As Kelly explains, "We're just a private enterprise operation."

They have opted out of the army's mission (winning the war) and created their own (getting the gold). They have become entrepreneurs of their own destiny.

This is a vital step in the Oddballist journey. Once you have rejected the labels and missions that the world has tried to impose on you, a vacuum is created. You must fill that vacuum with your own purpose. You must define your own "gold." The danger is that most people, terrified of the vacuum, rush to fill it with the next available label or mission—a new job, a new political cause, a new hobby that quickly becomes a rigid identity.

The Wave Rider resists this urge. They sit in the quiet of the vacuum, listening for the sound of their own engine.

The transition from being a labelled entity to a private enterprise operation is not a single leap, but a process with three distinct stages:

Sub-Section: The Three Stages of Oddballist Entrepreneurship

Case Study 2: The Mother and the Digital Label

Consider Sarah, a 45-year-old mother of three who had spent the last decade defined by the label "Stay-at-Home Mom."

This label, while noble, had become a psychological trap. In the digital age, it was compounded by the label "Ex-Marketing

Executive," a ghost of her former self that haunted her LinkedIn profile. She felt she had to perform the role of the perfect mother—the organic cook, the tireless chauffeur, the flawless event planner—a role amplified and judged by social media.

Her crisis came when her youngest started school. The world expected her to either return to her old, high-pressure career (re-embracing the "Executive" label) or double down on the "Mom" label by joining every school committee. She felt a profound sense of dread at both options. The labels paralysed her.
One afternoon, while scrolling through a feed of perfectly curated family photos, she felt the familiar shame of not measuring up.

The internal voice whispered, "You are a Stay-at-Home Mom, you should be doing more for the community."

She stopped. She thought of Oddball. No, baby, I ain't. I am not a Stay-at-Home Mom. I am not an Ex-Executive. I am Sarah.

Her "gold" was not a career or a committee. It was Creative Connection. She realised she missed the strategic problem-solving of her old job, but she also cherished the flexibility of her current life. Her private enterprise operation became a small, highly specialised consulting business helping local non-profits with their digital strategy, working only during school hours.

The world tried to label her "Freelancer," "Part-Timer," or "Hobbyist." She simply smiled. "I'm a private enterprise operation," she'd tell her husband. She had defined her own terms of engagement, rejecting the binary choice the world had offered her, and in doing so, she found a sustainable, fulfilling purpose.

Defining Your Gold: The Wave Rider's Treasure Map

What is your gold? It doesn't have to be $16 million in bullion. Your gold is whatever you decide is worth your time, your energy, and your risk. It is the self-authored mission that replaces the world's imposed mission.

Practical Application: The Gold-Definition Technique

To define your gold, you must first clear the noise. This is a step-by-step process of de-labelling and re-defining:

Step 1: The Label Audit (Rejection)

• List the five most common labels the world applies to you (e.g., "Accountant," "Single," "Overweight," "Introvert," "Failure").

• For each label, write the Oddball response: No, baby, I ain't.

• Then, write a single sentence that describes the function the label describes, without judgment. (e.g., "Accountant" becomes "I perform financial analysis for a living.") This separates your being from your doing.

Step 2: The Resentment Inventory (Definition)

• List the five things you most resent doing or being forced to do in your current life. (e.g., "Attending pointless meetings," "Pretending to care about my boss's golf game," "Always being the one to organise family events.")

• Resentment is a compass pointing toward a violation of your autonomy. The opposite of each resentment is a clue to your gold. (e.g., Resenting "pointless meetings" suggests a gold of Efficiency and Impact).

Step 3: The Three Tigers Test (Execution)

• Oddball's crew was willing to take on three Tiger tanks for the gold. What is the equivalent "Tiger" in your life?
This is the risk, the sacrifice, or the difficult thing you would willingly face for your self-defined mission.

• List three "Tigers" you would face for your potential gold.

• Tiger 1: The risk of financial instability.

• Tiger 2: The disapproval of your family/peers.

• Tiger 3: The long, lonely hours of building something from scratch.

• If you can honestly say, "Yes, I would face all three of those for this mission," you have found your gold. If you hesitate, the mission is not truly your own.
Your gold must be your gold. It cannot be something your parents, your spouse, or your society told you to want. You must find the thing that makes your heart say, "For that, I would take on three Tigers."

The Neuroscience of Self-Authorship

The power of Oddball's declaration is rooted in the brain's reward system. When we act in alignment with an externally imposed goal (a label's expectation), the reward is often extrinsic—a paycheck, a promotion, or social approval. This engages the brain's extrinsic motivation system, which is powerful but ultimately unsustainable and prone to burnout.

When we act in pursuit of a self-authored goal—our "gold"—we engage the intrinsic motivation system. This system, tied to the prefrontal cortex and the ventral tegmental area, releases dopamine not only upon achievement but also during the process of working toward the goal. This is the feeling of flow, of deep, satisfying engagement.

Oddball's crew, as a "private enterprise operation," is intrinsically motivated. They are not fighting for a flag or a general; they are fighting for their own gold. This is why they are so resourceful, so unconventional, and so effective. They are in a state of flow, a psychological state in which action and awareness merge, and the work itself becomes the reward.

The Wave Rider understands that the most powerful fuel for human action is not duty or fear, but self-directed purpose.

When you have defined your gold, you are no longer just a rebel. You are a revolutionary.

You are no longer just saying "no" to the world's missions; you are saying "yes" to your own.

You have become your own private enterprise operation. And that is the beginning of true freedom. The world will try to put a new label on you—"Visionary," "Eccentric," "Success Story"—but you will know the truth.

You are simply a Wave Rider, and you ain't nobody's baby but your own.

Chapter Thirteen:

The Private Enterprise Operation

Oddball: "We see our role as essentially defensive in nature. While our armies are advancing so fast and everyone's knocking themselves out to be heroes, we are holding ourselves in reserve in case the Krauts mount a counteroffensive which threatens Paris... or maybe even New York. Then we can move in and stop them. But for 1.6 million dollars, we could become heroes for three days."

This quote, delivered with a straight face to a sceptical Kelly, is a masterclass in creating a personal narrative that justifies your independence. It is the business plan for your "private enterprise operation." It is the philosophical foundation for a life lived on your own terms, a life where you are the sole CEO, strategist, and shareholder.

Let's be honest: Oddball's explanation is magnificent nonsense. The idea that his three beat-up Sherman tanks are a strategic reserve for the defence of New York is patently absurd. But it's a brilliant absurdity. It's a story he tells himself and others that allows him to do exactly what he wants to do: stay out of the main fighting and preserve his own life and the lives of his crew.

He is not rejecting the war; he is simply rewriting his role in it. He is not a deserter; he is a strategic asset, a reserve force, a private contractor with a very specific, high-value mission.

This is the Doctrine of the Personal Narrative. You cannot simply opt out of the world's systems; you must create a new system for yourself, complete with its own logic, its own mission statement, and its own justification.

Your personal narrative is the story you tell yourself about why you do what you do. It is the invisible shield that deflects the negative waves of societal expectation, family pressure, and self-doubt.

Notice the key elements of Oddball's narrative—the elements you must incorporate into your own:

• **It sounds plausible (if you don't think about it too hard):** A "defensive role," a "strategic reserve." He uses the language of the system he is rejecting to justify his rejection. He's not a deserter; he's a strategist. He borrows credibility from the very structure he is subverting.

• **It's grandiose and humorous:** The idea of defending New York is so over-the-top that it signals he's not taking any of this too seriously. Humour is a key ingredient in a successful personal narrative. It keeps you from becoming a self-important ideologue. It's the oil that keeps the gears of your independence from seizing up with self-seriousness.

• **It defines a clear boundary:** "While our armies are advancing so fast and everyone's knocking themselves out to be heroes, we are holding ourselves in reserve." He creates a clear distinction between "them" (the hero-seekers, the rule-followers) and "us" (the strategic, self-preserving elite). This boundary is crucial for maintaining focus and preventing mission creep.

• **It has a price:** "But for 1.6 million dollars, we could become heroes for three days." This is the most important part. His independence is not absolute. It can be bought, but only for a price that aligns with his real mission (getting the gold). He is not a slave to his own narrative; he is its master. He knows his value, and he is ready to negotiate.

To operate as a private enterprise, you must craft your own narrative. Let's look at a modern case study.

Case Study: The Architect and the Strategic Sabbatical

Meet Elias, a 38-year-old architect in a high-pressure firm in Chicago.

He was on the partner track, working 80-hour weeks, and his soul was slowly being paved over with concrete and glass. He knew he needed a break, a year to travel and study sustainable design in Scandinavia, but the corporate world would see this as a weakness, a derailment.

The negative wave was a tsunami: "You're throwing away a decade of work! You'll never get back on the partner track! You're being irresponsible!"

Elias didn't quit; he launched his "Strategic Sabbatical." His new personal narrative, which he articulated to his firm, his family, and most importantly, himself, was this:

"I am entering a phase of strategic intellectual and creative development. The firm's future depends on integrating world-class sustainable practices, and I am the only one willing to undertake the necessary deep-dive research. While others are focused on the immediate quarterly projects, I am holding myself in reserve to cultivate the cutting-edge knowledge that will secure our competitive advantage for the next decade. This is not a break; it is a high-value, self-funded R&D mission."

See the difference? It's the same action—he left his job for a year—but the story is better. It's a story that gives him dignity, purpose, and a shield against the negative waves of others.

He framed his self-care as a strategic business decision.

He used the language of the system (R&D, competitive advantage, strategic development) to justify his departure from the system's norms. He returned a year later, not as a prodigal son, but as a specialist with unique, in-demand knowledge, and he negotiated a new, more flexible role on his own terms. He became the master of his narrative, not its victim.

The Neuroscience of Self-Authorship

This is not just motivational fluff; it is grounded in how the human brain works. Modern psychology and neuroscience confirm the power of the personal narrative. Our brains are fundamentally storytelling machines.

The prefrontal cortex, the seat of executive function, constantly weaves a coherent story from our experiences, memories, and future projections. This story is what psychologists call the "self-concept."

When your external actions (like quitting a high-paying job) conflict with your internal story (e.g., "I am a responsible, successful person"), you experience cognitive dissonance, which is deeply uncomfortable and often leads to self-sabotage. Oddball's narrative, however absurd, is internally consistent. He is a strategist, and strategists hold themselves in reserve. His actions align perfectly with his self-concept.

To apply this, you must engage in Self-Authorship, a concept explored in developmental psychology. It means moving from being a character in a story written by others (society, parents, boss) to becoming the author of your own story.

Practical Application: Crafting Your Private Enterprise Narrative

Here is a step-by-step guide to writing your own Doctrine of the Personal Narrative:

1. Identify the Negative Wave: What is the societal or internal pressure you are trying to escape? (e.g., "I must work a 9-to-5 job," "I must be married by 30," "My worth is tied to my salary.") Write it down clearly.

2. Define Your True Mission (The Gold): What is the real, underlying goal of your independence? (e.g., "Creative freedom," "Time with family," "Mastery of a specific craft," "Financial self-sufficiency.")

3. Borrow the Language of the System: Find the high-status, strategic-sounding terms from the world you are leaving. (e.g., Optimisation, Strategic Reserve, Intellectual Property, Competitive Advantage, Deep Work, Portfolio Diversification).

4. Write the Absurdly Plausible Justification: Combine your True Mission and the borrowed language into a statement that justifies your action. It must be a little over-the-top, a little humorous, and entirely self-serving. Example: "I am not taking a gap year; I am engaging in a high-intensity, self-directed, global market research initiative to optimise my human capital for the next economic cycle."

5. Set the Price (The Boundary): Define what it would take for you to re-engage with the old system. This is your non-negotiable boundary. (e.g., "I will only take a full-time job if it offers 100% remote work and a 4-day work week. That is the price of my current freedom.")

This narrative is not a lie; it is a re-frame. It is the ultimate act of cognitive control, ensuring your internal story supports your external freedom.

Part Five:

The Doctrine of Competence & Creativity

We have now arrived at the pillar that separates Oddballism from simple, passive hedonism. A lesser philosophy might stop at rejecting negativity, enjoying simple pleasures, and declaring independence. This is the path of the stereotypical slacker, the lazy dropout. But Oddball is no slacker.

He is a master. His laid-back demeanour is not born of apathy; it is earned through deep, abiding competence.

This is the Doctrine of Competence and Creativity. It is the understanding that true calm, true freedom, and proper safety come from being exceptionally good at what you do. It's about loving your craft, mastering your tools, and using your imagination to create an unfair advantage. This is the pillar that gives Oddballism its power. It's what makes it a philosophy for winners, not just survivors.

Oddball's competence is not in following orders; it is in his mastery of his machine and his environment. He knows his Sherman tank, "The Private Enterprise," inside and out. He knows how to use the terrain, improvise, and keep his crew calm under pressure. His creativity is the application of that competence: the sound system, the paint job, the willingness to drive backwards to confuse the enemy. His competence gives him the right to his narrative. Without it, he's just a guy hiding in a tank. With it, he's a strategic reserve.

The Ancient Roots of Oddball's Mastery

This doctrine is not new; it echoes the wisdom of ancient philosophy. The Stoics, for instance, emphasised the importance of focusing only on what is within your control. Oddball doesn't control the war, the generals, or the supply lines. What he does control is his tank, his crew, and his attitude.

His mastery of his craft is his internal fortress.

- **Stoicism (Epictetus):** Focus on your prohairesis (moral purpose/will). For Oddball, his prohairesis is self-preservation and the acquisition of gold. His competence is the tool he uses to execute this purpose flawlessly.

- **Aristotle (Virtue Ethics):** The concept of techne (craftsmanship or art) and phronesis (practical wisdom). Oddball possesses both. His techne is his mechanical skill and driving ability; his phronesis is his ability to assess a chaotic situation and devise a creative, effective, and often unconventional solution.

The lesson is clear: Mastery is the prerequisite for true independence. You can't tell the world to leave you alone if you need the world to bail you out constantly. Your competence is your currency. Your creativity is your edge.

Case Study: The Freelancer and the Unfair Advantage

Consider Maya, a graphic designer who decided to go freelance. The initial negative wave was the fear of instability, the feast-or-famine cycle. She could have just been another designer on a crowded platform, constantly undercutting her price. Instead, she applied the Doctrine of Competence and Creativity.

1. Competence (Mastery): She didn't just master design software; she mastered the business of design. She became an expert in contract law for creatives, advanced SEO for portfolio sites, and the psychology of client communication. She didn't just deliver a logo; she offered a full, legally sound, strategically positioned brand identity package.

2. Creativity (The Edge): Her "unfair advantage" was her niche: she specialised in branding for sustainable food startups, a sector she deeply cared about. She developed a proprietary, 3-day "Brand Blitz" workshop that was expensive but guaranteed a full brand rollout. This was her sound system, her backward driving. It was a creative solution to the slow, drawn-out process of traditional design work.

Her personal narrative became: "I am not a freelancer; I am a high-value, rapid-deployment brand strategist. My competence allows me to charge a premium, and my creative process delivers faster, more effective outcomes than any agency. I have optimised my operation for maximum impact and minimum time-waste."

Maya's competence gave her the confidence to charge more, and her creative process gave her the time freedom she craved. She was no longer a commodity; she was a private enterprise operation, and her services were non-negotiable.

PRACTICAL APPLICATION: CULTIVATING COMPETENCE AND CREATIVITY

To build your own Private Enterprise Operation, you must actively cultivate both mastery and imagination.

1. The Competence Audit (Mastery):

- **Identify Your Core Tool:** What is the primary skill or tool of your operation? (e.g., coding, writing, public speaking, financial analysis).

- **The 10,000-Hour Myth Re-frame:** Forget the number. Focus on Deliberate Practice. Identify the 20% of your skill that yields 80% of the results, and dedicate focused, uncomfortable time to mastering only that 20%.

- **The "Can I Fix It?" Test:** Can you fix your own machine when it breaks? Can you troubleshoot the most complex problems in your field without calling for help? If not, your competence is incomplete.

Oddball could fix his tank. You must be able to fix your own operation.

2. The Creativity Engine (The Edge):

• **The Cross-Pollination Technique:** Creativity is often just connecting two things that don't belong together. Oddball put a sound system in a tank. What two disparate ideas can you combine in your field? (e.g., Financial analysis + Stand-up comedy = Engaging financial literacy course).

• **The "What If I Drove Backwards?" Question:** Always ask the opposite question. If everyone in your industry is moving forward (e.g., faster, cheaper, more features), what would happen if you drove backwards (e.g., slower, more expensive, fewer but higher-quality features)? This is where the unfair advantage is found.

• **The Play Imperative:** Oddball is always playing. He is not grimly executing a mission; he is enjoying the process. Dedicate time to "play" with your tools—use them in ways they weren't intended, just to see what happens. This is the wellspring of creative solutions.

The Private Enterprise Operation is the ultimate synthesis of these two doctrines. Your Personal Narrative is the story you tell the world, and your Competence and Creativity are the proof that makes the story true. You are not just surviving; you are thriving on your own terms, a strategic asset in a world of rule-followers, ready to move in and stop the counteroffensive—for a price, of course. And you'll be doing it with a smile, a good cigar, and a sound system blasting the perfect tune.

That is the Oddball way.

Chapter Fourteen:

Mastering the Mother Beautiful Tank

Oddball: "It's a mother beautiful tank."

This is not just a statement of aesthetic appreciation; it is a declaration of profound connection born from mastery. Oddball loves his tank because he knows his tank. He and his crew are not just operators; they are connoisseurs. They are artists whose medium is a 30-ton steel beast. This simple, profound statement—"It's a mother beautiful tank"—is the cornerstone of the Oddballist philosophy of competence. It signifies a relationship of deep respect, intimate knowledge, and earned confidence between a person and their chosen craft.

This chapter is about the spiritual necessity of being good at your job. And by "job," we mean your chosen craft, your primary function in the world, whether it's coding, carpentry, parenting, or painting. This is your "tank." The tank is the vehicle through which you express your unique value to the world. It is the crucible of your competence.

Why is competence so central to a philosophy of being laid-back? Because competence creates calm. Anxiety is born from uncertainty. When you don't know what you're doing, when you feel unprepared and out of your depth, your mind is a fertile ground for negative waves. You worry about failure, about being exposed as a fraud, about all the things that could go wrong. But when you have achieved mastery—when you know your craft inside and out—a deep sense of peace settles in.

You've seen it all before. You trust your skills. You know you can handle whatever comes your way. This is the difference between a frantic, reactive life and a deliberate, responsive one. The master is not immune to chaos, but they possess the internal architecture to navigate it with grace.

The Psychology of the Mother Beautiful Tank

The concept of the "mother beautiful tank" is deeply resonant with modern psychological and philosophical thought. It speaks to the human need for efficacy and flow.

Efficacy and the Reduction of Anxiety: In psychology, self-efficacy, a concept popularised by Albert Bandura, is the belief in one's capacity to execute behaviours necessary to produce specific performance attainments. Oddball's statement is not just a boast; it is an expression of high self-efficacy. He knows the tank is beautiful because he knows he can make it perform.

This belief is a powerful buffer against anxiety. When faced with a challenge, the person with high self-efficacy doesn't panic; they use the skills they've learned. The anxiety response, which is fundamentally a fear of being unable to cope, is short-circuited by the quiet, internal certainty of competence. The master doesn't need external validation; their confidence is an internal, verifiable fact, built on a mountain of successful repetitions.

The State of Flow: The feeling of "mother beautiful" is the feeling of being in a state of flow, a term coined by psychologist Mihaly Csikszentmihalyi. Flow is the mental state in which a person performing an activity is fully immersed in a feeling of energised focus, full involvement, and enjoyment of the activity itself. For Oddball, the tank is not a burden; it is an extension of his will, a perfect challenge that matches his high skill level. When you are in flow, the self disappears, time warps, and the work becomes its own reward. This is the ultimate expression of loving your tank—when the act of operating it becomes a meditation, a dance between intention and execution.

Ancient Wisdom on Craft: This modern psychological framework draws on ancient philosophy. The Stoics, for instance, emphasised *technē*, often translated as "craft" or "art." For them, a good life was one lived in accordance with nature, and a key part of that was the mastery of one's chosen domain.

The carpenter's virtue is in their carpentry; the philosopher's virtue is in their reasoning. Oddball's wisdom is a practical, modern Stoicism: the path to inner peace runs directly through the excellence of your external work. You cannot be a calm, effective human being if you are constantly failing at the thing you are supposed to be doing. Mastery is a moral imperative.

Case Study 1: The Calm Coder and the Legacy System

Consider David Chen, a senior software architect in San Francisco.

In his junior years, David was a wreck. Every new project filled him with dread. He was constantly afraid of being assigned a task he didn't know how to do, of being "found out" as an imposter. His days were filled with frantic Googling, anxiety-fuelled coding sessions, and the constant fear of breaking the build. He was a Moriarty at the keyboard, constantly over-complicating simple problems out of fear.

But David didn't quit. He embraced the Doctrine of Competence. He spent his evenings and weekends not just doing the work but also studying it. He read books on software architecture. He did online courses on new programming languages. He built his own small projects just for fun. He wasn't just trying to get through the day; he was trying to master his tank.

Years later, David is the lead on a critical, decades-old financial system—a true "legacy tank" held together by duct tape and sheer will. When a major crisis hits—a zero-day vulnerability is discovered, or a core database fails during a peak transaction window—everyone else panics. David is the one who quietly opens his laptop, takes a sip of his lukewarm coffee, and starts methodically diagnosing the problem.

His calm isn't a personality trait; it's the earned dividend of thousands of hours of practice. He is not afraid, because he has seen this problem, or a version of it, a hundred times before. He knows the system's quirks, its hidden dependencies, and its ancient, undocumented rituals. He knows exactly which piece of pipe to add to make the gun look bigger, or in his case, which line of code to comment out to keep the whole system from collapsing. He has mastered his mother, beautiful code. His competence is the team's anchor.

Case Study 2: The Freelance Writer and the Empty Page

Now consider Sarah Miller, a freelance content strategist and writer. Her "tank" is the ability to craft compelling narratives and persuasive arguments under tight deadlines. For years, Sarah struggled with the paralysing fear of the empty page. She would stare at the blinking cursor, convinced that her ideas were stale and her voice was inadequate. This anxiety led to procrastination, which led to rushed, mediocre work, which in turn reinforced her anxiety—a vicious cycle of incompetence breeding fear.

Sarah decided to apply the Oddball principle. She stopped focusing on the outcome (the perfect article) and started focusing on the process (the mastery of writing). She began a deliberate practice regimen: she committed to writing 500 words of pure, unedited prose every morning, regardless of topic. She studied the structure of great essays, not just their content. She learned the "mechanics" of her craft—the rules of grammar, the rhythm of sentences, the architecture of an argument.

The change was transformative. When a client now gives her a challenging brief, she doesn't feel dread; she feels a familiar, low-level hum of engagement. She knows the steps: research, outline, draft, revise. The empty page is no longer a void of potential failure, but a blank canvas for a process she has mastered. Her confidence is now a quiet, operational certainty. She can afford to be humorous and playful in her drafts because she knows the underlying structure is sound. Her work is not just good; it is beautiful because it is an expression of her mastery over the chaos of language.

She has built a mother, beautiful narrative.

THE PATH TO MASTERY: THREE STAGES OF TANK OWNERSHIP

The path to mastering your tank involves three stages, which move you from a novice operator to a true connoisseur.

1. Identify Your Tank and Its Terrain

First, you must identify your primary craft. What is the core skill set that you use to navigate the world? It's often, but not always, related to your profession. It's the thing you are, or want to be, exceptionally good at. It could be a broad skill, like "leadership," or a specific one, like "graphic design." Be honest with yourself. What is the "tank" you are currently riding? Is it the one you want to be in?

Crucially, you must also understand the terrain your tank operates on. A master tank commander knows the difference between a dry, hard-packed road and a muddy, soft field. For a financial analyst, the terrain is the market, its regulations, and its irrational human elements. For a parent, the terrain is the ever-changing emotional landscape of their child. Mastery is not just knowing your tool; it is knowing the environment in which your tool must perform. A beautiful tank is useless if its driver doesn't understand the map.

2. The Deliberate Practice of Refinement

Mastery is not a destination; it is a continuous process of learning and refinement. It requires dedication, but the Oddballist approach to mastery is playful, curious, and deeply deliberate.

- **Learn the Rules (The Manual):** You have to know the standard operating procedures before you can break them. Learn the fundamentals of your craft. Read the manuals. Study the greats. Put in the hours. This is the stage of foundational knowledge. For a chef, mastering the five mother sauces is the key. For a musician, this is mastering scales and chord theory. You must internalise the rules so deeply that they become subconscious.

- **Find the Edges (The Customisation):** Once you know the rules, start looking for the loopholes, the shortcuts, the unconventional techniques. Where can you add a piece of pipe to make the gun look bigger? Where can you tweak the engine for more speed? This is the stage of experimentation. It involves pushing the boundaries of your craft, trying new tools, and deliberately failing in low-stakes environments. This is where you move from following instructions to creating new instructions.

- **Develop Your Style (The Signature):** Mastery isn't just about technical skill; it's about developing your own unique voice and approach. Oddball's tanks are not just effective; they are expressions of his personality. They play music! They shoot paint! Your work should also become an expression of who you are. Your unique history, perspective, and humour should be visible in the final product. This is the difference between a competent technician and a true artist.

3. Cultivate Confidence Through Capability

True confidence is not a personality trait you're born with. It is a byproduct of proven capability. Every time you successfully complete a task, solve a problem, or receive positive feedback, you are depositing in your confidence account. The more you practice your craft, the more capable you become, and the more confident you feel. This confidence is the bedrock of the laid-back attitude.

Oddball can afford to relax while his tank is being fixed because he has absolute confidence in his crew's ability and his own ability to command them once it's running. His calm is not a façade; it is a logical conclusion drawn from a lifetime of successful execution. The confidence of the master is not a hope; it is a prediction based on historical data.

The Neuroscience of Competence: The Myelin Sheath

The physical reality of mastery is rooted in the brain. When you practice a skill, you are not just building muscle memory; you are literally wrapping the neural circuits responsible for that skill in a fatty white substance called myelin. Think of myelin as the insulation around an electrical wire. The thicker the myelin sheath, the faster and more efficiently the electrical signal—the thought or command—can travel down the axon.

Every time David the coder practices a complex algorithm, every time Sarah the writer structures a difficult paragraph, they are thickening the myelin around those specific neural pathways. This is the biological basis for flow and competence. When a crisis hits, the master's response is fast, clean, and effortless because the signal travels along a super-highway of thick myelin. The novice's signal, travelling along a bare wire, is slow, prone to interference, and requires immense conscious effort.

This is why mastery feels so good. It is the brain rewarding itself for building a more efficient machine. The "mother beautiful tank" is not just the external machine; it is the beautifully myelinated, highly efficient neural network inside the master's skull. The joy of competence is the joy of a perfectly tuned biological instrument.

Practical Application: The 5-Step Tank Tuning Technique

How do you start tuning your tank today? It doesn't require a full career change, just a shift in focus.

Step 1: The Competence Audit (Identify the Rust) Take an honest inventory of your primary craft. What are the three most common tasks you perform? For each task, rate your competence on a scale of 1 to 10. Be brutal. Now, identify the single most common point of failure or anxiety. This is the "rust" on your tank. For David, it was debugging legacy code. For Sarah, it was writing the first paragraph. This is your immediate target for deliberate practice.

Step 2: Isolate and Drill (The Engine Overhaul) Once you've identified the rust, isolate that specific skill and drill it relentlessly. Do not practice the whole task; practice the weakest link. If your weakness is public speaking, don't just give more presentations; practice the first two minutes of your talk in front of a mirror fifty times. If your weakness is a specific coding function, write 100 small programs that use only that function. This is not about being productive; it is about building myelin. It is focused, low-stakes repetition designed to make the difficult effortless.

Step 3: Find a Connoisseur (The Master Mechanic) Every master has a master. Find someone who has already built a mother beautiful tank in your field. This could be a mentor, a coach, or even a book or course by a recognised expert. You need a connoisseur to point out the flaws you can't see. Oddball didn't invent tank driving; he learned from others and then customised. Seek out the best feedback you can find, and treat it as the most valuable fuel for your tank.

Step 4: The Playful Experiment (Adding the Pipe) Once you have a solid foundation, introduce an element of play. Oddball's crew paints their tank and plays music. What is the equivalent in your craft? If you are a project manager, try running a meeting using a completely unconventional format. If you are a baker, try combining two ingredients that should never go together. The playful experiment is where you find the edges and develop your unique style. It's a low-stakes way to break the rules and discover a better way of doing things. This is where the work stops being a chore and starts being an art form.

Step 5: The Maintenance Mindset (Daily Polish) Mastery is not a one-time achievement; it is a maintenance schedule. You must commit to a small daily practice to keep the rust away. This could be 15 minutes of reading industry news, 10 minutes of journaling, or 5 minutes of reviewing a difficult concept. This daily polish is what separates the temporary expert from the lifelong master. It ensures that when the moment of crisis arrives, your tank is not just beautiful, but battle-ready.

Stop chasing the feeling of confidence. Chase the reality of competence, and confidence will follow, as surely as a tank follows its treads. Love your work. Know your tools. Master your craft. Turn your profession into a work of art.

Build yourself a beautiful tank, mother.

Chapter Fifteen:

Getting Out of Trouble Faster

Oddball: "These engines are the fastest in any tanks in the European Theatre of Operations, forwards or backwards. You see, man, we like to feel we can get out of trouble quicker than we got into it."

This single, deceptively simple statement is the prime directive of Oddballist innovation. It is not a philosophy of aggression, but a sophisticated doctrine of survival, self-preservation, and strategic prudence. The goal of modifying the engine is not to be a better attacker, but to be a better escape artist.

This is a crucial, often overlooked insight into the nature of creative problem-solving: true genius lies not in the ability to win every fight, but in the wisdom to avoid the unwinnable ones and the speed to survive the inevitable mistakes.

Oddball knows his reality. "All the tanks we come up against are bigger and better than ours."

He understands the brutal arithmetic of a head-to-head confrontation—he cannot win. Therefore, his entire strategy is predicated on asymmetry. He refuses to play the enemy's game, which is a game of armour, size, and brute force. Instead, he creates a new one, a game based on speed, surprise, psychological warfare, and, most importantly, the guaranteed exit.

This is the Doctrine of Asymmetric Advantage, the Wave Rider's manifesto for navigating a world where the odds are perpetually stacked against the individual. It's about using your creativity to turn perceived weaknesses into overwhelming strengths and to avoid a fair fight at all costs.

A fair fight, after all, is for suckers who haven't done the math.

A Wave Rider always looks for the unfair advantage, the angle the opposition hasn't even considered.

The Engine of Prudence: Why the Reverse Gear Matters

The modification to the tank engine—making the reverse gear as fast as the forward—is a profound metaphor for psychological resilience and strategic planning. Most people, when they plan, focus only on forward momentum: the launch, the growth, the success. They design a perfect path to victory, but they leave the retreat route as an afterthought, a slow, grinding process of failure and shame. Oddball's engine, however, is a physical manifestation of prudence. It is the wisdom of knowing that not every battle is worth fighting, and that the ability to execute a rapid, clean retreat is the highest form of strategic genius.

Consider the ancient philosophical roots of this idea. The Stoics, for instance, were masters of psychological retreat. They taught that while you cannot control external events—the "bigger tanks" of the world—you can absolutely control your response to them.

The fast reverse gear is the Stoic's mental discipline: the ability to instantly withdraw your emotional investment from a failing venture, a toxic relationship, or a dead-end job.

It is the immediate recognition that the cost of staying is higher than the cost of leaving. This is not pessimism; it is a clear-eyed assessment of reality. The ability to retreat quickly and efficiently is not a sign of weakness; it is a sign of strategic genius that allows you to survive a mistake and live to fight another day, on your own terms.

Case Study 1: The Startup and the Titan

Meet Amelia Chen, a brilliant software engineer who founded a niche social media platform called The Agora, focused on long-form, thoughtful discussion.

Her "tank" was small, agile, and specialised. Her competitor, the "bigger tank," was GlobalConnect, a trillion-dollar behemoth that dominated the market. Amelia knew she couldn't compete on features, user count, or advertising budget. A fair fight would mean certain death.

Amelia applied the Doctrine of Asymmetric Advantage.

First, she identified her disadvantage. GlobalConnect could copy any feature she built within a week and outspend her 10,000-to-1.

Second, she changed the rules of the game. GlobalConnect's weakness was its size and need to appeal to everyone; it was slow and bureaucratic, and its content was diluted by noise.

Amelia intentionally made The Agora small, invitation-only, and focused on a hyper-specific, high-value user base: academics, journalists, and policymakers.

Her advantage was quality over quantity and trust over reach. She wasn't trying to get a billion users; she was trying to get the thousand most influential users.

Third, she prioritised the escape route. She built her platform on a modular, open-source framework, ensuring that if GlobalConnect ever decided to crush her, she could quickly pivot.

Her "reverse gear" was a pre-planned, easy migration path for her users to a decentralised, self-hosted version of the platform. This wasn't a plan for failure; it was a survival plan.

When GlobalConnect launched a competing "thoughtful discussion" feature, Amelia didn't fight. She executed her retreat, immediately releasing the decentralised version and positioning The Agora not as a competitor, but as the spiritual home of the community, free from corporate control.

She got out of trouble quicker than she got into it, not by winning the battle, but by changing the battlefield. Her company survived, not as a billion-dollar unicorn, but as a profitable, highly respected, and resilient non-profit foundation.

Case Study 2: The Mid-Career Pivot

Consider David Miller, a forty-five-year-old marketing executive who had spent two decades climbing the corporate ladder at a major consumer goods company.

David's "tank" was a comfortable, well-armoured career, but it was slow and running on fumes.

The "bigger tank" he faced was the rapidly changing digital landscape and a new, younger CEO who valued disruption over loyalty.

David saw the writing on the wall; his traditional skill set was becoming obsolete, and a head-on confrontation with the new corporate culture would only lead to a painful, drawn-out firing.

David's application of the doctrine was internal and psychological.

He identified his disadvantage: his skills were siloed, and his professional identity was too tied to the company's brand. He changed the rules of the game. He stopped trying to prove his worth in the old system.

Instead, he quietly began using his corporate resources to build his own asymmetric advantage. He volunteered for every cross-departmental, future-focused project, not for promotion, but to learn new digital tools and network with younger, more agile teams. He was using the enemy's resources to train his own engine.

He prioritised the escape route: For eighteen months, he treated his job as a paid apprenticeship. He built a side portfolio of digital marketing consulting for small, non-competing businesses. When the inevitable restructuring came, David didn't wait for the axe. He executed a rapid, dignified retreat, resigning the day before the layoffs were announced.

He didn't leave as a victim of corporate downsizing, but as a consultant with a ready-made client base and a newly acquired, future-proof skill set. He got out of the trouble of professional obsolescence more quickly than he got into it, turning a potential career disaster into a successful, self-directed pivot.

The Psychology of the Fast Reverse Gear

Oddball's wisdom resonates deeply with modern psychology, particularly in the realm of decision-making and cognitive bias. The fast reverse gear is the antidote to the Sunk Cost Fallacy. This fallacy is the psychological trap of continuing to invest time, money, or effort in a failing endeavour simply because we have already invested so much.

It is the slow, grinding reverse gear of a standard tank—the emotional friction that prevents a quick, rational exit.

The Wave Rider, equipped with the fast reverse gear, understands that past investment is irrelevant to future success.

The only question that matters is: Does this path still serve my objective?

If the answer is no, the retreat must be immediate and without regret. This is a form of cognitive agility, a neurological ability to override the emotional pain of loss and execute a strategic withdrawal. Neuroscience suggests that this ability is linked to a well-regulated prefrontal cortex, which can suppress the emotional signals from the amygdala that scream, "Don't quit! You'll look like a failure!" Oddball's engine is a physical hack for a fundamental human psychological flaw.

To cultivate this psychological fast reverse gear, one must practice pre-mortem analysis.

Before starting any major project—a new business, a significant investment, a serious relationship—take an hour and assume the project has failed spectacularly a year from now. Then, write down all the reasons why it failed. This exercise forces you to identify the potential "bigger tanks" and, more importantly, to design the escape route before you are emotionally invested. It is the act of installing the fast reverse gear while the tank is still in the garage.

Practical Application: The Four Steps to Oddball's Advantage

The Doctrine of Asymmetric Advantage is not just a philosophical concept; it is a four-step operational manual for life.

1. Identify Your Disadvantage (The Brutal Honesty Check)

Be brutally honest about where you are outmatched. This requires a cold, objective assessment, free from ego. Are you a small business competing with a giant corporation? Are you an introvert in a world that rewards extroversion? Are you underfunded, understaffed, or underestimated? Good.

This is not a moment for despair; it is a moment for clarity. Your disadvantage is simply the constraint that defines your creative solution. The constraint is the mother of invention. Oddball didn't complain about his tank; he accepted its limitations and then innovated around them.

• **Technique:** The "Enemy's Whiteboard" Exercise. Imagine your main competitor or challenge has a whiteboard listing your weaknesses. What are the top three items on that board? These are your disadvantages. Now, how can you make those three items irrelevant? If they list "low budget," your goal is to make the battle one that money cannot win.

2. Change the Rules of the Game (The Creative Pivot)

Don't try to beat your opponent at their own game. They have more resources, more power, more experience in that specific arena. You will lose. You must create a new game. If they are bigger, you must be faster. If they are stronger, you must be smarter. If they are more formal, you must be more agile and personal. This is the core of asymmetry. It is the judo flip of strategy, using the opponent's weight and momentum against them.

• **Technique:** The "Unfair Advantage" Matrix. List your opponent's top three strengths and your top three unique, non-scalable assets (e.g., niche expertise, personal network, speed of execution, unique voice). The intersection of your unique assets and their strengths is where you find the new game. If their strength is mass production, your new game is bespoke craftsmanship. If their strength is distribution, your new game is direct, personal community building.

3. Prioritise the Escape Route (The Prudent Pre-Mortem)

In every project, every venture, every relationship, always build in an escape route. This is the "backwards" part of Oddball's engine design. It is the contingency plan for when the Wave breaks the wrong way. This is not pessimism; it's prudence. It is the wisdom of knowing that not every battle is worth fighting. The escape route is your insurance policy against the Sunk Cost Fallacy. It defines the point of no return before you start.

• **Technique:** The "Tripwire" Protocol. Before you commit, define three clear, objective tripwires. These are non-negotiable conditions that, if met, trigger an immediate, pre-planned retreat. For a business, a tripwire might be: "If monthly burn rate exceeds X for three consecutive months." For a relationship: "If a core value is violated twice." When the tripwire is hit, the decision is already made.

You simply execute the retreat plan.

4. Embrace the "Good Enough" Solution (The Effectiveness Imperative)

Oddball's modifications are not factory-perfect. They are improvised, field-tested solutions that get the job done. A piece of pipe, a loudspeaker, and some paint. He is not striving for perfection; he is striving for effectiveness. Don't let the perfect be the enemy of the good.

An 80% solution that you can implement today is infinitely better than a 100% solution that never gets finished. Get it running, get it moving, and get out of trouble. Perfectionism is a slow, heavy tank; effectiveness is a light, fast dune buggy.

• **Technique:** The "Minimum Viable Retreat." When you are in the middle of a project, constantly ask: What is the absolute minimum I need to do right now to survive the next week? What is the simplest, fastest, most improvised solution that will get me to the next safe harbour? Focus on function over form, speed over polish.

Nuances and Edge Cases: When to Stay and Fight

Does the Doctrine of Asymmetric Advantage mean you should always run? Absolutely not. The wisdom lies in the choice to run, not the compulsion. There are times when the only way out is through, but even then, the Oddballist approach applies.

The edge case is the Strategic Stand. This occurs when the cost of retreat is demonstrably higher than the cost of a calculated, asymmetric engagement.

For example, if Amelia Chen's platform, The Agora, was the only place where a critical, life-saving piece of information could be shared, a retreat would be a moral failure. In this scenario, the fight is not about winning the market but about achieving the mission.

When a Strategic Stand is necessary, the Doctrine still provides the framework:

1. The Fight Must Be Asymmetric: You still don't fight on their terms. You use your speed, your surprise, and your psychological advantage. You don't try to out-tank the bigger tank; you use the terrain, the darkness, and the element of surprise to disable its tracks and blind its vision.

2. The Retreat Must Be Ready: Even in the stand, the fast reverse gear is idling. The moment the mission is accomplished or the cost becomes truly existential, the retreat is executed. The Strategic Stand is a surgical strike, not a siege.

The true Wave Rider understands that the goal is not victory in a specific skirmish, but the longevity of the mission. The ability to get out of trouble faster ensures that the mission survives the failure of any single tactic.

Your life is your European Theatre of Operations. You will always come up against tanks that are bigger and better than yours—financial crises, health scares, professional rivals, and personal heartbreaks. Don't try to match their armour or their firepower. Modify your engine. Be faster, be smarter, be weirder. And always, always make sure you can get out of trouble quicker than you got into it. That is the secret to a long, successful, and gloriously oddball life.

Chapter Sixteen:

Pretty Pictures & Righteous Tunes

Oddball: "We got our own ammunition; it's filled with paint. When we fire it, it makes... pretty pictures. Scares the hell outta people! We have a loudspeaker here, and when we go into battle, we play music, very loud. It kind of... calms us down."

This is the heart of Oddball's creative genius. It is where the Doctrine of Competence and Creativity blossoms into pure, joyful art. He has taken the grim, violent tools of war and repurposed them for psychological and aesthetic ends.

This is the highest form of mastery: turning your weapons into paintbrushes and your battle cries into music.

This chapter is about the tactical application of beauty and joy. It's about understanding that the softest powers—art, music, humour, and style—are often the most effective instruments of change, influence, and self-mastery. They are the ultimate expression of control, not over the external world through brute force, but over the internal world through intentional design.

The Paint Shell Philosophy: The Strategic Power of Perception

Oddball's paint-filled shells are a work of surrealist genius. They do no physical damage, but they are immensely powerful. They are a masterclass in psychological warfare, demonstrating that reality is less important than its perception. The shell's kinetic energy does not defeat the enemy; instead, it creates cognitive dissonance.

1. The Weapon of Confusion

An enemy tanker, trained for the sound and shock of high-explosive impact, instead sees a splash of bright yellow or blue paint. The sheer absurdity of the event causes a moment of mental paralysis. In that fraction of a second, the enemy's pre-programmed response—fight or flight—is interrupted.

They are forced to ask, "What was that?" Is this a new weapon? Are they playing with us? In that moment of confusion, they are vulnerable.

This is the essence of the Paint Shell Philosophy: disrupt the expected pattern to create a strategic opening.

Case Study: The Architect and the Absurd Proposal

Consider Elias, a brilliant but perpetually overlooked architect in a cutthroat firm.

He was competing for a massive, career-defining contract against two established rivals. His initial proposal was technically perfect but lacked the "wow" factor. Applying the Paint Shell Philosophy, Elias didn't just submit a better design; he submitted an absurdly beautiful design.

He commissioned a local street artist to hand-paint the cover of his final presentation binder with a vibrant, abstract mural that had nothing to do with the building itself, but everything to do with the building's feeling—joy, light, and unexpected colour.

His rivals presented their standard, leather-bound, corporate-blue binders. When Elias's presentation was placed on the table, it was a splash of "paint" in a sea of grey. The clients, a conservative board of directors, were initially confused, then intrigued, and finally delighted.

Elias didn't win on technical merit alone; he won because he broke the pattern. He used an aesthetic choice—a "pretty picture"—to signal a creative confidence and a willingness to challenge norms that his competitors, stuck in their predictable routines, could not match. The paint shell didn't destroy the competition; it simply made them irrelevant by shifting the entire context of the battle.

2. The Illusion of Power and the Fear of the Unknown

Oddball understands that fear is a function of imagination. As he explains, the pipe on the gun makes the enemy think it might be a 90mm. The paint shell, being an unknown type of ammunition, reinforces this fear of the unknown. The enemy doesn't know what you're capable of, and their imagination fills in the blanks with something terrifying.

This taps into a core psychological principle: uncertainty is often more frightening than a known threat.

In modern life, this translates to maintaining a degree of strategic ambiguity. When you are always predictable, you are easily countered. When you introduce an element of the unexpected—a sudden, bold move in a negotiation, a radical pivot in a business strategy, or an uncharacteristic act of generosity—you create the illusion of a deeper, more complex strategy at play. You become the tank that might be firing a 90mm, or might be firing paint, but either way, you are not to be trifled with.

3. Creative Expression as Self-Regulation

Crucially, the paint shells are an act of creative expression. Oddball is not just shooting at them; he's making "pretty pictures." This keeps him and his crew in a creative, playful mindset, which is the opposite of the fearful, aggressive mindset of their opponents. He is an artist; they are just soldiers.

This is the profound connection to modern neuroscience. When we engage in creative play, we activate the prefrontal cortex, the part of the brain responsible for complex decision-making, planning, and emotional regulation. By turning a life-or-death situation into an artistic performance, Oddball is literally changing his crew's brain chemistry, making them calmer, more focused, and more adaptable.

Practical Application: The Creative Counter-Attack

To apply the Paint Shell Philosophy, ask yourself: Where can I use perception, humour, and style to achieve my goals instead of brute force?

- **In Conflict:** Instead of escalating an argument with a colleague, use a well-timed, self-deprecating joke. The humour is the paint shell—it disarms the tension, forces a cognitive shift, and opens the door for a productive conversation.

- **In Personal Branding:** Don't just present your qualifications; present your style. Your resume, your website, your social media presence—these are your tanks. Are they firing boring, grey facts, or are they firing "pretty pictures" that showcase your unique personality and creative approach?

- **In Problem Solving:** When faced with a seemingly intractable problem, stop trying to solve it with the same tools. Introduce an element of play, a ridiculous suggestion, or a completely different medium (e.g., drawing the problem instead of talking about it). This creative disruption is the paint shell that breaks the mental deadlock.

The Loudspeaker Principle: The Mastery of Internal State

The loudspeaker is even more profound than the paint shells.

Oddball explicitly states its purpose: "It kind of... calms us down." This is a radical act of self-mastery. In the heat of battle, when every instinct is screaming for high alert and adrenaline, Oddball's priority is to keep his crew calm. He knows that a calm crew is an effective crew. A panicked crew makes mistakes.

1. Emotional Regulation as a Tactical Advantage

Oddball uses music as a tool for emotional regulation. He is actively curating the soundtrack of his own experience. He is not a passive victim of the sounds of war; he is the DJ of his own battlefield. This is the ultimate act of environmental control; a concept deeply rooted in Stoic philosophy and modern psychology. The Stoics taught that we cannot control external events, but we can control our judgment and response to them.

Oddball takes this a step further: he actively introduces a controllable external element (the music) to regulate the internal state of his team.

Connection to Neuroscience and Ancient Philosophy

The Loudspeaker Principle is a perfect synthesis of ancient wisdom and modern science.

- **Ancient Philosophy (Pythagoras & Plato):** The Greeks understood the ethos of music—its power to shape character and mood. Pythagoras used music to heal and purify the soul, and Plato argued that the right kind of music was essential for the education of the ideal citizen. Oddball is applying this ancient knowledge to a modern context: music is not just entertainment; it is a vital tool for cultivating the perfect state of mind for high-stakes performance.

- **Modern Neuroscience (The Vagus Nerve):** The music, especially the "righteous tunes" that are loud and rhythmic, engages the vagus nerve, the main component of the parasympathetic nervous system. This system is responsible for the "rest and digest" state. By stimulating the vagus nerve, the music actively counteracts the adrenaline and cortisol flooding the crew's system, literally calming them down and allowing the prefrontal cortex to remain online for clear, rational decision-making. The music is a physiological anchor.

2. The Step-by-Step Guide to Becoming Your Own DJ

To apply the Loudspeaker Principle, you must become the DJ of your own life, curating your internal and external soundscape with intention.

Step 1: Curate Your Audio Environment (The Input).

What are you listening to? Is it the negative waves of the 24-hour news cycle, the constant stream of social media outrage, or is it a playlist of righteous tunes that makes you feel powerful and calm?

Your choice of music, podcasts, and audiobooks is not trivial; it is a primary tool for managing your energetic state. Be ruthless in eliminating audio clutter that induces anxiety or negativity.

Step 2: Create Your "Battle Music" (The Anchor). Identify the music that calms you down under pressure, the music that makes you feel focused and capable, and the music that makes you feel unstoppable. Create three distinct playlists:

• **The Calm:** For pre-stress moments (e.g., before a major presentation). Slow, rhythmic, and familiar.

• **The Focus:** For deep work and concentration. Often instrumental, repetitive, and driving.

• **The Unstoppable:** For moments when you need a surge of confidence and energy. Loud, triumphant, and emotionally resonant.

Use these playlists intentionally. Before a difficult meeting, a stressful conversation, or a challenging task, put on your battle music. Let it set the tone.

Step 3: Project Your Vibe (The Output). The loudspeaker works on the enemy, too. It's unnerving. A tank blasting music is not afraid. Your own calm, your own positive energy, your own playful humour—these are your loudspeakers. When you project this vibe, it unnerves the Moriartys of the world. It shows them you are playing a different game, and it scares the hell outta them. This is the concept of emotional contagion—your calm, intentional state is contagious, and it can either elevate your allies or destabilise your opponents.

Case Study: The CEO and the Quarterly Crisis

Dr Anya Sharma, the CEO of a rapidly growing tech startup, faced a quarterly earnings call that threatened to tank the company's stock.

A key product launch had failed, and the media was circling. The atmosphere in the executive suite was one of pure panic. Dr Sharma, a student of Oddball's philosophy, knew she couldn't control the market, but she could control the vibe of her team and the call itself.

Instead of a tense, silent prep session, she walked into the boardroom with a portable speaker and put on a playlist of 1970s funk—her "Unstoppable" battle music. She started the meeting not with a grim review of the numbers, but with a self-deprecating joke about her terrible dance moves. The absurdity was her paint shell. It broke the tension.

During the call, she maintained an unflappable, almost cheerful confidence. She didn't minimise the failure; she reframed it as a necessary, high-cost lesson that had already been integrated into a superior, forward-looking strategy.

Her calm, projected through her voice and body language, was her loudspeaker. The analysts, expecting a defensive, panicked CEO, were instead met with a leader who seemed to be enjoying the challenge. Her intentional vibe controlled the narrative, calmed the investors, and stabilised the stock far better than any purely rational explanation could have. She used her internal state as her most powerful external tool.

The Nuance of the Mother Beautiful Tank

Competence is not just about being good with the hardware. It's about being good with the software—the human, emotional, and psychological elements of any situation. By mastering the arts of the paint shell and the loudspeaker, you move beyond being a mere technician and become a true artist of life, a maestro of the mother beautiful tank.

The Edge Case: When the Paint Shell Fails

What happens when the enemy is not confused, but simply angry? What if the paint shell is seen not as a creative act, but as an insult? This is the edge case where Oddball's wisdom shines brightest. The philosophy is not about avoiding conflict; it's about choosing the terms of the conflict.

If the paint shell fails to disarm, it has still served its purpose: it has confirmed the enemy's mindset.

It tells you that you are dealing with a purely brute-force opponent who is incapable of creative thought or humour. This knowledge is a tactical advantage in itself. You now know exactly what you are up against, and you can adjust your strategy from psychological disruption to pure, focused competence. The paint shell is a diagnostic tool as much as it is a weapon.

The Ancient Connection: Lao Tzu and the Soft Power

Oddball's philosophy finds a profound echo in the ancient Chinese text, the Tao Te Ching.

Lao Tzu wrote:

"The softest thing in the universe overcomes the hardest thing in the universe. That which has no substance enters where there is no space."

The paint shell is soft. The music is soft. They are the water that wears away the stone. They are the "no substance" that enters the "no space" of the enemy's rigid, fear-based mindset.

The hard power of the enemy—their armour, their guns, their aggression—is brittle. It can be shattered by a force it doesn't know how to fight: joyful, creative competence.

The ultimate lesson of Chapter 16 is that true power lies in the ability to define your own reality, even in the most hostile environments.

You cannot control the war, but you can control the music you play. You cannot control the enemy's reaction, but you can control the picture you paint. By choosing beauty over brutality, humour over hostility, and calm over chaos, you don't just survive the battle—you win the war for your own soul, and in doing so, you become an unstoppable force.

You become the mother, beautiful tank, rolling to the righteous tunes of your own making.

Chapter Seventeen:

I Only Ride 'Em

Big Joe: "Well, then, why the hell aren't you up there helping them?"

Oddball: [chuckles] "I only ride 'em, I don't know what makes 'em work."

We return to this sacred exchange one last time, for it contains the final, crucial teaching of this doctrine: the wisdom of knowing your limits and the power of trusting your crew.

This is the Doctrine of Delegation. It is the philosophical counterpoint to the modern cult of the "do-it-all" hero, a radical acceptance of interdependence that frees the Wave Rider from the crushing weight of unnecessary responsibility.

Big Joe, the traditional, hierarchical leader, believes the commander should be involved in everything. He sees Oddball's relaxation as a failure of leadership, a dereliction of duty. But Oddball operates on a higher level of understanding.

His response, "I only ride 'em, I don't know what makes 'em work," is not an admission of ignorance; it is a statement of profound strategic wisdom, a declaration of his highest-leverage role.

The Wave Rider understands that energy is finite, and attention is the most precious currency.

To spend your unique, high-value attention on a low-value task is not diligence; it is sabotage. The Doctrine of Delegation is built on three foundational pillars, each a necessary step toward true, sustainable effectiveness.

1. Know Your Circle of Competence: The Art of Ruthless Self-Assessment

Oddball is a brilliant tank commander. His skills are in strategy, morale, navigation, and the uncanny ability to generate a positive wave in the direst circumstances. He is not a mechanic. Moriarty is the mechanical genius. For Oddball to "help" Moriarty would be like a world-class conductor trying to "help" the first violinist by grabbing their bow.

It would be clumsy, insulting, and counterproductive. The first step to effective delegation is a ruthless self-assessment. What are you truly great at? What is your unique contribution? This is your Circle of Competence. Stay inside it.

This concept, often discussed in modern business strategy, has deep roots in ancient philosophy. The Stoics, particularly Marcus Aurelius, spoke of focusing only on what is within your power—your judgments, your actions, your intentions—and letting go of the rest.

Oddball's wisdom is the practical application of this principle. He is saying, "My power is in commanding this tank; the mechanics of the engine are outside my sphere of influence, and thankfully, they are squarely within Moriarty's."

Case Study: The Architect and the Spreadsheet

Consider Elias, a brilliant architect who runs his own boutique firm.

Elias is a visionary; his designs win awards, and his clients adore his creative process. However, he is terrible at bookkeeping and project management spreadsheets. For years, he spent his evenings wrestling with pivot tables and expense reports, tasks that took him four hours to complete and often contained errors. This time spent was time not spent designing, time not spent with his family, and time that drained his creative well.

His Circle of Competence is spatial design and client relations.

His Circle of Incompetence includes financial administration.

The moment Elias hired Sofia, a freelance virtual assistant with an accounting background, his firm transformed. Sofia, who could complete the same tasks flawlessly in one hour, was operating within her Circle of Competence. Elias, freed from the tyranny of the spreadsheet, designed two major projects in the time he would have spent on admin. His unique contribution was amplified by delegating his weakness. The lesson is clear: your time is best spent where your unique skills create the highest value. Everything else is a distraction, a negative wave you must deflect.

2. Delegate Everything Else: The Humility of Letting Go

Everything outside your Circle of Competence should be delegated to someone whose Circle of Competence it falls within.

This requires two things: having a crew you trust (which we will cover in the next section) and having the humility to let go of control.

Micromanagement is the **enemy** of a positive wave.

It signals a lack of trust, and it creates anxiety for everyone involved. When you delegate a task, you must also delegate the authority and the responsibility. You cannot give Moriarty the job of fixing the tank and then stand over his shoulder telling him how to do it. That is not delegation; that is simply performing the task with extra steps and a witness.

The psychological barrier to delegation is often the fear of failure or the ego-driven belief that "no one can do it as well as I can." This is a lie the ego tells itself to maintain a false sense of indispensability. Neuroscience shows that micromanaging triggers stress responses in both the manager and the subordinate, flooding the system with cortisol and inhibiting the prefrontal cortex—the very part of the brain responsible for creative problem-solving.

Oddball, by contrast, is calm. He trusts Moriarty's expertise implicitly, which allows Moriarty's brain to operate at peak performance.

Practical Application: The 3-Step Delegation Technique

To delegate effectively and maintain the positive wave, follow this step-by-step guidance:

A. Define the Outcome, Not the Process: Clearly articulate what success looks like (e.g., "The tank must be fully operational and ready to move in one hour," or "The client presentation needs to be visually stunning and uploaded by 5 PM"). Do not dictate how the person should achieve it. The "how" is their domain, their Circle of Competence.

B. Verify Resources and Authority: Ensure the person has all the necessary tools, information, and authority to complete the task without needing to come back to you for permission. Oddball doesn't just tell Moriarty to fix the tank; he gives him the keys to the toolbox and the freedom to work.

C. Establish the Check-in Rhythm: Agree on a single, non-intrusive check-in point. This is not to check on them, but to check in with them. A simple, "Let me know when you're 80% done so that I can review the final details," is sufficient. This provides a safety net without becoming a leash. Once the rhythm is set, step back and let the wave carry them.

3. Understand that Rest is Your Job: The Strategic Pause

When Oddball is relaxing, he is not "doing nothing." He is performing a vital part of his job as commander: conserving his mental and emotional energy.

A tired, stressed-out leader makes bad decisions.

A calm, rested leader makes good ones.

By trusting his crew to handle their tasks, he frees himself to perform his unique role at the highest possible level. Your job is not to do everything; your job is to do your specific thing brilliantly and to create the conditions for others to do theirs. And sometimes, that means drinking wine, eating cheese, and catching some rays.

This is the profound connection between Oddball's wisdom and modern neuroscience. The brain's Default Mode Network (DMN), which is active when we are resting, daydreaming, or not focused on a specific task, is crucial for creativity, self-reflection, and consolidating memories.

When Oddball is "riding 'em," he allows his DMN to process the strategic landscape, to see patterns and connections that hyperfocus would obscure. His rest is not a luxury; it is a strategic necessity that allows him to maintain the positive wave and make the high-stakes, intuitive decisions that only a rested mind can make.

EXTENDED NARRATIVE EXAMPLE: THE CASE OF THE BURNED-OUT CEO

Dr Lena Sharma was the CEO of a fast-growing tech startup. She embodied the "super-mom" and "do-it-all" entrepreneur cult. She insisted on reviewing every line of code, writing every major press release, and even personally approving the office supply orders. Her rationale was sound: she cared deeply about quality and efficiency. But her method was a negative wave generator. She was perpetually exhausted, snapping at her team, and her decision-making was becoming erratic. She was a world-class rider trying to be the mechanic, the gunner, the loader, and the driver all at once.

The turning point came during a critical product launch. A minor bug was discovered hours before the announcement. Lena, in her exhausted state, panicked and tried to fix the code herself, introducing a far worse error. Her Head of Engineering, Javier, a calm and brilliant mechanic, had to step in, fix both errors, and delay the launch by a day.

In the aftermath, Javier quoted Oddball to her: "Dr Sharma, you're the rider. You see the whole battlefield. You tell us where to go. But you don't know what makes the engine work, and that's okay. That's my job. When you try to fix the engine, you're not helping; you're just distracting the mechanic and exhausting the commander."

Lena realised her exhaustion was not a badge of honour; it was a failure of delegation. She implemented a "Strategic Pause" policy for herself, scheduling two hours of "no-work" time every afternoon for reading, walking, or simply staring out the window. She ruthlessly delegated all tasks outside her Circle of Competence—vision, investor relations, and high-level strategy.

The result was immediate: her team's productivity soared, her stress levels plummeted, and her strategic decisions became sharper and more intuitive. She learned that the highest form of leadership is not doing, but being—being rested, being clear, and being the calm centre of the storm.

Part Six:

The Doctrine & The Crew

No tank is a one-man operation. You can have the most positive vibe, the deepest presence, the fiercest independence, and the most brilliant skills, but without a crew, you are just a lonely nut in a metal box. The final pillar of Oddballism is arguably the most important, for it is the one that makes all the others sustainable. This is the Doctrine of the Crew.

This is a philosophy of radical, chosen family. It's about understanding that who you surround yourself with is the single most crucial factor in determining the quality of your life and the success of your mission. Your crew is your support system, your sounding board, your engine room, and your defence against the endless negative waves of the world.

Building and nurturing this crew is the most sacred work a Wave Rider can do.

1. The Ancient Roots of the Crew: Aristotle and the Polis

The idea of the Crew is not new; it is as old as civilisation itself.

Aristotle, in his Nicomachean Ethics, argued that man is a political animal—a creature meant to live in a polis, or community. He believed that true happiness (eudaimonia) could only be achieved in the context of deep, meaningful friendships and a supportive community.

Oddball's crew—Moriarty, the mechanic; the unnamed gunner; the driver—is his modern polis. They are not just employees or subordinates; they are co-creators of the positive wave.

The Wave Rider must actively cultivate a crew that possesses three essential qualities: Competence, Trust, and Vibe Alignment.

- **Competence:** They must be masters of their own Circle of Competence. You need a Moriarty who knows what makes the engine work, not a pretender.

- **Trust:** This is the bedrock. You must trust their skill, their judgment, and their loyalty. Trust is the silent contract that allows you to relax and "only ride 'em."

- **Vibe Alignment:** They must be people who contribute to the positive wave. A brilliant mechanic with a perpetually negative attitude will poison the entire mission.

The crew must share a fundamental, if unspoken, agreement on the mission's purpose and the spirit in which it is to be executed.

2. The Modern Challenge: Building a Crew in the Age of Isolation

In the modern world, the "tank" is often a startup, a family, a creative project, or even just one's own mental health. The challenge is that modern life often encourages isolation and hyper-individualism. The Wave Rider must be intentional about crew-building.

Case Study: The Freelancer and the Virtual Crew

Marcus is a freelance graphic designer who works from home. For years, he felt the loneliness of the solo entrepreneur, struggling with self-doubt and procrastination. He was a one-man tank, constantly trying to be the rider, the mechanic, and the gunner. His productivity was inconsistent, and the negative wave of isolation was starting to pull him under.

Marcus decided to apply the Doctrine of the Crew to his virtual life. He didn't hire employees, but he intentionally cultivated a network of three key people:

A. The Navigator (The Accountability Partner): Sarah, a fellow freelancer in a different industry. They meet every Monday for a 30-minute "Mission Briefing" to set goals and every Friday for a "Debrief" to review progress. Sarah is his external strategist, helping him stay on course.

B. The Mechanic (The Technical Expert): Ben, a web developer, pays for one hour a month. Ben handles all the technical issues Marcus doesn't understand (website updates, server maintenance). Marcus delegates his technical incompetence to Ben.

C. The Gunner (The Creative Critic): Chloe, a former colleague who provides honest, high-level feedback on his designs. She is the one who ensures his creative "shots" are on target.

By building this virtual, distributed crew, Marcus transformed his solo operation into a high-performing "tank." He was finally free to "only ride 'em," focusing his energy entirely on the creative design work he excelled at, knowing his trusted crew protected his periphery.

3. Nurturing the Crew: The Rituals of the Positive Wave

A crew is not a static entity; it is a living system that requires constant nurturing. Oddball doesn't just trust his crew; he cultivates them. He shares his wine, his cheese, and his positive vibe. He creates an environment where competence is respected and rest is valued.

Step-by-Step Guidance for Nurturing Your Crew:

1. The Shared Feast (The Vibe Check): Create regular, non-work-related rituals. This could be a weekly lunch, a monthly virtual coffee, or simply five minutes of non-task-related conversation at the start of a meeting. This is where the positive wave is generated and maintained. It reinforces the human connection that underpins the professional one.

2. The Competence Shield (Respect and Autonomy): When a crew member is operating in their Circle of Competence, your job is to run interference. Shield them from unnecessary distractions, bureaucratic nonsense, and micromanagement. Defend their autonomy fiercely. When you trust them, you must show it by protecting their ability to work.

3. The Open Channel (Honest Feedback): Establish a culture where feedback flows freely and without fear of reprisal. The Wave Rider must be the first to admit a mistake and the most gracious in receiving constructive criticism. The tank cannot function if the gunner is afraid to tell the commander that the target has moved.

The Doctrine of the Crew is the ultimate expression of the Wave Rider's humility and wisdom. It is understood that the most significant strength is not self-sufficiency but the ability to form powerful, synergistic alliances. Identify your role. Master it. Build your crew. Trust them. And then, with a chuckle and a deep sense of peace, trust your crew to handle the rest. You've earned it.

Chapter Eighteen:

Building The Tank Squad

Crapgame: "It's a top-line outfit, I personally recommend these guys."

Oddball doesn't command a random assortment of soldiers assigned to him by the army. He leads a hand-picked team of specialists, a "top line outfit" that operates with a unique synergy.

They are his crew. They understand his eccentricities, they trust his leadership, and they share his general philosophy of survival and enrichment. This is not an accident; it is a deliberate act of team architecture.

The army, with its rigid hierarchy and bureaucratic inertia, would have assigned him a group of square pegs for his round hole.

Oddball, the ultimate pragmatist, knew better. He understood that the success of any mission, whether it's stealing gold or simply navigating the minefield of modern life, hinges on the quality and composition of the crew.

This is the first, most critical lesson in the Wave Rider's doctrine: you must consciously build your own tank squad.

This is not about networking or accumulating followers. It is about identifying and cultivating deep, trusting relationships with a small number of essential people. A whole crew has several key roles, and you may find one person fills multiple roles, or that you have several people in one category. The key is to recognise the functions, the archetypes of support that you need to maintain your equilibrium and execute your grandest plans. Your crew is your external nervous system, your reality check, and your emergency response team all rolled into one.

Without them, you are just a single, vulnerable tank on a vast, hostile battlefield.

The Four Pillars of the Tank Squad: Archetypes of Support

The original crew from the mission to Clermont is a perfect microcosm of the balanced life. Each member brings a vital, non-negotiable function to the table. To build your own squad, you must first understand these roles and honestly assess where your own life is lacking in these specific forms of support.

1. The Moriarty (The Mechanical Genius & Grounding Force)

Every crew needs a Moriarty.

This is the person who knows how things work. They are the pragmatists, the realists, the ones who understand the nuts and bolts of reality. They are the master of the how.

They may be prone to what Oddball calls "negative waves," but their pessimism is often rooted in a deep, almost prophetic understanding of potential problems, mechanical failures, and logistical nightmares. They are the voice that says, "That won't work because the axle will snap at that speed," or "You haven't accounted for the new regulatory change."

Your Moriarty is the one you call when your car breaks down, your computer crashes, or your plan has a fatal flaw. You must love them not in spite of their negativity, but for the vital, grounding perspective it provides.

Their function is to pressure-test your positive waves. They force you to move from abstract vision to concrete, executable steps. The psychological term for this is "Defensive Pessimism," a strategy in which an individual anticipates a wide range of negative outcomes to motivate them to take preventive action. Your job is to manage their waves, not to dismiss their wisdom.

A crew without a Moriarty is a crew that is flying blind, mistaking enthusiasm for competence. They are the anchor that keeps the tank from floating away on a cloud of pure optimism.

2. The Crapgame (The Quartermaster & Resource Navigator)

Every mission needs resources.

The Crapgame is the hustler, the deal-maker, the one who knows how to get things. They are the master of the what. They can find you the sixty feet of bridge, the extra supplies, the inside information. They are worldly, cynical, and opportunistic, but their opportunism is in service of the crew. They understand that the world runs on deals, on favours, and on the strategic deployment of assets, and they are not afraid to make them. Crapgame is the ultimate connector, the one who can translate the crew's needs into the language of the market.

Your Crapgame is the friend who always knows a guy who can get you a discount, who can find a way to make things happen. They are your bridge to the material world, your access point to the hidden economy of favours and opportunities. In modern terms, they are your expert negotiator, your venture capitalist contact, or the friend who has a brilliant, if slightly unorthodox, solution to a supply chain problem. They remind you that while the spirit is willing, the flesh— and the tank—requires fuel, parts, and a clear path.

3. The Kelly (The Strategist & Visionary Leader)

Every crew needs a leader with a vision.

The Kelly is the one who finds the gold. They are the master of the why. They are the strategist, the planner, the one who sees the big picture and charts the course. They may not be as laid-back as you, but their focus and drive are essential. They provide the mission, the raison d'être for the whole operation. It is Kelly who brings the plan to

Oddball, who provides the positive wave so powerful that it can overcome the fear of three Tiger tanks. He is the one who dares to dream of the impossible score.

Your Kelly is the mentor, the partner, or the friend who inspires you, who pushes you, and who shows you which way to go. They are the embodiment of your ambition, the one who holds the map to the future you want to build. They are the source of the initial spark, the strategic genius that transforms vague desire into a concrete objective.

A Wave Rider needs a Kelly to give their positive waves a direction, a target to aim at.

4. The Oddball (The Vibe Master & Commander)

This is you.

As the Wave Rider, your primary role in the crew is to be the centre of gravity. You are the master of the when and the mood. You are the commander, the morale officer, the keeper of the vibe. You manage the group's energy. You keep Moriarty from despairing, you keep Crapgame from becoming too cynical, and you provide Kelly with the calm, creative firepower needed to execute the plan. You are the soul of the operation, the one who ensures that the process of getting the gold is as enjoyable and low-stress as possible.

Your unique contribution is the ability to maintain a state of flow and non-attachment to the outcome. You are the one who can pivot when the plan fails, who can see the opportunity in the chaos, and who can remind everyone that, ultimately, it's just a game. You are the psychological lubricant that keeps the crew's gears turning smoothly.

Case Study: The Startup Squad

Consider the case of Anya, a brilliant software engineer who decided to launch a sustainable fashion tech company.

Her initial team was composed entirely of other engineers—a squad of Moriartys. They had the technical know-how down cold, building a flawless, bug-free platform. But they were failing. Why? Because they lacked the other three pillars.

1. The Missing Kelly: Anya found her Kelly in Marcus, a former brand strategist. Marcus didn't know how to code, but he saw the why—the potential for a global, ethical brand. He gave technical perfection a strategic target and a clear vision of market dominance and impact. He provided the mission.

2. The Missing Crapgame: They were burning through cash and couldn't secure ethical sourcing deals. They needed a Crapgame. They brought in Sofia, a veteran of the textile industry. Sofia was a master negotiator, a little rough around the edges, but she knew what to ask for and who to ask. She secured the supply chain and negotiated the seed funding, the "sixty feet of bridge" they desperately needed.

3. The Missing Oddball: Anya herself was a high-strung perfectionist, a Kelly who was trying to be an Oddball. The team was constantly stressed. She realised her true role was to step back from the day-to-day coding and focus on the vibe. She started implementing "No-Stress Fridays," encouraging creative detours, and, most importantly, modelling non-attachment to minor setbacks. She became the commander, trusting her Moriartys (the engineers) to handle the how, her Kelly (Marcus) to handle the why, and her Crapgame (Sofia) to handle the what.

The moment she embraced her role as the Vibe Master, the company's negative waves dissipated, and the mission began to succeed.

The Nuance: Managing Edge Cases and Negative Waves

The relationship between the Oddball and the Moriarty is the most delicate and, arguably, the most important. It is the philosophical tension between Stoicism (Oddball's calm acceptance and focus on what he can control) and Existential Dread (Moriarty's focus on the absurd, often negative, reality of the world).

Oddball's genius is not in ignoring the negative waves, but in transmuting them.

When Moriarty says, "The bridge is out, man, the bridge is out," a lesser leader would panic or dismiss him. Oddball listens, acknowledges the reality, and then immediately pivots to a creative solution: "No sweat, we'll build a bridge." The negative wave is not a stop sign; it is a data point that informs the next creative move.

This is a practical application of the psychological concept of Cognitive Reappraisal. Instead of suppressing the negative emotion (Moriarty's fear), the Oddball reinterprets the situation. The bridge being out is not a disaster; it is an opportunity to demonstrate ingenuity and resourcefulness.

The Moriarty provides the raw, unvarnished truth, and the Oddball provides the frame through which that truth is viewed. You must actively seek out people who will give you the unvarnished truth, even if it's unpleasant, and then practice the art of reframing their input into actionable intelligence.

Practical Application: Step-by-Step Crew Cultivation

Finding your crew is not a passive process; it is a deliberate, multi-stage operation.

Phase 1: The Self-Assessment (Identifying Your Gaps)

Before you can recruit, you must know what you lack. Take a moment to analyse your current life mission—your career, your major project, your personal growth goal.

• Where is your mission stalling? Is it a lack of resources (Crapgame gap)? A lack of technical know-how (Moriarty gap)? A lack of clear direction (Kelly gap)? Or is it a lack of motivation and persistent stress (Oddball gap)?

• What is your dominant archetype? Most people naturally lean into one or two roles. If you are a natural Kelly, you need more Moriarty and Crapgame. If you are a natural Moriarty, you need a Kelly to give you a target and an Oddball to keep you from burning out.

Phase 2: The Mission is the Audition (Active Recruitment)

The best way to find your crew is to go on a mission. Start a project, plan a trip, try to build something. The people who show up, who contribute their skills, and who stick with it when things get tough—those are your potential crew members.

• **The Crapgame Test:** Propose a problem that requires resourcefulness. "I need to get this rare item by tomorrow, but all the stores are closed." The person who immediately starts calling contacts, checking obscure online marketplaces, and offering creative solutions is your Crapgame.

• **The Moriarty Test:** Present a half-baked idea and ask for honest feedback. "I'm going to launch this product with zero marketing budget." The person who systematically dismantles your plan, pointing out every single flaw in the logistics and execution, is your Moriarty.

• **The Kelly Test:** Share a vague, ambitious dream. "I want to be financially independent in five years." The person who immediately starts asking about timelines, milestones, and specific action steps is your Kelly.

Phase 3: Invest in Trust (The Fuel of the Crew)

Trust is the fuel of the crew. It is built through shared experience, mutual respect, and keeping your word. This is where the Oddball's role as the Vibe Master is paramount.

• **Be Reliable:** Do what you say you will do, especially the small things. Reliability builds the foundation of trust.

• **Be Loyal:** Defend your crew members against outsiders. If someone criticises Moriarty's negativity, you must step in and explain that his perspective is a vital asset, not a flaw. Make them feel safe to be their authentic, eccentric selves.

• **Practice Mutual Vulnerability:** Share your own failures and doubts. This is the ancient philosophical concept of Parrhesia, or "speaking truth to power." When the commander admits a mistake, it gives the rest of the crew permission to be honest about their own struggles.

The Philosophical Underpinnings: Oddball And Ancient Wisdom

The Oddball doctrine of the Tank Squad is not new; it is a modern, tank-flavoured take on ancient philosophical and psychological principles.

• **Aristotle's Philia (Friendship):** Aristotle distinguished between three types of friendship: utility, pleasure, and virtue.

The Tank Squad is a blend of all three, but it is fundamentally a Friendship of Utility and Virtue. The crew members are useful to one another (Crapgame gets the supplies, Moriarty fixes the tank), but their bond ultimately rests on a shared commitment to a virtuous life—a life of autonomy, resourcefulness, and self-determination.

They are not just friends; they are co-conspirators in the pursuit of a better, more authentic existence.

- **Jungian Archetypes:** The four roles map neatly onto Jung's psychological functions.

The Kelly is the Thinking function (strategy, logic).

The Crapgame is the Sensing function (material reality, resources).

The Moriarty is the Intuition function (seeing potential problems, the "negative waves" of the future).

And the Oddball, the Vibe Master, is the Feeling function (managing morale, emotional intelligence, the mood of the operation).

A balanced psyche, like a balanced tank squad, requires all four functions to be integrated and respected.

Extended Narrative: The Architect and the Algorithm

David, a brilliant but socially awkward architect, was stuck.

He had designed a revolutionary, sustainable housing project, but he couldn't get it past the city council. He was a pure Moriarty—he knew the structural engineering, the zoning codes, and the material science better than anyone. But his negative waves were suffocating the project. Every meeting was a detailed recitation of all the ways the project could fail.

His friend, Elena, a high-energy, politically savvy community organiser, was his Kelly. She saw the why—the social impact, the legacy. She told him, "David, the design is perfect. The mission is sound. But you're presenting a blueprint for failure, not a vision for success." She took over the presentation strategy, focusing on the positive wave of the future, the gold they were seeking.

They were still missing the Crapgame. The city council demanded a complex, custom-built algorithm to predict the project's long-term energy consumption. David could build it, but it would take six months. Elena knew a guy: Omar, a freelance data scientist with a reputation for delivering impossible solutions overnight. Omar was their Crapgame. He was expensive, demanded a cut of the future profits, and was completely unorthodox, but he delivered the algorithm in three weeks. He got the "sixty feet of bridge" they needed to cross the bureaucratic river.

David, the Moriarty, was horrified by Omar's messy, non-standard code, but Elena, the Kelly, and the newly emerging Oddball in David's own consciousness said, "It works. It got us across the river. We can clean up the code later." David learned the final lesson: Perfection is the enemy of the mission. The Oddball's role is to accept the necessary imperfection of the Crapgame's hustle and the Moriarty's gloom, and to keep the tank rolling toward the Kelly's vision.

Your crew is your sanctuary. They are the people you can be your weird, authentic self with. They are the ones who will help you fix the tank, find the bridge, and get the gold.

Choose them wisely, respect their unique brand of crazy, and remember that the most powerful force in the universe is a well-oiled, slightly eccentric tank squad rolling in the same direction.

The wave is always there; your crew just helps you ride it without wiping out.

Chapter Nineteen:

The Sharing of The Loaf

Oddball: "I'm drinking wine and eating cheese, and catching some rays, you know."

We have examined this parable from the perspective of personal rest, the necessity of the "time-out" for the individual soul. But to stop there is to miss the profound communal doctrine embedded in Oddball's casual declaration.

While he is enjoying this ritual alone, Big Joe finds him; the act of sharing simple, quality provisions is the primary, unspoken bonding ritual of the entire crew. It is the social contract of the Oddballist.

This is the Doctrine of the Shared Loaf. It is the understanding that a true, resilient connection is forged not in grand, transactional gestures, but in small, repeated, and intentional moments of shared pleasure.

The modern world, with its relentless pace and digital distractions, tries to make connection another form of work: networking events, scheduled "check-ins," and transactional interactions designed to yield a specific professional or social return.

Oddballism rejects this frantic, utilitarian approach. It teaches that true community, the kind that can withstand the pressure of a Tiger tank or a market crash, is built around a campfire, a dinner table, or a picnic blanket, where the only agenda is the shared moment itself.

The Core Principles of the Shared Loaf

The Shared Loaf is more than just a meal; it is a philosophical stance against the tyranny of productivity. It is a deliberate act of deceleration.

1. Simplicity and Quality: The Signal of Respect

The ritual does not need to be elaborate. It is not about impressing each other with culinary feats or expensive trappings. It is about sharing something simple and good. A loaf of fresh bread, a decent bottle of wine, a good cup of coffee, or even just a perfectly ripe piece of fruit.

The simplicity ensures accessibility—anyone can participate. The quality, however, matters immensely because it signals respect for the ritual and, more importantly, for the people you are sharing it with.

It says, "This moment is important, so we will use the good stuff."

This is not extravagance; it is reverence. It is the difference between mindlessly grabbing a fast-food burger and intentionally selecting a quality ingredient to share. The quality elevates the mundane act of eating into a sacred, shared experience.

2. Presence Over Production: The Anti-Agenda

The goal of the gathering is not to accomplish anything. It is not a meeting, a strategy session, or a therapy group. There is no agenda, no measurable outcome, and no action items. The goal is to be together.

To talk, to laugh, to argue, to enjoy the silence. It is a time to put away the mission, to shed the roles of "soldier," "employee," or "parent," and enjoy the company of the crew as fellow human beings.

This is the radical core of the doctrine: the value of the time is intrinsic, not extrinsic. It is a space where the pressure to perform is lifted, allowing genuine connection to surface.

3. A Celebration of the Now: The Antidote to Anxiety

The Shared Loaf is a ritual of radical gratitude for the present moment. It is a way of saying, "We are alive today. We have food and drink. We have each other. And that is enough." It is a powerful antidote to the anxiety of what comes next.

For a few moments, you are not worried about the next bridge, the next Tiger tank, the next quarterly report, or the next bill. You are just enjoying the cheese. This practice grounds the crew in the tangible reality of the present, strengthening their bond by reminding them that their shared survival and enjoyment is the highest immediate priority.

Case Study: The Architect and the Algorithm

Consider the case of Sarah, a 35-year-old architect in a major metropolitan firm.

Her life was a relentless cycle of deadlines, client pitches, and email triage. Her "crew"—her closest friends from college—had devolved into a group chat that mostly exchanged memes and apologies for missed calls. Sarah felt profoundly lonely, despite being constantly "connected."

One day, Sarah remembered a story her grandfather, a veteran, used to tell about sharing a single can of peaches with his squad during a long, cold night.

Inspired by the Doctrine of the Shared Loaf, she instituted a new rule: "Sunday Supper." It wasn't a fancy dinner party; it was a simple, non-negotiable ritual. Every Sunday at 6 PM, she would make a large pot of something simple—chilli, pasta, stew—and invite her friends. The only rule was "No Shop Talk, No Phones."

Her friend Mark, a software engineer, initially resisted. He saw it as a waste of time that he could be using to optimise his side hustle. But Sarah insisted. The first few weeks were awkward. People kept glancing at their pockets. But slowly, the ritual took hold.

They started talking about their childhoods, their fears, their ridiculous dreams. Mark stopped talking about his code and started talking about his passion for restoring vintage motorcycles. The simple act of sharing a meal, a physical loaf of bread, and a bottle of cheap wine, with no goal other than being there, began to rewire their relationships. They moved from being a network of contacts to a crew of companions. The Shared Loaf became their anchor, a weekly declaration that their humanity was more important than their productivity.

The Neuroscience of the Shared Table

Oddball's wisdom, as is often the case, finds deep resonance in modern science. The act of sharing food is a powerful trigger for oxytocin release, often called the "bonding hormone." When we eat together, especially when the food is simple and the atmosphere is relaxed, our parasympathetic nervous system—the "rest and digest" system—is activated. This state of calm and safety is the optimal environment for trust to develop.

The Shared Loaf is a direct application of Polyvagal Theory, which suggests that our social engagement system is deeply tied to our sense of safety. When we are physically present, sharing a meal, and making eye contact (not looking at a screen), our vagus nerve signals to our brain that we are safe.

This down-regulates the fight-or-flight response, allowing for a genuine, vulnerable connection. Oddball, the master of calm under pressure, intuitively understood that a crew that shares a loaf is a crew that trusts each other, because they have repeatedly signalled safety to one another in the most primal way possible.

Connecting to Ancient Philosophy: Koinonia and Symposium

The Doctrine of the Shared Loaf is not new; it is a rediscovery of ancient wisdom.

The Greeks had the concept of koinonia, which roughly translates as "fellowship, sharing, or common possession." It was the idea of a deep, spiritual communion, often expressed through shared meals. Their famous Symposium was not merely a drinking party; it was a structured social ritual in which men gathered to drink, dine, and engage in philosophical discussion. The physical act of sharing the cup and the food was the foundation for the sharing of ideas and the forging of civic bonds.

Oddball's ritual is the modern, pragmatic, and less formal version of the Symposium. It strips away the intellectual pretence and gets straight to the human core: the shared experience. He understood that you don't need Plato to have a meaningful conversation; you just need a decent piece of cheese and a willingness to be present. The Shared Loaf is the koinonia of the modern warrior, a necessary pause for the soul to reconnect with its tribe.

Practical Applications: The Step-by-Step Guidance

To truly practice the Shared Loaf, one must move beyond the abstract idea and implement specific techniques. This is the Oddballist way: practical application is everything.

1. The Intentional Invitation: Do not issue a vague, open-ended invitation like, "We should get together sometime."

That is a social obligation, not a ritual. Instead, be specific and intentional. "Every Tuesday at 7 PM, I am making tacos. No need to RSVP, just show up. I'll have enough for three extra people. The only rule is you have to stay for at least an hour." This low-pressure, high-consistency approach makes the ritual a reliable anchor in a chaotic world.

2. The Sensory Anchor: Choose a specific, simple element that will become the sensory anchor for your ritual.

For Oddball, it was the wine and cheese. For you, it might be a specific type of coffee, a particular scent (like burning cedar or a certain candle), or a specific album of music.

This anchor, repeated every time, conditions the crew to immediately enter the "Presence Over Production" mindset. The moment the anchor is introduced, the mission is paused.

3. The Phone Basket Protocol: The most critical step for the modern Shared Loaf is the removal of digital distraction.

Before the loaf is broken, a designated "Phone Basket" is placed in a neutral, inconvenient location. Every person places their phone in the basket.

This is not a suggestion; it is a non-negotiable rule. The physical act of separating from the device is a powerful, symbolic commitment to the present company. The digital world can wait; the crew cannot.

4. The Conversation Prompt: While the goal is not an agenda, sometimes a crew needs a gentle nudge to move past surface-level talk.

Have a simple, open-ended prompt ready, but do not force it.

Something like, "What is one thing you learned this week that surprised you?" or "What is a small victory you had today that no one else knows about?" These prompts encourage vulnerability and storytelling, the true currency of the Shared Loaf.

Nuances and Edge Cases: The Solitary Loaf

What about the times when the crew is scattered, or when one is intentionally alone? Oddball himself is alone when Big Joe finds him. This introduces the concept of the Solitary Loaf.

The Solitary Loaf is the practice of applying the principles of the Shared Loaf to oneself. It is the intentional, high-quality, present-moment ritual of self-care. If the communal loaf is about koinonia with the tribe, the solitary loaf is about koinonia with the self. It is the recognition that you, too, are part of the crew that needs tending.

Imagine David, a long-haul truck driver who spends weeks on the road. He can't have a Sunday Supper. But he can practice the Solitary Loaf. Instead of mindlessly eating a convenience store meal while driving, he pulls over, sets up a small folding table, and prepares a simple, high-quality meal—a good sandwich, a thermos of excellent coffee, and a piece of dark chocolate.

He puts his CB radio on standby and his phone on silent. For thirty minutes, he is present. He is not a driver; he is a man enjoying his provisions. This ritual prevents the slow erosion of the soul that comes from constant, unacknowledged labour. It is a moment of self-respect, a declaration that even when alone, he is worthy of the good stuff and the present moment.

The Real Gold

In the end, the gold in the movie is just a MacGuffin. The real treasure is the journey with your crew. The moments you will remember are not the battles, the promotions, or the quarterly bonuses, but the quiet times in between. The laughter, the arguments, the shared silence. The breaking of the bread.

Oddball's Doctrine of the Shared Loaf is a powerful, subversive philosophy for the 21st century. It tells us to stop chasing the next big thing and to start cherishing the small, repeatable things. It reminds us that our deepest human need is not for more productivity or more wealth, but for authentic, non-transactional connection.

It is a call to action: find your crew, find your loaf, and make the time to enjoy the cheese. This is the stuff of life. This is the real gold.

The Shared Loaf is the ultimate expression of Oddball's wisdom: the only way to survive the chaos of the world is to create small, intentional pockets of peace, quality, and community.

And it all starts with a simple invitation to share.

Chapter 20:

When the Tank Breaks Down

Moriarty: "The tank's broke and they're trying to fix it."

No crew is perfect. No tank runs forever. There will be conflict. There will be breakdowns.

The absence of problems does not measure the strength of a crew, but by how it responds to them. This is the Doctrine of Repair, and it is the philosophical engine that keeps the Wave Rider moving when the road gets rough. The world is full of people who believe that a perfect life is one free of friction, but the Oddballist knows better. Friction is the necessary heat that forges steel; it is the tension that makes the music. The real art is not in avoiding the breakdown, but in mastering the repair.

Conflict within the crew is inevitable. You have a collection of eccentric, independent, and often cynical individuals working together under pressure. They are going to clash.

Moriarty's pessimism will clash with Oddball's optimism.

Crapgame's opportunism will clash with Kelly's strategic focus.

This is not a sign of failure; it is a sign that you have a crew of passionate individuals, not mindless drones. A crew that never argues is a crew that has stopped caring. The silence of a team is often more dangerous than its noise. The key is to transform the noise of disagreement into the constructive sound of a wrench turning a bolt.

The Oddballist Approach to Conflict Resolution: The Four Tools of Repair

The Oddballist doesn't run from conflict; he treats it like a mechanical failure—a problem to be diagnosed, not a moral failing to be judged. This approach is built on four practical, repeatable steps that turn a crisis into a cohesion-building exercise.

1. Acknowledge the Vibe Shift: The Diagnostic Phase

The first sign of a breakdown is a change in the energy. The easy banter stops. The air gets thick with negative waves.

As the Vibe Master, your first job is to notice and name this. You must develop a radar for the subtle shifts in emotional climate. Is the normally talkative team member silent? Is the usually punctual one suddenly late? These are not just isolated incidents; they are dashboard warning lights. The classic mistake is to ignore these signals, hoping the problem will fix itself.

The Oddballist knows that a small leak ignored becomes a catastrophic failure.

Case Study: The Architect and the Coder.

Consider the case of Anya, a brilliant but highly sensitive software architect, and Ben, a pragmatic, deadline-driven coder.

Anya spent weeks designing an elegant, complex system. Ben, under pressure, bypassed a key component of her design to meet a tight deadline, using a simpler, less elegant solution.

Anya felt personally betrayed; Ben felt Anya was being precious about code that "just needed to work."

The vibe shift was palpable: Anya started communicating only via terse emails; Ben began eating lunch alone. The Vibe Master, their project lead, didn't wait for the blow-up. She called a five-minute "vibe check" meeting.

Her opening line: "The vibe feels a little off today. What's happening? I feel a tension that's slowing us down, and I want to fix it."

By naming the tension without assigning blame, she created a safe space for the diagnosis to begin.

2. Humour as a Disinfectant: Lowering the Emotional Temperature

Oddball's primary tool for dealing with interpersonal tension is humour. When Big Joe confronts him with hostility, Oddball's dog imitation is so absurd that it makes the anger seem ridiculous. Humour is not about dismissing the problem; it's about lowering the emotional temperature so the problem can be addressed calmly.

Anger is a hot, sticky emotion that prevents clear thinking. Humour is the cool, dry air that allows the parts to separate and be examined.

This is not about making light of a serious issue, but about introducing perspective.

A well-timed joke can be the grease that gets a stuck gear moving again. It reminds everyone that they are human, that the problem lies outside their core values, and that the stakes, while important, are not life-or-death. It's the difference between saying, "You messed up the whole project!" and saying, "Well, that's a spectacular way to break the internet. Let's see if we can un-break it before the aliens notice."

The latter acknowledges the gravity while inviting collaboration over confrontation. The absurdity of Oddball's actions—like driving a tank backwards or painting it in psychedelic colours—is a constant, subtle reminder that the rules of engagement are flexible, and a little bit of fun is always a tactical advantage.

3. Respect the Specialist: The Principle of Distributed Expertise

When the tank breaks down, Oddball doesn't tell Moriarty how to do his job. He trusts his expertise. When there is a conflict, respect the other person's perspective and expertise. Don't assume you know their motivations or their internal state.

Ask questions. "Help me understand why you see it that way."

This is the philosophical core of Oddballism applied to conflict: everyone is a specialist in their own experience. You are the specialist in your feelings; they are the specialists in theirs.

You may disagree with their conclusion, but you must respect the data they are presenting—their reality.

In the case of Anya and Ben, the Vibe Master didn't take sides.

She asked Anya, "What part of the design did you feel was most compromised, and what was the long-term risk you were trying to mitigate?"

She asked Ben, "What was the specific pressure point that made you choose speed over the original design, and what was the immediate mission you were trying to save?"

By focusing on their expertise—Anya's long-term vision, Ben's immediate execution—she validated both. The conflict shifted from "You are wrong" to "We have two competing, valid priorities." This is the essence of the Doctrine of Repair: understanding the function of the broken part before attempting to fix it.

4. Focus on the Mission: The Unifying Goal

Ultimately, the crew is united by a shared goal. When conflict arises, bring the focus back to the mission.

"Okay, we disagree here. But we all still want to get the gold. How can we resolve this so we can get the tank moving again?"

A shared purpose is the most powerful solvent for interpersonal friction. This step leverages a deep-seated psychological principle: humans are wired for cooperation, especially when facing an external challenge.

By reframing the conflict as an internal obstacle to an external goal, you shift the energy from "me vs. you" to "us vs. the problem."

For Anya and Ben, the mission was the launch date.

The Vibe Master concluded: "Anya, your design is the long-term gold standard. Ben, your quick fix saved the immediate mission. The new mission is to integrate Anya's component into Ben's working code after the launch, turning a temporary fix into a permanent solution. Ben, you will lead the integration, and Anya, you will be the technical advisor."

This not only resolved the immediate tension but also created a new, shared objective that utilised both of their strengths, reinforcing their interdependence.

The Neuroscience of Repair: From Amygdala Hijack to Prefrontal Peace

Oddball's methods, though seemingly intuitive, are deeply aligned with modern neuroscience.

Conflict often triggers an "amygdala hijack," where the brain's emotional centre takes over, shutting down the rational prefrontal cortex. When this happens, people cannot think clearly; they can only react defensively.

• Acknowledge the Vibe Shift is the first step in mindfulness—it brings the prefrontal cortex back online by simply observing the emotional state. By naming the feeling, you begin to regulate it.

• Humour as a Disinfectant is a powerful cognitive reframing technique. Laughter releases endorphins and shifts the nervous system from a sympathetic (fight-or-flight) state to a parasympathetic (rest-and-digest) state. It literally calms the body, making rational dialogue possible.

• Respect the Specialist is an exercise in empathy and perspective-taking. This engages the parts of the brain responsible for social cognition, forcing a shift away from self-centred defence toward understanding the other.

• Focus on the Mission leverages the brain's goal-directed behaviour circuits. It provides a positive, future-oriented focus that overrides the negative, past-focused rumination of the conflict.

The Oddballist is an applied neuroscientist who uses social tools to regulate the crew's collective nervous system and ensure optimal performance.

When a Crew Member Must Be Left Behind: The Necessary Amputation

Sometimes, a breakdown is terminal. A crew member may consistently generate negative waves, refuse to trust the crew, or betray the mission. This is the hardest part of the Doctrine of Repair, the point where maintenance turns into necessary amputation. Your primary responsibility is to the health and vibe of the whole. One consistently toxic member can poison the entire operation.

Oddball demonstrates this with Bellamy, the engineer who constantly makes the same "stinking awful stupid joke" about the nut ward.

Oddball gives him a chance, but when Bellamy continues to be unhelpful and disrespectful, the verdict is swift and final: "You don't want in this thing... You don't get in this thing... I cut you out of everything... I don't need you."

This is a painful but necessary part of managing a crew, whether it's a business team, a friendship circle, or a family unit. The decision to cut someone out should never be taken lightly. It must follow a clear, repeated pattern of violation of the core mission and the crew's vibe. Before the final cut, the Oddballist follows a three-step protocol:

1. The Clear Warning: The toxic behaviour must be named explicitly, and the consequences of its continuation must be stated. This is not a threat, but a statement of reality. "When you constantly criticise the plan in front of the whole team, it creates doubt and slows us down. If this continues, we cannot have you on the team."

2. The Final Opportunity: A specific, time-bound chance for the individual to re-engage with the mission and the crew's values. This is the moment of truth. If they choose to change, the repair is successful. If they double down on the negativity, the decision is made for you.

3. The Clean Break: The cut must be clean, final, and without lingering guilt. The Oddballist understands that carrying dead weight is a betrayal of the rest of the crew who are pulling their weight. Your tank cannot carry dead weight forever. The mission is paramount, and the collective vibe's health is the engine of the mission.

Case Study: The Friend Who Drained the Fuel.

Liam had a friend, Mark, who was a constant source of negative waves.

Every conversation was a complaint about his job, his partner, or his life choices, but he refused to take any advice or make any changes.

Liam, a budding Wave Rider, initially applied the Doctrine of Repair, using humour and respect to try to shift the dynamic. He acknowledged the vibe shift ("You seem really down, Mark, what's the core issue?"). But Mark refused to engage in problem-solving, preferring to wallow.

After months of feeling emotionally drained after every interaction, Liam realised Mark was not a broken part to be repaired, but a hole in the fuel tank.

The final cut was not a dramatic confrontation, but a slow, firm fade. Liam stopped initiating contact, declined invitations politely, and when Mark finally asked why, Liam used the Oddballist principle: "Mark, I respect your path, but the vibe we create together is consistently negative, and it's slowing down my mission. I need to focus my energy on people who are moving forward. I wish you well, but I need to cut this out for now."

It was honest, mission-focused, and final. The immediate relief was a clear sign that the necessary amputation had saved the whole.

The Ancient Wisdom of the Crew

The Doctrine of Repair is not new; it is a modern articulation of ancient philosophical wisdom.

The Stoics spoke of the Dichotomy of Control, teaching us to focus only on what we can influence. In a conflict, you cannot control the other person's reaction, but you can control your own diagnosis, your use of humour, your respect, and your focus on the mission. Oddball's wisdom is Stoicism with a sense of humour and a tank.

Similarly, the concept of the crew as a living organism echoes the Buddhist principle of interdependence. No one exists in isolation. The health of the whole depends on the health of the parts, and the failure of one part affects all. The Doctrine of Repair is simply the maintenance manual for that interdependence. It teaches that when a part breaks, the rest of the system must rally to fix it, not to blame it.

Your crew is a living organism. It needs maintenance, fuel, and repair. It will break down. But by approaching conflict with the four tools of repair—acknowledging the vibe shift, using humour as a disinfectant, respecting the specialist, and focusing on the mission—you can fix almost any problem, get the engine running again, and continue your journey toward the gold, together.

The breakdown is not the end of the road; it is merely a scheduled stop for a necessary, powerful repair.
The Wave Rider is defined not by the perfection of their journey, but by the tenacity of their repair.

Part Seven:

Living the Oddball Life

We have explored the Five Pillars. We have dissected the parables.

We have established the theoretical framework of Oddballism.

Now, we must move from the philosophical to the practical. A philosophy that you don't live is just a collection of interesting ideas. A tank that stays in the garage is just a heavy sculpture.

The purpose of this knowledge is not to be admired, but to be used. This is the part of the book where the rubber treads meet the road.

This section is your field manual. It's about integrating the doctrines into the messy, beautiful, and often frustrating reality of your daily existence.

We will cover how to structure your day like a Wave Rider, how to apply the principles at work and in love, and how to hold onto your righteous vibe when the world around you is exploding.

This is where you stop being a student of Oddballism and start becoming Oddball.

Chapter Twenty-One:

The Daily Practice of the Wave Rider

A righteous life is not built on grand, heroic gestures, but on small, consistent, daily practices.

It's the rhythm of your days that determines the quality of your life. A Wave Rider's day is structured around a simple goal: to maximise positive waves, minimise negative ones, and find moments of beauty and joy along the way.

This is not a rigid, unforgiving schedule, but a template, a rhythm. Some days you will hit every beat; other days the tank will break down and you'll spend the whole afternoon drinking wine and eating cheese. That's fine. The goal is not perfection. The goal is a life lived with more intention, more joy, and a whole lot more positive waves.

The Morning (06:00 - 09:00): Protecting the Vibe

Your first ninety minutes are the most sacred of the day. They set the energetic tone for everything that follows. The goal here is defence. You must protect your newly awakened consciousness from the world's barrage of negativity. This period is your personal demilitarised zone, a sanctuary where you fortify your mind before the day's engagement. The quality of your morning determines the resilience of your afternoon.

1. Wake Up and Hydrate: The Foundational Act of Self-Respect

Before anything else, drink a large glass of water. Your body is a machine that needs fuel.

Hydration is the most basic form of self-respect, a simple, non-negotiable act of maintenance. Think of your body as the tank you'll be riding all day. You wouldn't send a tank into battle with a dry radiator.

This is a physical act with a profound psychological effect: it is the first conscious and positive decision you make, a small victory that sets the tone for a day of intentional living. The ancient Stoics spoke of living in accordance with nature; what is more natural than tending to your physical needs with immediate, simple care?

2. The Morning Declaration: The Shield of Positive Intent

Find a quiet spot. Stand, stretch, and perform the sacred declaration: "Don't hit me with them negative waves so early in the morning."

Say it with intent. Feel the shield of positivity forming around you. This is more than a humorous mantra; it is a powerful psychological anchor. In modern neuroscience, this is a form of priming in which a specific thought or action influences the response to subsequent stimuli.

By declaring your boundary, you are actively programming your subconscious to filter out incoming negativity. It is a moment of self-sovereignty, a clear statement that you, and not the external world, are in charge of your emotional state.

3. No Screens: The Spiritual Self-Defence

This is the most important and most difficult rule. For at least the first hour of your day, do not look at your phone, your computer, or your television. Do not check email. Do not check social media. Do not check the news.

To do so is to invite a thousand Moriartys into your brain before you've even had your coffee.

It is an act of spiritual self-harm. The modern screen is a portal to a world of manufactured urgency, comparison, and anxiety. By delaying this exposure, you give your prefrontal cortex—the part of your brain responsible for planning and decision-making—a chance to wake up fully before the reactive, fear-driven amygdala hijacks it.

This practice is a modern echo of ancient contemplative traditions, a brief, deliberate withdrawal from the saṃsāra of the digital world to establish inner peace.

4. The First Pleasure: Savouring the Small Victory

Engage in a simple, sensual pleasure. This is your personal version of wine and cheese. It could be savouring a cup of coffee in silence, stretching, meditating, or simply sitting by a window and watching the world wake up.

This is your first act of "digging it." This is a direct application of hedonic psychology, focusing on the small, accessible joys that accumulate into a sense of well-being. It is a moment of pure, non-productive enjoyment, a reminder that life is not merely a series of tasks to be completed, but a collection of moments to be experienced.

The Wave Rider understands that a day begun with a moment of genuine pleasure is a day already won.

5. Set the Mission: The Clear, Simple Sortie Plan

Briefly review your plan for the day. What is your "gold" for the next 12 hours? Identify your top one to three priorities. This is not a stressful to-do list; it is a clear, simple mission.

This practice aligns with the Pareto Principle, or the 80/20 rule, focusing your limited energy on the few tasks that will yield the greatest return. By defining your mission early, you prevent decision fatigue later in the day.

You are telling your subconscious exactly what to aim for, giving your tank a clear heading before you leave the garage.

Case Study: The Architect and the Morning Wave

Consider Elias, a 42-year-old architect in Chicago.

Elias was a high performer, but his mornings were a disaster. He would wake up, immediately check his phone, and within five minutes be drowning in emails from his demanding firm, a news headline about a global crisis, and a social media post from a rival architect.

By the time he sat down to work, he was already running on a cocktail of cortisol and resentment. His creativity was stifled, and he often snapped at his junior staff.

Elias adopted the Wave Rider's morning practice.

He started leaving his phone in the kitchen overnight. His first hour was spent drinking water, performing the declaration while looking out over Lake Michigan, and then savouring a single, perfectly brewed cup of tea while reading a physical book.

The change was immediate. He wasn't reacting to the world; he was entering it on his own terms. The simple act of delaying screen time gave him the mental space to identify his "gold" for the day—the one critical design problem he needed to solve.

Within a month, his productivity soared, his stress levels dropped, and his team noticed a profound shift in his demeanour. He wasn't just a better architect; he was a better captain of his own ship.

He learned that the morning is not for catching up, but for getting ahead—ahead of the negative waves, ahead of the noise, and ahead of his own reactive tendencies.

The Day (09:00 - 18:00): Riding the Wave

This is the main part of the battle. You are now engaging with the world. The goal is to be effective, creative, and energetically resilient.

The Wave Rider does not fight the current; he uses it. This requires a constant, subtle awareness of the flow of energy—both internal and external.

1. Start Your Engines with Righteous Tunes: Controlling the Sonic Environment.

As you begin your work, put on your "battle music." Choose a playlist that makes you feel calm, focused, and powerful. Use your loudspeaker to control your audio environment. This is a practical application of auditory entrainment, using rhythm and melody to synchronise your brainwaves for optimal focus.

The Wave Rider knows that the environment is not a given; it is a variable to be controlled.

By curating your soundscape, you are building an invisible wall against distraction and a sonic launchpad for deep work. Your music is your personal soundtrack to the mission, a constant, positive wave you generate yourself.

2. Master Your Tank: The Competence Account.

Do your work, and do it well. Apply yourself with focus and skill. This is where you build your confidence account. Be a professional. Be competent.

Oddball's wisdom here is simple: mastery is the ultimate form of self-respect and the most effective shield against self-doubt. When you know your craft, you are less susceptible to the negative waves of imposter syndrome or external criticism.

This concept is deeply rooted in Aristotelian ethics, where *arete* (excellence or virtue) is achieved through consistent, skilful action. Every successful task, every problem solved, is a deposit in your competence account, making you more resilient for the next challenge.

3. Practice the Mid-Day Dig: The Nervous System Reset

Sometime around noon, take a deliberate pause. Step away from your work. Go outside if you can. Perform a Five-Sense Dig.

Notice the weather, the sounds, the feeling of the air. This resets your nervous system and reminds you that there is a world beyond your mission. This is a form of mindfulness, a deliberate shift from the abstract, conceptual world of work to the concrete, sensory reality of the present moment.

Psychologically, this brief pause helps to replenish your attentional resources, preventing the afternoon slump and the inevitable drop in decision quality.

It is a moment to remember that you are a human being, not a human doing, and that the mission is served best by a mind that is fresh and connected to the source of life.

4. Share the Loaf: The Ritual of Replenishment

Lunch is a sacred ritual. Do not eat at your desk while working. If you can, share the meal with a crew member. If you are alone, savour the food.

Pay attention to the taste and texture.

This is a moment of replenishment, not just refuelling. The Wave Rider understands that communal eating is a fundamental human bonding ritual. Sharing the loaf reinforces the crew's cohesion, builds trust, and provides a much-needed break from the mission's intensity.

Even when eating alone, savouring the food is a powerful anti-anxiety technique, grounding you in the physical reality of nourishment. It is a small, daily rebellion against the modern tendency to treat food as a mere utility.

5. Wave Rejection Practice: The Art of Internal Shielding

You will be hit with negative waves—a stressful email, a complaining coworker, a frustrating setback.

Practice naming the wave internally ("Negative wave detected"). Use a verbal shield if appropriate ("Let's focus on solutions for now"). Take a deep breath and visualise the wave dissipating against your shield. This is the core of the Wave Rider's philosophy in action. It is a cognitive-behavioural technique known as cognitive diffusion, in which you distance yourself from the thought or emotion by labelling it, thereby reducing its power over you. By naming the wave, you are acknowledging its existence without allowing it to become your reality.

The deep breath activates the parasympathetic nervous system, the body's natural "rest and digest" mode, physically counteracting the stress response triggered by the negative wave.

Deeper Exploration: Oddball's Wisdom and Modern Psychology

Oddball's philosophy of "Don't hit me with them negative waves" is a surprisingly sophisticated precursor to several key concepts in modern psychological science.

His intuitive wisdom about managing one's internal state aligns perfectly with the principles of Acceptance and Commitment Therapy (ACT) and Stoicism.

The Stoics, particularly Epictetus, taught that we are disturbed not by things, but by the views we take of them. Oddball's "Wave Rejection Practice" is a practical, humorous application of this. The external event—the stressful email—is the "thing." The internal reaction—the anxiety, the anger—is the "negative wave."

By naming the wave, the Wave Rider is essentially saying, "I see this emotional reaction, but I choose not to identify with it or be controlled by it."

This is the essence of Stoic detachment and of ACT's concept of mindfulness, in which one observes thoughts and feelings as passing events rather than absolute truths.

Furthermore, the emphasis on controlling the environment (righteous tunes, no screens) is a powerful lesson in neuroscience. The brain is a prediction machine, constantly seeking patterns and safety. A chaotic, reactive environment (like checking the news first thing) floods the system with unpredictable, threat-based information, leading to chronic low-level stress.

The Wave Rider's structured day creates a predictable, positive environment that calms the nervous system, conserves cognitive energy, and enables higher-level creative and problem-solving work. Oddball, the intuitive philosopher, understood that the best way to win the battle is to choose the terrain.

Extended Narrative Example: The Case of the Complaining Coworker

Maria, a project manager at a mid-sized tech firm, was constantly being hit by negative waves from her coworker, Gary.

Gary was a talented but deeply cynical engineer who saw every new project as a catastrophe waiting to happen. Every morning, Gary would stop by Maria's desk to deliver a five-minute monologue about the incompetence of management, the impossibility of the deadline, and the general futility of their work.

Maria, a natural empath, would absorb this negativity like a sponge, leaving her drained and anxious before 10 AM.

Maria decided to apply the Wave Rejection Practice.

The next morning, as Gary approached, she internally named the wave: "Negative Wave: Gary's Cynicism."

As he launched into his usual tirade about the new server migration, Maria didn't argue or try to fix his mood. Instead, she used a verbal shield, delivered with Oddball's gentle, practical humour.

"Gary, I hear you, man," she said, holding up a hand. "That sounds like a real mess. But listen, I'm in the middle of my morning 'Master Your Tank' session, and I need to keep my focus tight. How about you shoot me a quick, bullet-point email with the top three technical risks you see? That way, I can put it on the mission plan for this afternoon, and we can focus on solutions then. Sound like a plan?"

By doing this, Maria achieved three things:

1. She deflected the emotional wave: She didn't let his mood infect hers.

2. She validated the core concern: She acknowledged the technical problem, showing respect for his competence.

3. She redirected the energy: She converted his formless complaint into a structured, actionable task, shifting the focus from problem-dwelling to solution-finding.

Gary, disarmed by the unexpected boundary and the request for concrete action, simply nodded and walked away. The negative wave had been detected, named, and dissipated without a fight.

Maria was able to get back to her work, her vibe intact, proving that the Wave Rider's practice is not about avoiding conflict, but about managing energy.

The Evening (18:00 - 22:00): The After-Action Report

The mission for the day is over. The goal now is to power down the tank, connect with your crew, and prepare for tomorrow's mission. This is the crucial period for restoration and integration, ensuring that the day's stress is metabolised and the lessons are learned.

1. The Shutdown Ritual: Creating a Clear Boundary

Create a clear end to your workday. It could be closing your laptop, changing your clothes, or saying a specific phrase. This signals to your brain that it's time to switch from "mission mode" to "rest mode." This is a psychological trick to prevent "task residue"—the tendency for work thoughts to bleed into personal time.

The ritual serves as a symbolic close to the day's file, allowing your mind to relax. For some, it might be a 15-minute walk around the block; for others, it's a simple, ceremonial wiping down of the desk. The key is consistency.

2. Connect with the Crew: Reinforcing the Bonds

This is the prime time for connection. Have dinner with your family. Call a friend. Engage in a shared activity. This is where you reinforce the bonds that give your life meaning. Social connection is the single greatest predictor of long-term happiness and health. The Wave Rider knows that no tank operates alone.

The crew—family, friends, partners—are the support system that makes the mission possible. This time is not a luxury; it is a vital part of the maintenance schedule. Put the phone away, look people in the eye, and share the stories of the day.

3. The Beauty Log: Priming for Gratitude and Sleep

Before you go to sleep, open your Tank Journal. Write down three beautiful things you "dug" today. This primes your brain to enter sleep with a sense of gratitude and positivity. This simple practice is a form of cognitive restructuring. Throughout the day, the brain has a natural negativity bias, focusing on threats and problems.

The Beauty Log forces a deliberate search for positive data points, retraining the brain to notice the good. This shift in focus reduces rumination and anxiety, leading to a faster onset of sleep and more restorative rest. It's the final, positive wave of the day.

4. Plan the Next Sortie: Offloading the Mental Load

Spend five minutes—and no more—planning the next day's mission. This gets the plan out of your head so you don't lie awake thinking about it. It tells your subconscious that everything is under control. This is a powerful technique for managing intrusive thoughts at night.

By externalising the plan—writing down the "gold" for tomorrow—you free up your working memory. Your brain can then safely transition into its restorative sleep cycles, knowing that the mission is organised and ready to go.

5. Power Down with Pleasure: The Screen-Free Sanctuary

The last hour of your day should be screen-free. Read a book. Listen to calm music. Take a bath. Engage in a simple, relaxing pleasure that prepares your body and mind for restorative sleep. The blue light emitted by screens suppresses melatonin, the hormone that regulates sleep. The Wave Rider respects the body's natural rhythms.

This final hour is a return to the self, a gentle, analogue transition into the unconscious, ensuring that the tank is fully recharged and ready to ride the waves of the next day. The simple, non-digital pleasure is the final, perfect piece of cheese before the lights go out.

Practical Application: The 5-Step Wave Rider's Daily Audit

To ensure you are consistently riding the wave, perform this quick audit at the end of each week. This is your tank maintenance check.

1. The Screen Test: How many days this week did you successfully avoid screens for the first hour? (Score 1 point per day). If your score is below 5, you are letting the enemy into the camp too early.

Technique: Move your charging station to a different room.

2. The Dig Ratio: How many times did you take a true, sensory-focused Mid-Day Dig? (Aim for 5). If you missed more than two, you are running on fumes.

Technique: Set a recurring, non-negotiable alarm on your phone labelled "Go Outside."

3. The Loaf Quality: How many meals did you eat away from your work desk, truly savouring the food and connecting with others?

(Aim for 10, or 2 per workday). If this number is low, you are treating yourself like a utility rather than a Wave Rider.

Technique: Schedule a 30-minute lunch block with a coworker or friend.

4. The Shield Count: Can you recall at least three instances where you successfully used a verbal or internal shield to deflect a negative wave? If you can't, you were likely absorbing them.

Technique: Practice the phrase, "That's an interesting perspective, but I'm focused on X right now."

5. The Beauty Tally: How many entries are in your Beauty Log? (Aim for 21, or 3 per day). If your tally is low, you are missing the joy in the details.

Technique: Keep a small notebook and pen next to your bed, and write down the three things you did immediately before turning off the light.

The Wave Rider's life is a constant, joyful adjustment. It is the art of being present, of being competent, and of being kind—to yourself and to your crew. Keep riding, keep digging it, and keep those negative waves at bay.

The mission continues tomorrow.

Chapter Twenty-Two:

Oddball At Work:

The Mother, Beautiful Tank of Professional Life

The modern workplace is a negative wave factory. It is a battlefield of deadlines, egos, bureaucracy, and fluorescent lighting.

To survive, let alone thrive, you must be a master Wave Rider.

Applying the Five Pillars of Oddballism to your career can transform it from a source of stress into a field for creative expression and personal satisfaction. Oddball understood that the true professional is not a cog in a machine, but a self-contained, highly optimised unit—a mother beautiful tank—moving with purpose and efficiency through the chaos.

1. Dealing with Corporate Moriartys: The Art of Validation and Redirection

Every office has a Moriarty. They're the ones who say, "That will never work," "We've tried that before," and "I'm just being realistic." They are the human embodiment of the negative wave, and you cannot escape them. Your job is not to fight them, but to manage their waves, to let their negativity wash over your tank without penetrating the hull.

The Psychology of the Moriarty: From a psychological perspective, the Corporate Moriarty often operates from a place of fear—fear of change, fear of failure, or fear of losing their perceived status. Their resistance is a defence mechanism. Arguing with them reinforces their position as an obstacle you must overcome, only strengthening their resolve.

Oddball's wisdom here aligns perfectly with the principles of Motivational Interviewing and Aikido: use their energy against them.

Case Study: The Architect and the Sceptic.

Consider Elara, a brilliant but young architect who proposed a radical, sustainable design for a new corporate campus.

Her Moriarty was Mr Harrison, the long-tenured Head of Facilities, a man whose career was built on concrete and steel. When Elara presented her plan, Harrison immediately launched a barrage of budget and timeline concerns.

"That will never work, Elara. The cost of those materials alone will sink the project before we even break ground. We've tried 'green' before; it's a pipe dream."
Elara, channelling her inner Oddball, did not argue.

She used the technique of Validate and Redirect: "That's a valid point, Mr Harrison, and I appreciate you flagging the budget risk. You have decades of experience navigating these costs, and I respect that. Now, assuming we can find the resources—perhaps through the new government sustainability grants I've identified—how would you suggest we phase the construction to minimise disruption? Your expertise on logistics is exactly what we need to make this ambitious project realistic."

By validating his concern and, more importantly, his expertise, she shifted his role from adversary to consultant. She didn't dismiss his wave; she rode it, steering the conversation away from if it could be done to how he, the expert, could help her do it.

The Moriarty, now feeling respected and necessary, began offering solutions rather than roadblocks.

The Humorous Shield: When a coworker is complaining endlessly, hit them with a gentle, Oddball-esque absurdity.

"Man, that sounds like a tidal wave of negativity. We're gonna need a bigger boat."

It's friendly, but it sends a clear message: I hear you, but I refuse to be pulled under. This is a form of cognitive reframing—using humour to break the pattern of negative rumination and introduce a lighter, more solution-oriented perspective.

It's a social lubricant that prevents conflict while protecting your own mental space.

2. Your Desk is Your Tank: Creating the Optimal Command Centre

Your workspace, whether it's a corner office, a cubicle, or a kitchen table, is your command centre.

It must be a mother, beautiful tank.

This is not about aesthetics; it is about environmental mastery, a concept deeply rooted in both ancient Stoicism and modern neuroscience. The Stoics believed in controlling what you can control; your immediate environment is the most tangible thing within your sphere of influence. Neuroscience confirms that a chaotic environment leads to a chaotic mind, increasing cortisol levels and decreasing focus.

Master and Modify: Are your tools working for you? Have you customised your software, organised your files, and created a system that is fast and efficient? Or are you fighting with the standard-issue equipment? Take the time to master your tools and make them your own.

This means more than just a clean desk. It means:

- **Software Customisation:** Learning keyboard shortcuts, writing simple scripts to automate repetitive tasks, and configuring your applications to minimise friction. If you spend 15 minutes a day fighting your tools, that's 60 hours a year lost. Oddball would never tolerate a poorly maintained engine.

- **Information Architecture:** Your digital files should be as organised as the inside of a tank turret. Use a consistent naming convention. Implement a "Zero Inbox" policy for email. The gold is in the information; if you can't find it instantly, you don't own it.

Control the Vibe: The Sensory Firewall. Use your loudspeaker if you can, play righteous tunes on your headphones. Put up pictures that make you happy. Have a plant. Your desk should be an island of positive energy in a sea of corporate grey.

This is your sensory firewall. The corporate environment is designed for conformity and control; your tank is a declaration of autonomy. The plant, the music, the personal photos—these are all anchors to your true self, reminding you that you are a human being with a mission, not just a resource.

Practical Application: The 5-Minute Vibe Check. At the start of every workday, spend five minutes performing a "Vibe Check."

1. Clear the Decks: Put away anything left over from the previous day's chaos.

2. Tune the Frequency: Put on your chosen music (or noise-cancelling headphones for silence).

3. Set the Anchor: Look at your personal item—the photo, the plant, the small sculpture—and take three deep breaths, grounding yourself in your command centre.

4. Tool Check: Open the first application you need and ensure it's ready to go.

This small ritual reinforces the boundary between the external negative waves and the internal sanctuary of your tank.

3. The Art of Strategic Laziness: The High-Leverage Wave

Oddball's greatest lesson for the workplace is that being busy is not the same as being effective.

The cult of productivity often leads to burnout, not brilliance. This is the core of The Pareto Principle (the 80/20 rule) applied to professional life. Oddball was never lazy; he was strategically efficient. He conserved his energy for the moments of highest leverage, the moment the bridge needed to be crossed or the gold needed to be retrieved.

Know Your Role: Rider vs. Mechanic. What is the unique, high-value skill that only you can provide? Oddball was a Rider—a master of the tank, a strategist, a motivator. He was not the mechanic who changed the oil. Focus 80% of your energy on your unique, high-value skill. Delegate or de-prioritise the rest.

Case Study: The Marketing Director and the Metrics Trap.

Marcus was a Marketing Director who was drowning in "mechanical" work. He spent his mornings compiling weekly performance reports, a task that took four hours and could be automated. He felt busy, but his high-leverage work—developing the next quarter's creative strategy—was being done late at night, exhausted and rushed. His Moriarty was his own guilt, the belief that a good director must be across every detail.

His Oddball shift was to recognise his role; he was a Rider of the Creative Wave, not a Mechanic of the Spreadsheet.

He politely but firmly handed the report generation to a junior analyst, framing it as a "development opportunity" for them. He used the time he gained to go for a walk, clear his head, and sketch out a campaign that increased engagement by 40%.

His "laziness" in refusing to do low-value work was the most productive decision he made all year.

Embrace the Picnic: The Productive Pause.

When you are waiting for someone else to do their part, do not fill the time with busywork. This is your moment to drink wine and eat cheese. Go for a walk. Read an interesting article. Meditate. Rest is a productive act that prepares you for your next moment of high-leverage work.

This concept is supported by neuroscience on the Default Mode Network (DMN). The DMN is the brain network that becomes active when we are not focused on the outside world—when we are daydreaming, mind-wandering, or resting. Far from being "lazy," the DMN is crucial for consolidating memories, integrating information, and, most importantly, creative problem-solving. The solution to a complex problem often emerges not when you are staring intently at the screen, but when you are "on a picnic." Oddball's picnic is your brain's DMN activation time.

4. Finding Your Gold: The Private Enterprise Operation

Is your current job aligned with your personal mission? Is the "gold" the company is offering (salary, status) the same as your gold? This is the most important question. Many people confuse the company's mission with their own, leading to profound misalignment and burnout.

The Private Enterprise Operation: View yourself not as an employee, but as a consultant. You are "You, Inc." and your current employer is your client. This mental shift gives you a sense of autonomy and power. You are not a subordinate; you are a valued vendor. This perspective aligns with the Existentialist view of radical freedom and responsibility. Your job title does not define you; you are defined by the value you choose to create.

Step-by-Step Guide to Running "You, Inc.":

1. Define Your Product: What is the core value you provide? (e.g., "I solve complex data architecture problems," not "I am a Senior Engineer.")

2. Define Your Client's Needs: What specific problem is your current employer paying you to solve? Be ruthless in this assessment.

3. Set Your Terms: What are your non-negotiables (work-life balance, creative freedom, compensation)? These are the terms of your contract with the client.

4. Deliver Value, Not Time: Your focus shifts from clocking hours to delivering the highest possible value for the client's investment. If you can solve their problem in two hours instead of eight, you have delivered maximum value and earned yourself a picnic.

Know Your Price: The Liberation Point. Oddball's crew would become heroes for three days, but only for $1.6 million. What is your price? What is the point at which the stress and negativity of a job are no longer worth the compensation? Know this number. It is your liberation point.

This is not just a financial number; it's a holistic calculation that includes:

- **Financial Freedom:** The amount of savings or passive income required to cover your essential expenses for a defined period (e.g., two years).

- **Skill Mastery:** The point at which you have mastered the skills this job offers, and further time there offers diminishing returns on your personal growth.

- **Psychological Cost:** The daily toll on your mental and physical health.

When the psychological cost exceeds the value of the gold, you have reached your liberation point, and it is time to find another bridge.

5. The Nuance of the Wave: The Edge Cases of Oddballism

Oddball's philosophy is not a license for anarchy; it is a blueprint for intelligent, self-directed action. There are nuances to the wave that must be understood to avoid becoming a negative wave yourself.

The Difference Between Strategic Laziness and Negligence: Strategic laziness is a deliberate choice to conserve energy for high-leverage work. Negligence is a failure to meet your agreed-upon obligations.

The distinction lies in intent and outcome. If your "picnic" results in a missed deadline or a failure to deliver on your core value proposition, you are not Oddball; you are simply a bad consultant. Oddball always delivered the gold. His methods were unconventional, but his results were impeccable.

The Ethical Line of the Private Enterprise Operation: While you view your employer as a client, you must maintain professional ethics. You are not there to sabotage or steal. You are there to fulfil the contract you have implicitly or explicitly agreed to.

The autonomy of "You, Inc." is earned through impeccable delivery and professional integrity. Your tank must be a force for good, not just for personal gain.

Connecting to Ancient Philosophy: Oddball and the Tao. The Oddball approach to work is a modern echo of the ancient Chinese philosophy of Taoism, specifically the concept of Wu Wei, or "non-action." Wu Wei does not mean doing nothing; it means acting in alignment with the natural flow of things, exerting effort only when necessary, and avoiding unnecessary struggle.

"The greatest efficiency is achieved not through frantic effort, but through finding the path of least resistance. The water does not fight the rock; it flows around it. The Wave Rider does not fight the wave; he rides it."

This is the essence of Strategic Laziness. It is not about avoiding work; it is about avoiding unnecessary work. It is about being so attuned to the project's flow that your actions are minimal, precise, and maximally effective.

If you find that your job is a constant source of negative waves, that it does not allow you to master your craft, and that the gold it offers is not the gold you seek, then it may be time to find another bridge.

A career lived in the spirit of Oddball is not about climbing the ladder; it's about finding the right wall to put your ladder against. It is about building a mother, a beautiful tank that can navigate any terrain, secure in the knowledge that you are the master of your own professional destiny.

The true Oddball at work is not the loudest, the busiest, or the most stressed. He is the one who is calm, effective, and always seems to be enjoying a quiet picnic while everyone else is running in circles. He is the one who knows where the gold is and how to get it without breaking a sweat. He is the master of the high-leverage wave.

Chapter Twenty-Three:

Oddball in Relationships:

The Art of Curating Your Crew and Navigating the Waves

Love, family, and friendship are the ultimate crew. They are the people we share the loaf with, the ones we trust to help us fix the tank. They are the essential infrastructure of a righteous life, the very ground upon which we build our mobile command post.

But here's the rub, the great paradox of human connection: they can also be the most powerful source of negative waves in our lives. They can be the friendly fire that cripples the engine, the well-meaning advice that steers the tank into a ditch.

Applying Oddballism to your personal relationships is not just a delicate art; it is a critical survival skill, essential for maintaining the integrity of your vibe and the clarity of your mission.

The core principle is simple, yet profoundly difficult to execute: You are the commander of your own emotional tank.

Your relationships should be a force multiplier, not a constant drain. If you find yourself perpetually exhausted, defensive, or anxious after spending time with your closest people, you are taking on too many of their negative waves.

Oddball's wisdom teaches us that the best defence is not a wall, but a clear, honest, and well-maintained boundary.

Romantic Partnership: Finding Your Co-Commander and Aligning the Turret

A romantic partner is the most important member of your crew. They are not your Moriarty, the brutally honest critic, nor are they your Crapgame, the fixer who gets you out of a jam.

They are your co-commander, the person in the seat next to you, with their hand on the other set of controls. You are piloting a two-person tank, and this requires a unique level of alignment and trust that goes beyond mere affection. It requires a shared philosophy of movement.

Shared Vibe is Everything: The Resonance Test

You can have different hobbies, different opinions on the best kind of music, and different careers, but you must be on the same energetic wavelength.

This is the Resonance Test.
Does your partner lift you up, or do they drain you?

Do they hit you with negative waves in the morning, or do they help you build your shield?

A partnership with a fundamental vibe mismatch is a tank with two drivers trying to go in opposite directions, or worse, one driver constantly slamming the brakes while the other accelerates.

This isn't about being identical; it's about being complementary and mutually supportive. The Oddball philosophy recognises that energy is a finite resource, and a relationship should be a net positive energy exchange. If you are constantly giving and they are constantly taking, or vice versa, the tank will eventually run out of fuel.

The Mission Must Align: Compatible Trajectories

You and your partner don't need the exact same "gold," but your missions must be compatible.

Suppose your gold is a life of travel, adventure, and building a global non-profit, and their gold is a quiet, stable life in their hometown, focused on a predictable career path. In that case, you are on fundamentally different missions.

This is not a judgment on either goal; it is a logistical reality. The tank cannot be in two places at once. Oddball would advise a clear-eyed assessment of these trajectories. Are they parallel, converging, or diverging? Diverging missions require a level of sacrifice and compromise that often leads to resentment, which is the rust that eats away at the tank's armour. Compatible missions, however, mean that even when you are pursuing separate goals, the overall direction of the relationship—the "we"—is moving forward together.

Case Study: The Diverging Missions of Leo and Clara

Consider Leo, a software engineer who found his "gold" in the freedom of remote work, dreaming of living in a different country every six months.

His co-commander, Clara, a talented architect, found her deepest satisfaction in the tangible, long-term process of designing and overseeing the construction of physical buildings in their city. Their love was deep, their vibe was good, but their missions were diverging.

Leo's tank was packed and ready to roll; Clara's tank was dug in for the long siege.

For years, they tried to compromise, with Leo taking shorter trips and Clara feeling resentful of the time apart. The negative waves weren't malicious; they were the friction of incompatible missions.

The Oddball solution, which they eventually embraced, was not to break up but to redefine their partnership.

They acknowledged the divergence, choosing to remain deeply connected friends and occasional co-conspirators, but they released each other from the obligation of the co-commander role.

They traded the two-person tank for two parallel, supportive jeeps, each free to pursue their own gold without dragging the other down.

This is the ultimate Oddball move: recognising reality and choosing peace over a forced, painful alignment.

PRACTICAL APPLICATION: THE WEEKLY VIBE CHECK

To keep the co-commander relationship running smoothly, Oddball would prescribe a weekly maintenance ritual: the Weekly Vibe Check.

This is not a time for airing grievances, but for a strategic assessment. Set aside one hour, distraction-free.

The conversation should be structured around three questions:

1. What are the positive waves I'm sending you? (What did I do this week that made you feel supported, loved, or happy?)

2. What are the negative waves I'm sending you? (What did I do this week that created friction, anxiety, or made you feel drained?)

3. What is the next objective for our tank? (What is one small, shared goal for the coming week—a date, a household task, a financial decision—that moves our shared mission forward?)

This structured, non-confrontational approach turns emotional issues into logistical problems that can be solved together, rather than personal attacks that lead to entrenched positions.

Friendship: Curating Your Crew and Identifying the Roles

As we get older, we have less time and energy. We cannot afford to spend it on friendships that are a net negative on our vibe. You must curate your crew with the same care that Oddball chose his. Every member of the crew has a function, and if a person's role is to consistently lower your morale, they are a liability, not an asset.

The Oddball Crew Archetypes

It is helpful to categorise your friends not by how long you've known them, but by the role they play in your life's mission.

• **The Kelly:** The ambitious, driven one. They inspire you to be better, but their intensity can sometimes feel like judgment. They push you to take the hill.

• **The Moriarty:** The brutally honest one. You call them for a reality check, not for sympathy. They cut through your self-deception like a hot knife through butter. Their loyalty is to the truth, which is a rare and valuable thing.

• **The Crapgame:** The well-connected fixer. They know a guy who knows a guy. They can get you out of a jam, find the impossible part, or open a door you didn't know existed. They are the network.

• **The Fellow Oddball:** The ones you can relax and be weird with. They don't judge your mission; they appreciate your style. They are the pure, unadulterated positive vibe.

The problem arises when you miscast a role.

If you call your Crapgame for deep emotional support, you will be disappointed.

If you ask your Moriarty for a gentle pep talk, you will get a lecture.

Understanding the role allows you to manage your expectations and appreciate the specific value each person brings to your life.

STARVE THE NEGATIVE WAVES: THE ENERGY AUDIT

If you have a "friend" who consistently complains, gossips, and drains your energy, you must lovingly and firmly reduce their role in your life. This is the Energy Audit. You don't need a dramatic breakup, which only creates more negative waves.

Just invest less time and energy consistently.

Your vibe is too precious to waste on a relationship that serves as an emotional siphon. This is not selfishness; it is self-preservation. Oddball understood that you can't fight a war on an empty tank. You must protect your fuel reserves.

CONNECTING TO MODERN PSYCHOLOGY: THE LAW OF RECIPROCITY AND SOCIAL CONTAGION

Oddball's wisdom here aligns perfectly with modern psychological concepts.

The principle of "Starve the Negative Waves" is a practical application of the concept of Emotional Contagion. Studies in social neuroscience show that emotions—both positive and negative—are highly contagious.

When you spend time with someone who is constantly anxious or pessimistic, their emotional state literally begins to affect your own brain chemistry. You are, in effect, absorbing their negative waves. Furthermore, the Law of Reciprocity suggests that we feel an obligation to return favours, including emotional ones. If a friend constantly uses you as a therapist, you feel obligated to continue that role, even if it harms you. The Oddball move is to break this cycle by gently, but firmly, changing the terms of the engagement. You can still be kind, but you must stop being the receptacle for their unmanaged negativity.

Family: The Original, Unchosen Crew and the Art of the Loving Shield

Family is the trickiest terrain in the Oddball doctrine. You don't choose your family. They are your original crew, the people who loaded the first fuel into your tank. But you may not be on the same mission, and they can be powerful sources of negative waves, often rooted in love and concern.

This is what makes it so difficult: the negative waves are disguised as affection.

Love the Crew Member, Reject the Wave: The Boundary Protocol

The key is to separate the person from the wave. You can love your family deeply while still refusing to absorb their negativity. When your mother says, "Are you sure that's a good idea? It sounds risky. You should just get a safe job," she is not trying to sabotage you. She is expressing her love through her own fear. She is sending a negative wave, but the intent behind it is positive.

The Boundary Protocol is the Oddball response:

1. Acknowledge the Love: "I know you're worried because you love me, and I appreciate that."

2. Shield the Wave: "But I've got a good feeling about this one, and I've done my homework. I'm moving forward."

3. Redirect the Conversation: "Now, tell me about your garden."

You acknowledge the love but shield yourself from the fear. You refuse to argue the point because arguing invites the negative wave into your tank. You state your position and move on. This is not disrespectful; it is a healthy act of self-preservation and relationship-preservation. It is the most loving thing you can do, because it preserves your ability to be the best version of yourself for them.

> EXTENDED NARRATIVE EXAMPLE: THE CASE OF SOFIA AND THE FAMILY BUSINESS

Sofia, a brilliant young designer, had left a high-paying corporate job to start her own sustainable fashion line. Her family, which owned a successful but traditional manufacturing business, saw this as a catastrophic mistake.

Every Sunday dinner was a barrage of "Are you sure you can pay your rent?" and "When are you going to come back to the real world?" Her father, in particular, was a powerful source of negative waves, convinced she was throwing away her future.

Sofia tried to argue, explain her business plan, and show them her early successes. It only made things worse. She was letting the negative waves breach her armour. Then she remembered the Oddball principle: Love the crew member, reject the wave.

She implemented the Boundary Protocol.

The next time her father started, she didn't argue. She smiled and said, "Dad, I know you're asking because you care about my security, and I love you for that. But my business is my mission, and I'm not going to discuss the financials at the dinner table. It's not up for debate. Tell me, how is the new production line running?"

She held the boundary with a calm, unwavering smile. The first few times, her father was frustrated. But Sofia was consistent. She refused to engage in the argument, always acknowledging the love, shielding the wave, and redirecting. Slowly, the waves subsided. Her father realised that his questions no longer had the power to derail her. He couldn't deny her peace. He may never fully understand her philosophy, but he came to respect her resolve, which is the highest form of respect an Oddball can earn.

Deeper Exploration: Oddballism, Stoicism, and the Neurobiology of Boundaries

The Oddball approach to relationships is not new; it is a modern, humorous articulation of ancient wisdom, particularly Stoicism, filtered through the lens of modern neurobiology.

The Stoic philosophers, such as Epictetus and Marcus Aurelius, taught the fundamental distinction between what is within our control and what is outside it. Oddball's "negative waves" are simply the things outside our control: other people's opinions, fears, and emotional states.

The Oddball move—to "shield yourself from the fear"—is the Stoic practice of dichotomy of control. You cannot control your mother's anxiety about your career, but you can absolutely control your response to it.

You can control whether you let that anxiety into your own emotional tank.

Furthermore, the concept of the "loving shield" finds a fascinating echo in neuroscience. When we are confronted with criticism or emotional pressure, our amygdala—the brain's fear centre—activates, triggering a fight-or-flight response.

This is the moment the negative wave hits the tank. By using the Boundary Protocol, particularly the step of "Acknowledge the Love," you are engaging your prefrontal cortex, the centre for rational thought and emotional regulation.

You are consciously reframing the perceived threat (the criticism) as an act of love (the concern). This cognitive reframing de-escalates the amygdala's response, allowing you to respond calmly and strategically, rather than reacting defensively. The loving shield is, in fact, a neurobiological hack for emotional self-regulation.

The Edge Case: The Toxic Crew Member

What about the truly toxic relationship—the friend or family member whose negative waves are not rooted in love, but in genuine malice, envy, or deep-seated dysfunction?

Oddball is wise, but he is not a martyr.

The Oddball doctrine is clear: If a relationship is a persistent, unfixable leak in your tank, you must seal it off. This is the edge case where gentle reduction is not enough. If a person's presence consistently compromises your mission, your peace, and your self-worth, they are not a crew member; they are an enemy agent.

Step-by-Step Guidance: The Oddball Severance

1. The Final Audit: Conduct a final, brutally honest audit. Have you clearly communicated the problem? Have you set and maintained boundaries that were ignored? Is the relationship a net negative 90% of the time? If the answer is yes, proceed.

2. The Quiet Exit: Do not announce your departure. Do not write a dramatic letter. Do not engage in a final argument. The Quiet Exit is the most powerful move. You simply stop engaging. You do not return calls, you decline invitations with simple, non-negotiable phrases ("I'm unavailable," "That doesn't work for me"), and you do not explain.

3. The Vibe Vacuum: The goal is to create a vacuum where the negative waves used to be. This is not about punishing them; it is about protecting yourself. The lack of engagement is a clear, non-verbal boundary that requires no defence.

4. Refuel and Re-Crew: Immediately fill the space with positive, supportive connections. The tank abhors a vacuum. Use the newfound energy to invest deeply in your Kellys, your Moriartys, and your Fellow Oddballs.

This is the hardest move, but sometimes, the only way to save the tank is to jettison the part that is dragging you down. It is a practical, not a moral, decision. Your mission is paramount, and your peace is the engine that drives it.

Practice the Shared Loaf Daily: The Micro-Rituals of Connection

The most important ritual in a relationship is the daily sharing of the loaf.

It's the quiet cup of coffee in the morning, the "how was your day" conversation in the evening, the shared silence while watching a movie. It's the small, consistent moments of connection that keep the engine running. These micro-rituals are the equivalent of a daily maintenance check on the tank. They are low-stakes, high-frequency opportunities to align the vibe and ensure there are no small leaks that could become major problems.

Oddball understood that grand gestures are fleeting, but consistency is the true measure of commitment. The daily loaf-sharing is the practice of presence. It is putting down the phone, turning off the noise, and truly seeing the person in front of you. It is the moment you confirm that your co-commander is still in the seat, still aligned, and still ready to roll. This is where the real gold of a relationship is found: not in the grand mission, but in the quiet, shared moment of being a crew.

Relationships are the terrain where Oddballism is most tested. It requires immense patience, compassion, and strong boundaries. But by curating a crew that shares your vibe, lovingly managing the waves from those who don't, and consistently performing the daily maintenance, you can build a personal life that is a true sanctuary—a mobile command post of positive energy and righteous fun.

You will find that when your crew is right, the mission becomes not just possible, but a genuine pleasure.

Now, let's fire up this engine and roll.

Chapter Twenty-Four:

Oddball in Crisis:

The Art of Surfing the Tiger Wave

Oddball: "The only way I got to keep them Tigers busy is to LET THEM SHOOT HOLES IN ME!"

Sooner or later, the bridge gets bombed. The tank breaks down. And sometimes, three Tiger tanks roll into the town square of your life.

Crisis is not a possibility; it is an inevitability. It is the ultimate, non-negotiable test of a philosophy. A system of belief that only works when the sun is shining, when the market is up, or when your health is perfect, is no system at all—it is a fair-weather fantasy.

Oddballism, the philosophy of the Wave Rider, shines brightest in the dark, in the blinding, terrifying glare of the Tiger's headlights.

When faced with a genuine, life-altering crisis—a sudden job loss, a devastating health scare, a profound betrayal, or a public failure that seems to redefine your very existence—the untrained mind panics.

It is instantly flooded with a tidal wave of negative energy: fear, despair, self-recrimination, and a paralysing sense of helplessness.

The Wave Rider, however, has been training for this moment, perhaps without even knowing it. They have the tools, the discipline, and the quiet, unshakeable faith that the wave, no matter how large, can be ridden. The crisis is not a wall to be hit, but a massive, terrifying wave to be surfed.

Here is the Oddballist protocol for crisis management, a five-step process for turning a moment of existential dread into a masterclass in resilience and creative problem-solving.

Step 1: Acknowledge the Tigers (Radical Honesty and Emotional Inventory)

Oddball's first reaction to the news of the Tigers is not denial, nor is it a bravado-fuelled charge.

It is a moment of blunt, honest assessment: "It's a wasted trip, baby. Nobody said nothing about locking horns with no Tigers."

He doesn't pretend the threat isn't real, nor does he engage in the corrosive practice of "toxic positivity." He looks the crisis square in the eye and names it for what it is: a very, very bad situation.

This is the first and most crucial step in any crisis: Radical Honesty. Do not attempt to sugarcoat the situation, minimise the damage, or immediately try to find the "silver lining."

The mind, in its protective state, will try to negotiate with reality, to bargain away the pain.

Resist this urge. Acknowledge the brutal fact: "I have been diagnosed with a serious illness." "I have lost my life savings, and the business is gone." "This relationship is over, and the future I planned is cancelled."

Stating the brutal fact cuts through the fog of panic and gives you a solid, if terrifying, place to stand. This is the moment you stop fighting the reality of the wave and start preparing to ride it.

The Neuroscience of Naming: Modern neuroscience supports this ancient wisdom. When we name an emotion—a process called affect labelling—it activates the ventrolateral prefrontal cortex, which, in turn, dampens the amygdala's activity, the brain's fear centre.

By saying, "I am terrified because I just lost my job," you are literally turning down the volume on your panic button. You are shifting from a purely reactive, limbic state to a more rational, executive state.

Oddball's blunt assessment is a neurological hack for immediate emotional regulation.

Step 2: Feel the Wave, Don't Become the Wave (The Observer's Stance)

Fear is a natural, primal response to a Tiger tank. It is a powerful wave of energy, a surge of adrenaline and cortisol designed to prepare you for fight or flight. You are going to feel it, and it will feel overwhelming. The key, the absolute core of the Wave Rider's discipline, is to let that feeling wash over you, not through you, and certainly not to let it define you.

Acknowledge the feeling: "I am feeling immense, gut-wrenching fear right now."

But do not identify with it: "I am a fearful person."

You are the sky; the fear is a storm cloud passing through. You are the ocean; the fear is a single, powerful wave.

The storm cloud will pass. The wave will break. Your fundamental nature remains unchanged. This is the Observer's Stance; a concept deeply rooted in Stoicism and modern Cognitive Behavioural Therapy (CBT).

The Stoics taught that we are not disturbed by things, but by the view we take of them. The crisis is the thing; your interpretation of it is the view. By observing the fear without judgment, you create a vital space between the stimulus (the crisis) and your response (the action).

Case Study: The Architect and the Earthquake.

Consider Elias, a 45-year-old architect whose firm was his life's work. A major economic downturn—his "Tiger Tank"—led to the sudden, irreversible collapse of his business. The first week was a blur of panic, shame, and self-hatred. He felt like a failure, a fraud. His wife, a Wave Rider in her own right, simply said, "Elias, you are not the firm. The firm is a thing that happened to you. The fear is a feeling you are having. Let's sit with the feeling for ten minutes."

By permitting himself to feel the fear—to let the wave wash over him—he stopped fighting the reality of his emotions. He realised, "I am a man who lost a firm," not "I am a lost man." This subtle but profound shift in identity was the moment he regained his footing and began to see the crisis as a challenge, not a final verdict.

Step 3: Find Your Still Point (The Picnic in the Panic)

Remember Oddball, calmly eating cheese and sipping wine while his tank is broken down and the enemy is closing in? This is the crisis application of that doctrine. In the midst of chaos, you must find a small, inviolable island of calm, a "still point in the turning world."

You cannot operate effectively from a place of pure, sustained panic. Your prefrontal cortex—the part of the brain responsible for planning, creativity, and strategic thinking—shuts down when the amygdala is screaming. You must find a way to regulate your nervous system and bring your executive function back online.

This is not about ignoring the crisis; it is about creating a moment of psychic space to think clearly and creatively.

Practical Applications for the Still Point:

1. The 4-7-8 Breath: The simplest and most powerful tool. Inhale deeply through your nose for a count of four. Hold your breath for a count of seven. Exhale completely through your mouth with a whoosh sound for a count of eight. Repeat this cycle three times. This sends a direct, physiological signal to your panicked brain via the vagus nerve that you are not, in fact, currently being eaten by a Tiger.

2. The Sensory Anchor: Engage one of your five senses with a simple, deliberate pleasure. Make a cup of high-quality coffee and savour the aroma and the heat. Listen to one, calming, righteous tune—something without lyrics that allows your mind to settle. Step outside and feel the sun on your face or the wind on your skin for sixty seconds. This simple act of presence pulls you out of the abstract terror of the future and into the concrete reality of the present moment, where you are safe.

3. Connect with Your Crew (The Borrowed Stability): Make one phone call to the calmest, most solid person on your crew. The purpose is not to solve the problem, but just to hear their voice and borrow their stability. A brief, non-judgmental connection with a trusted human can rapidly lower stress hormones.

The crisis is yours, but the calm can be shared.

The Ancient Philosophy Connection: This concept is a direct echo of the Taoist principle of Wu Wei, or "effortless action." By pausing, by finding the still point, you are not being passive; you are allowing the correct, non-reactive action to emerge naturally from a place of clarity, rather than forcing a panicked, likely incorrect move.

Step 4: Look for the Asymmetric Advantage (The Paint Shell Solution)

Once you have achieved a measure of calm, once the still point has been established, you can begin to think strategically. The initial, panicked thought is always to fight the Tiger tanks head-on. You will lose. You must look for a creative, unconventional solution. You must find your paint shells—the unexpected, non-lethal, psychological weapon that changes the rules of engagement entirely.

Oddball's genius was not in superior firepower, but in superior psychology. He didn't have a better tank; he had a better idea. He understood that the goal was not to destroy the enemy, but to neutralise the threat by confusing, distracting, or outmanoeuvring it.

Ask yourself the Oddball Questions:

• "How can I change the rules of this game? What is the unwritten assumption I can violate?"

• "How can I use psychology, humour, or style to my advantage? What is the element of surprise?"

• "What is the one, weird, unexpected thing I could do that nobody—especially the 'Tigers'—would see coming?"

• "How can I scare this problem away instead of fighting it to the death? How can I make the crisis irrelevant?"

EXTENDED NARRATIVE EXAMPLE: THE ENTREPRENEUR AND THE LAWSUIT.

Meet Sarah, a brilliant software entrepreneur whose small, successful startup was suddenly hit with a massive, frivolous lawsuit from a much larger competitor—a classic corporate Tiger Tank. Her lawyers advised a long, expensive, and draining defence. Her initial reaction was to fight fire with fire, to spend every dollar she had on legal fees. This was the head-on fight.

But Sarah, a devoted Wave Rider, paused. She found her still point, went through the Oddball Questions, and realised the competitor's goal wasn't to win the lawsuit, but to bleed her dry and acquire her technology cheaply.

The unwritten rule was "we must fight this in court." Her paint shell solution was asymmetric: she didn't fight the lawsuit; she changed the narrative.

She used her last remaining capital to launch a highly stylised, humorous, and deeply personal documentary-style video on social media, detailing the Goliath-vs-David struggle, focusing not on the legal details, but on the human cost and the competitor's history of predatory behaviour.

She framed the lawsuit as an attack on innovation itself.

The video went viral. The public outcry was immediate and intense. Within 48 hours, the competitor's stock took a hit, and their PR department was in full damage-control mode.

They didn't want a legal fight; they wanted a quiet acquisition. They certainly didn't want a public relations disaster. Sarah had successfully scared the problem away. The lawsuit was quietly dropped, and she negotiated a fair, profitable exit for her company. The paint shell was not a legal brief, but a viral video.

Sub-Section: The Nuance of the Edge Case (The Broken Tank)

What happens when the crisis is not a Tiger Tank you can outmanoeuvre, but a broken tank you cannot fix? What about the edge cases where the problem is purely internal, like a chronic illness or a profound, non-negotiable loss?

The Oddballist principle still holds, but the focus shifts from external action to internal acceptance and redirection.

- **Radical Honesty:** Acknowledge the permanence of the broken tank. "This is a chronic condition I must manage, not a temporary illness I can cure."

- **Feel the Wave:** Allow the grief, the frustration, and the anger to be felt, but do not let them become your identity. The Wave Rider accepts that some waves are simply too big to surf, and the only move is to dive deep and let them pass over.

- **Still Point:** The still point becomes even more critical. It is the daily, non-negotiable practice of self-regulation that allows you to live with the broken tank without being consumed by it.

- **Asymmetric Advantage:** The paint shell here is not an external solution, but an internal one: Redefinition of Success. If you cannot win the old game, you must invent a new one. The asymmetric advantage is the realisation that your value is not tied to your physical capacity or your past achievements, but to your resilience, your wisdom, and your ability to connect with others.

The crisis forces a necessary, painful, but ultimately liberating re-evaluation of what truly matters.

Step 5: Have a Little Faith, Baby (The Benevolence of the Universe)

This is the final and most important step, the philosophical bedrock upon which the entire protocol rests. In the heart of a crisis, when the way forward is unclear, when the fear is still a dull ache in your stomach, you must fall back on your deepest training. You must trust that there is another bridge. You must believe that a solution will present itself, not through magic, but through the clarity and creativity that your preceding four steps have unlocked.

You must have faith in your own resilience and in the fundamental, if sometimes hidden, benevolence of the universe. This is not a naive belief that everything will be easy, but a deep-seated conviction that the universe is not fundamentally hostile. It is a chaotic, beautiful, and ultimately neutral system, and your job is to find the path of least resistance through the chaos.

The Connection to Ancient Philosophy: This faith is the modern echo of the ancient Greek concept of Areté—excellence or moral virtue. The crisis is the arena where your Areté is tested. The faith is the belief that the character you have built, the wisdom you have accumulated, and the tools you have practised will be sufficient. It is the ultimate self-trust.

Crisis is the fire that forges a true Wave Rider. It burns away your ego, your attachments, and your illusions. It leaves you with nothing but your core philosophy, your raw, unvarnished self.

It asks you one question, the only question that matters: Do you really believe this stuff? Do you really believe in the power of a positive wave? Do you really have faith in your own ability to adapt and create?

When you can look three Tiger tanks in the face and, after the initial shock, take a deep breath, find your still point, look for your paint shells, and trust that you will find a way through—then you are no longer just a student of Oddballism.

You are a master. You have not just survived the crisis; you have used the crisis to become more fully yourself.

You have surfed the Tiger Wave, and you are ready for the next one.

The picnic is over, the cheese is gone, and the engine is running.

Time to move.

Chapter Twenty-Five:

The Oddball Revolution

This book, this philosophy, is not just about individual self-improvement. It is a quiet, joyful, and deeply subversive revolution. It is a revolution against the tyranny of negativity, the cult of busyness, and the soul-crushing machinery of modern life.

Every time a Wave Rider chooses a positive thought, enjoys a simple pleasure, or rejects a weird sandwich, they are casting a vote for a different kind of world. The world, as we know it, is a beautifully complex and often absurd place, and the Oddball Revolution is the only sensible response to its inherent chaos: a commitment to radical, joyful sanity.

An Oddball Revolution is not fought with protests, with anger, or with violence. It is fought with a well-timed joke. It is fought with a shared loaf of bread. It is fought with a loudspeaker blasting righteous tunes in the face of despair. It is a revolution of the vibe, a shift in the collective consciousness that begins with a single, well-adjusted mind.

It is the realisation that the greatest act of rebellion in a world obsessed with suffering is to choose happiness, to choose connection, and to choose a life lived fully in the present moment. This is the ultimate "mother, beautiful tank" of our philosophy—a powerful, unstoppable force of good humour and clear-eyed perspective.

The Psychology of the Quiet Uprising

To understand the power of this revolution, we must look beyond the surface-level humour and into the deep wells of human psychology. Oddball's wisdom, often delivered in a casual aside, aligns uncannily with modern neuroscience findings and ancient philosophical traditions. The rejection of "negative waves," for instance, is a profound psychological technique.

Neuroscientists have mapped the brain's negativity bias, a hardwired tendency to give more weight to negative experiences, which was an evolutionary advantage in the savanna but is a psychological burden in the modern office.

The Oddball approach—to acknowledge the negative wave and then banish it with a conscious, positive counter-thought—is a form of cognitive reframing that actively rewires the brain. It is Stoicism with a sense of humour; a practical application of cognitive-behavioural therapy (CBT) principles delivered with a wink.

Ancient philosophy, particularly Stoicism, taught the importance of distinguishing between what you can control and what you cannot. Oddballism takes this a step further: you cannot control the chaos of the battlefield, but you can absolutely control the vibe you bring to it. You can control the quality of your thoughts, the kindness of your actions, and the tunes you choose to blast. This is the Oddball Locus of Control, a practical framework for mental resilience.

When the world throws a "weird sandwich" at you—an unexpected crisis, a toxic colleague, a crushing deadline—the Wave Rider does not try to control the sandwich itself. They reject it, or perhaps, turn it into a joke, thereby controlling their reaction and maintaining their inner peace. This is the true power of the quiet uprising: it is a revolution fought entirely within the confines of one's own skull, and therefore, it is a revolution that can never truly be defeated.

Case Study: The Architect and the Negative Waves

Consider the story of Elias Vance, a brilliant but perpetually stressed architect in a high-pressure firm.

Elias was a classic victim of the "cult of busyness," equating his self-worth with the number of all-nighters he pulled.

His firm was a breeding ground for negative waves: constant fear of layoffs, backstabbing colleagues, and a pervasive sense that nothing was ever good enough. Elias was drowning in cortisol, his creativity stifled by anxiety.

One day, a junior architect, a quiet Wave Rider named Maya, left a small, hand-drawn sketch on his desk: a tiny, smiling tank with a surfboard, captioned, "Why don't you knock it off with them negative waves? Why don't you dig how beautiful it is out here?"

Elias, initially annoyed, found himself staring at the drawing. He realised his entire mental landscape was dominated by the fear of failure.

Maya's subtle intervention led Elias to the core Oddball doctrine. He didn't quit his job; that would be a retreat. Instead, he began his own quiet revolution. He started setting firm boundaries, leaving the office at 5:30 PM twice a week, even if it meant leaving a project unfinished until the next morning.

He used the time to bake bread—his personal "Shared Loaf." He started a "Righteous Tunes" playlist, playing softly upbeat 60s soul music through his noise-cancelling headphones, creating a personal sonic sanctuary.

When a colleague tried to pull him into a toxic gossip session, he would smile and say, "I'm not picking up that weird sandwich today, friend. I'm on a carb-loading mission." The change was slow but profound. Elias became more effective, not less. His calm became a shield, and his humour, a scalpel. He had not changed the firm, but he had changed his relationship to it, and in doing so, he had planted a seed of sanity in a deeply insane environment.

He became a beacon, and soon, other stressed architects started asking him about his "bread-baking habit."

The revolution had begun.

Building a Community of Wave Riders

While your core crew is small and intimate, the broader Wave Rider community is vast and global. We are a scattered tribe, often operating behind enemy lines in corporate offices, suburban neighbourhoods, and bustling cities. The time has come for us to begin recognising each other, not through formal organisation but through shared vibe and subtle signals.

The Symbols and Signals: A Modern Apocrypha

The symbols of Oddballism—the Wave and Turret, the Banished Wave, the Shared Loaf—are our calling cards. A sticker on a laptop, a doodle on a notebook, a t-shirt worn with ironic calm. These are the signals we can use to find each other in the wild. A knowing nod to someone wearing a "Negative Waves" t-shirt. A shared chuckle over a weird sandwich. These are the secret handshakes of our tribe.

But the symbols are not static; they evolve. In the digital age, the symbols of the Wave Rider include:

• **The Perfectly Timed GIF:** The ability to deploy a piece of media that perfectly captures the absurdity of a situation, defusing tension with a flash of humour. This is the digital equivalent of the well-timed joke.

• **The Unsolicited Compliment:** A random, genuine, and specific compliment in a public forum or social media thread. This is a small, positive wave cast into the digital ocean, a direct counter to the prevailing tide of cynicism.

- **The "Mother, Beautiful Tank" Emoji:** The use of a specific, non-obvious emoji (perhaps a sunflower, a vintage car, or a simple, serene face) as a subtle sign-off, a way of saying, "I see the beauty in this chaos."

These are not rules; they are invitations to connect. They are low-stakes ways to test the waters and see if the person across the table or across the internet is also digging the beautiful picture.

Gatherings of the Crew: Decentralised Picnics

We must begin to gather. Not in formal, hierarchical churches, but in loose, decentralised "picnics." A Wave Rider meetup in a park. A local chapter dedicated to the sharing of bread and cheese. An online forum for the exchange of righteous tunes and paintball strategies.

The goal of these gatherings is not to worship, but to connect, to recharge, and to amplify our collective positive wave. The structure of these gatherings is crucial: they must be low-friction and high-joy.

Step-by-Step Guide to a Wave Rider Picnic:

1. The Low-Stakes Invitation: The invitation should be casual and non-committal. "I'm going to be at the park with a loaf of bread and some righteous tunes. If you're in the area, stop by." No RSVPs, no agenda, no pressure.

2. The Shared Loaf Principle: The core activity is the sharing of simple, good things. Bread, cheese, good coffee, and a decent beer. The focus is on the act of sharing, not the quality of the goods. This grounds the gathering in the simple, material joy of the present.

3. The Righteous Tunes Veto: The music is a non-negotiable element of the vibe. It must be upbeat, soulful, and free of unnecessary angst. Crucially, anyone can veto a song that brings in a negative wave, but a suggestion for a better tune must accompany the veto. This is a practical application of the "banish the negative" doctrine in a social setting.

4. The No-Agenda Rule: The conversation should be allowed to flow naturally. The moment a gathering becomes a "meeting" with bullet points and action items, the revolution is lost. The purpose is to be together, to share the vibe, and to remember that you are not alone in your sanity.

SPREADING THE POSITIVE WAVE: THE ART OF ATTRACTION

Our mission is not to convert the world through argument or proselytisation. You cannot convince a Moriarty to become an Oddball by hitting him with logic.

Our method of evangelism is attraction. We spread the philosophy by living it, so joyfully and so effectively that others become curious. They will see your calm in the midst of chaos, your humour in the face of absurdity, your quiet confidence in a world of anxiety.

And they will eventually ask you, "What's your secret?"

This is where the deeper philosophical connection to ancient wisdom comes into play. The Oddball method of attraction is a modern echo of Aristotle's concept of Eudaimonia, often translated as "flourishing" or "living well."

The ancient Greeks believed that virtue was its own reward, and that a truly virtuous life was so visibly good that it naturally drew others to it. The Wave Rider's life is a demonstration of flourishing. It is a life that works, not because it is free of problems, but because the Wave Rider has developed an internal operating system to handle the issues of grace and humour.

Narrative Example: The Digital Nomad and the Vibe

Take the example of Chloe, a freelance graphic designer who embraced the Oddball philosophy while travelling the world as a digital nomad.

Her life, on the surface, was the envy of her peers: exotic locations, flexible hours, no boss. But the reality was a constant grind of client demands, unreliable Wi-Fi, and the profound loneliness of perpetual motion. She was constantly on edge, her "vibe" a brittle shell of forced positivity.

After reading the sacred texts, Chloe realised she was trying to force the positive wave, which is a form of negative wave in disguise. She started to practice Radical Acceptance of the Chaos.

When the Wi-Fi in a small Italian cafe failed for the third time, instead of panicking, she simply packed her laptop, found a sunny spot, and spent an hour sketching in her notebook, listening to her righteous tunes. She accepted the delay as a gift of time.

A local cafe owner, Marco, a man who had seen a thousand stressed-out tourists, watched her.

He saw the shift from frustration to serene calm. The next day, he approached her, not to complain, but to ask, "You are the only one who does not scream at the internet. What is your secret?"

Chloe didn't launch into a philosophical treatise. She smiled, pointed to her notebook where she had drawn a tiny, smiling tank, and said, "I just decided to dig how beautiful it is out here, Marco. Even when the internet is a weird sandwich."

Marco laughed, and from that moment, he became an ally, offering her a special, hidden corner of the cafe with a dedicated, stable connection. Chloe's calm had not only spread a positive wave; it had materially improved her circumstances. She didn't preach; she attracted. She didn't convert; she invited him into her reality.

And you will smile and tell them about the negative waves. You will tell them about the mother, beautiful tank. You will invite them to share your bread and cheese.

You will not preach; you will share. You will not convert; you will invite.

The Future of Oddballism: An Open-Source Operating System

The world is getting noisier, faster, and more anxious. The need for a philosophy of calm, creative survival has never been greater.

Oddballism is a timeless operating system perfectly suited for the challenges of the 21st century. It is open-source, adaptable, and deeply humane. It is a philosophy that understands that the most effective way to change the world is to change the way you see it.

Nuances and Edge Cases: The Necessary Fight

A common misconception is that the Oddball Revolution is a call to passivity. This is a dangerous misreading of the sacred texts.

The Wave Rider is not a pacifist; they are a strategist. Oddball was a soldier, a man who understood that sometimes, you have to fight. But the fight must be necessary, strategic, and executed with style.

The edge case is this: What if the "weird sandwich" is a genuine injustice? What if the negative wave is a real threat to your crew or your values? The Oddball response is not to ignore it, but to engage with it from a position of calm power. You banish the internal negative wave (fear, anger, panic) so you can address the external problem with a clear-eyed strategy.

The Oddball Engagement Protocol:

1. Acknowledge the Threat (The Weird Sandwich): Do not deny the reality of the problem. Acknowledge the injustice, the threat, or the crisis.

2. Banishing the Internal Wave: Before acting, take a moment to banish the fear and anger. Remind yourself: "I will not let this situation control my internal state." This is the moment of the deep breath, the quick joke, the mental blast of a righteous tune.

3. The Mother, Beautiful Tank Strategy: Engage the problem with the most effective, stylish, and decisive action possible. This is not about brute force; it is about precision. It is the difference between blindly charging a target and knowing exactly where to put the paint shell. The action is taken not out of rage, but out of a calm commitment to a better outcome.

4. The Shared Loaf Aftermath: Win or lose, the engagement is followed by a return to the simple joys. A shared meal, a moment of genuine connection. This is the necessary ritual to prevent the fight from poisoning the soul. The fight is over; the vibe must be restored.

This book is just the beginning. It is the first bridge. It is up to you, the new generation of Wave Riders, to build the next ones. To find new parables, to develop new techniques, to apply the core doctrines in ways we haven't even imagined yet. The revolution will not be televised. It will be lived. Quietly, joyfully, and with a hell of a lot of style. Your mission, should you choose to dig it, is to become a beacon of the positive wave. To build a life so beautiful, so effective, and so much fun that you become a living argument for a better way.

The world is a battlefield. Go make some pretty pictures.

Part Eight:

The Sacred Texts

At the heart of any great philosophy, there is a collection of core teachings—the stories, parables, and koans that contain the seeds of its wisdom. In Oddballism, our sacred texts are the words of the Prophet himself.

These are not just witty lines from a movie; they are profound spiritual teachings, each one a multi-faceted gem of insight. In this section, we will perform a deep exegesis of Oddball's most important parables, unpacking the layers of meaning contained within his deceptively simple words.

We will also explore the Apocrypha—the wisdom of the supporting characters who, in their own way, illuminate the path of the Wave Rider. The next chapter will begin this deep dive, starting with the most fundamental of all teachings: the nature of the "mother, beautiful tank."

Chapter Twenty-Six:

The Parables of the Prophet

Let us now sit at the feet of the master and study his words. Each of these parables should be read, contemplated, and revisited often.

They are the keys to the kingdom of the righteous vibe, the fundamental laws of a life lived with maximum freedom and minimum friction.

Oddball's wisdom is not academic; it is a philosophy forged in the crucible of chaos, a practical guide to navigating a world that is, more often than not, trying to sell you a weird sandwich.

His pronouncements are not mere quips; they are condensed spiritual prescriptions, each one a complete lesson in self-mastery, strategic inaction, and the power of a well-placed joke.

Parable 1: The Sermon on the Hill

"Always with the negative waves, Moriarty, always with the negative waves. Why don't you knock it off with them negative waves? Why don't you dig how beautiful it is out here? Why don't you say something righteous and hopeful for a change?"

Exegesis: The Physics of Vibe.

This is the foundational text, the Genesis of Oddballism. It contains the entire philosophy in microcosm. It begins with a diagnosis—the existence of negative waves—which are not just bad moods, but a tangible, destructive force in the universe, a kind of spiritual entropy.

It provides a clear commandment: knock it off.

This is not a gentle suggestion; it is an imperative to self-correct, to take immediate, radical responsibility for the energy you are generating and absorbing.

It then offers an alternative practice: dig how beautiful it is out here.

This is the call to radical presence, to find the inherent, unvarnished beauty in the immediate environment, regardless of the surrounding chaos.

Finally, it gives a final, actionable instruction: say something righteous and hopeful.

This is the ultimate act of creation, the verbal manifestation of a better reality. It is a complete spiritual prescription in four sentences, moving from awareness to action, from diagnosis to cure.

Deeper Exploration: The Neuroscience of Negativity.

Modern psychology and neuroscience confirm Oddball's intuitive wisdom.

The brain's negativity bias—our tendency to register negative stimuli more readily and dwell on them—is an evolutionary survival mechanism. But in the modern world, this mechanism often becomes a self-sabotaging loop.

Oddball's command to "knock it off" is a direct challenge to the default setting of the amygdala, the brain's fear centre. By consciously choosing to "dig how beautiful it is," we engage the prefrontal cortex, the seat of higher-order thinking, and initiate a cognitive reframing.

The act of "saying something righteous and hopeful" is a form of positive self-talk that physically rewires neural pathways, strengthening the connections associated with optimism and resilience. Ancient Stoic philosophy, particularly the teachings of Epictetus, echoes this, emphasising that it is not events themselves that disturb us, but our judgments about them.

Oddball provides a more colourful, jazz-infused vocabulary for this ancient truth.

Case Study: The Architect and the Echo Chamber.

Consider Elias, a talented but perpetually frustrated architect in his late thirties.

Elias was trapped in a cycle of negative waves, constantly complaining about his firm, his clients, and the state of the industry. His office had become an echo chamber of cynicism, a breeding ground for Moriartys. The negative waves were so thick you could cut them with a knife.

He was a master of the "what-if-it-fails" scenario, paralysing his own creativity.

Following the Parable of the Prophet, Elias began a radical experiment.

Every time a colleague started a complaint, he would gently interrupt with a genuine observation: "That's a tough one, but did you notice the light hitting the atrium this morning? It's incredible." Or, "Before we dive into that problem, let's just appreciate that we're building something that will last a hundred years."

The shift was subtle but profound. By actively choosing to speak hope, Elias didn't just change his own mood; he became a focal point of positive energy. His team's productivity rose, and his own creative block dissolved.

He learned that the most effective way to "knock off" the negative waves is to drown them out with a righteous, hopeful sound.

Application: The Vibe Check Technique.

This parable should be your constant companion. Use it as a diagnostic tool for your environment and your internal state.

1. Identify the Source: Are you generating the negative waves, or are you absorbing them from a Moriarty?

2. The Knock-Off: If you are the source, stop the thought immediately. If you are absorbing them, physically remove yourself from the source if possible, or mentally put up a shield.

3. The Dig: Find three things in your immediate sensory experience that are genuinely beautiful or interesting—the smell of coffee, the texture of your shirt, the pattern of light on the wall.

This grounds you in the present.

4. The Righteous Word: Speak or write one sentence that is righteous and hopeful. This is your active contribution to the universal vibe. It is a compass that will always point you back to the true north of the positive wave.

Parable 2: The Weird Sandwich

"To a New Yorker like you, a hero is some type of weird sandwich, not some nut who takes on three Tigers."

Exegesis: The Deconstruction of Glory.

This is the great deconstruction of ego and societal expectation. It teaches us that the world's definition of "glory," "success," or "heroism" is often an artificial, unappetizing, and dangerous construct—a weird sandwich.

The world, in its desperation for drama and spectacle, will try to sell you a mission that is not yours, a sacrifice that is not worth the cost, or a title that comes with a hidden price tag of misery.

Oddball permits us to reject the world's suicidal missions in favour of our own well-being and strategic goals.

The wisdom here is twofold: first, to recognise the "weird sandwich" when it is offered to you, and second, to have the courage to say, "No, thank you."

The true hero is the one who defines their own mission, not the one who blindly accepts the world's pre-packaged, unfulfilling destiny.

Deeper Exploration: The Psychology of External Validation.

The concept of the "weird sandwich" speaks directly to the psychological trap of external validation.

We are conditioned to chase titles, accolades, and challenges that look good on a resume or sound impressive at a party, even if they lead to profound personal unhappiness. This pursuit is driven by the ego's need for social status, a phenomenon explored in depth by modern behavioural economics.

The weird sandwich is the high-status job that demands 80 hours a week and destroys your family life; it is the toxic relationship you stay in because it "looks good" to outsiders; it is the pointless, high-risk endeavour undertaken purely for bragging rights. Oddball's parable is a radical call to internalise your value system. Your worth is not determined by the size of the tank you take on, but by the quality of the life you are living.

Case Study: The Executive and the Promotion.

Meet Sarah, a rising star in a global tech firm.

She was offered the "hero" promotion: Vice President of a failing division, a job everyone knew was a career-killer, but which came with a massive title and a huge salary bump.

Her peers called it a "challenge," a chance to be a "saviour." Sarah recognised the smell of the weird sandwich.

She saw the ingredients: impossible deadlines, a demoralised team, and a guaranteed public failure. Instead of accepting the high-status, high-risk role, she politely declined, citing a desire to focus on a smaller, more innovative project within a stable division.

Her colleagues were confused, but Sarah had protected her energy, her reputation, and her sanity.

Two years later, the VP division was dissolved, and the "hero" who took the job was laid off.

Sarah, meanwhile, had successfully launched her small project, which became a core product, and she was promoted to a position of genuine influence and stability. She chose the picnic over the weird sandwich.

Application: The Sandwich Test.

Before you accept any challenge, before you say "yes" to any request that involves significant sacrifice, ask yourself: "Is this a genuine opportunity that aligns with my gold, or is it a weird sandwich?"

1. Analyse the Ingredients: What is the true cost of this endeavour (time, stress, relationships, health)?

2. Check the Flavour: Does this challenge genuinely excite and fulfil you, or does it only satisfy an external need for approval?

3. Consult the Chef: Who is offering this sandwich? Is it a trusted mentor, or is it a system that profits from your sacrifice? This simple test is the guardian of your life force, saving you from burnout, resentment, and pointless heroism.

Parable 3: The Declaration of Independence

"No, baby, we ain't."

Exegesis: The Sacred Mantra of Self-Definition.

This is the shortest, most powerful parable, the sacred mantra of self-definition.

It is the calm, firm rejection of all labels, boxes, and categories that the world tries to impose upon you. It is a declaration of sovereignty. When the world tries to define you by your past mistakes, your job title, your social status, or your perceived limitations, this phrase is the ultimate defence.

It affirms that you are not a cog in a machine, not a demographic, not a job title, but a free and complex individual operating under your own authority. It is the sound of a soul refusing to be pigeonholed. It is the quiet, unshakeable power of being.

Deeper Exploration: Existential Freedom and Identity.

This parable is a direct echo of existential philosophy.

Jean-Paul Sartre argued that "existence precedes essence," meaning we are born without a predetermined nature and must define ourselves through our choices and actions. The world constantly tries to assign us an "essence"—a fixed identity—but Oddball reminds us that we are always free to reject that assignment.

"No, baby, we ain't" is the ultimate expression of this radical freedom.

It is the refusal to be bound by others' expectations. It is the recognition that your identity is a verb, not a noun, a continuous process of becoming, not a static state of being.

Case Study: The Artist and the Algorithm.

Consider Maya, a digital artist whose early work was highly successful because it fit neatly into a trending aesthetic.

The algorithms loved her, and the critics loved the algorithm. But Maya felt stifled, her creativity constrained by the expectation to keep producing the same "brand." She was constantly being told, "You're the one who does the neon-noir cityscapes."

She felt like a machine, not an artist.

One day, she looked at her canvas and whispered, "No, baby, I ain't." She abandoned the neon-noir, lost a few thousand followers, and began painting vibrant, abstract landscapes. Her income dipped, but her joy soared. She had rejected the label the world had given her and reclaimed her artistic sovereignty.

Her new work, born of genuine freedom, eventually found a deeper, more appreciative audience. She learned that true success is measured not by external metrics, but by the integrity of your self-definition.

Application: The Internal Rejection.

Use this phrase internally whenever you feel yourself being pigeonholed, limited, or defined by a past version of yourself.

1. Identify the Label: What is the limiting belief or external expectation being placed on you? ("I'm just a failure," "I'm too old for this," "I'm only a [job title]").

2. The Whisper: Whisper to yourself, "No, baby, I ain't."

3. The Re-Definition: Immediately follow the rejection with a positive, self-chosen affirmation of who you are becoming.

("I am a learner," "I am a creator," "I am free to choose my next move.")

It is a powerful reminder of your freedom to be authentically, complicatedly, and gloriously you.

Parable 4: The Faith in the Bridge

"There you go, more negative waves! Have a little faith, baby... Have a little faith."

Exegesis: The Two Kinds of Faith.

This parable teaches the two kinds of faith essential for a life of action.

The first is the faith of manifestation: "Think the bridge will be there and it will be there."

This is the power of positive focus, the belief that your intention and preparation will be met by opportunity. It is the necessary, initial leap of optimism. But the deeper, more resilient faith is revealed after the bridge is bombed.

It is the faith in the process, not the outcome. It is the unshakeable belief that another bridge is always available, that resources are infinite, and that a setback is merely a change of route, not a dead end.

This is the faith that can withstand any crisis, the faith that understands that the universe is fundamentally on your side, even when it seems to be actively blowing up your plans.

Deeper Exploration: Resilience and Antifragility.

This deeper faith is what modern thinkers call resilience or, even better, antifragility. Resilience is the ability to bounce back; antifragility, a concept coined by Nassim Nicholas Taleb, is the ability to get better because of a setback.

When Oddball's bridge is bombed, he doesn't despair; he acknowledges the new reality and starts looking for the next bridge. The crisis forces him to be more creative, more resourceful, and ultimately, more powerful. The bombing of the bridge is not a failure of faith; it is an opportunity for a higher-order faith to emerge.

It is the belief that the universe is not punishing you, but providing you with a necessary challenge to unlock a superior solution.

Case Study: The Startup Founder and the Failed Launch.

David, a tech startup founder, had spent two years building his product, pouring all his resources and belief into a single, massive launch event.

He had the faith of manifestation: "Think the bridge will be there."

On the day of the launch, a critical server failed, and the entire event was a public disaster. His bridge was bombed. His initial reaction was despair, a flood of negative waves.

But then he remembered the Parable of the Bridge. He realised his faith had been in the outcome (the perfect launch) rather than in the process (his ability to build, pivot, and solve problems).

He took a breath, publicly owned the failure with humour and grace, and immediately started a small, private beta test with a few dedicated users. The forced intimacy of the small group yielded invaluable feedback that completely improved the product.

The failed launch, the "bombed bridge," was the catalyst for a superior product and a more resilient company. He found a better bridge because the first one was destroyed.

Application: The Bridge Test.

When you suffer a setback, do not see it as a failure of your faith. See it as a test of your faith.

1. Acknowledge the Bombing: State the setback clearly and without emotional judgment. ("The funding fell through," "The client rejected the proposal," "The relationship ended.")

2. Reject the Negative Waves: Immediately stop the spiral of self-blame or external complaint.

3. Activate Deeper Faith: State with certainty: "Another bridge exists."

4. Begin the Search: Take a breath, and begin the search for the next bridge, knowing with absolute certainty that the crisis has sharpened your focus and prepared you for a superior route.

Parable 5: The Picnic of Power

"I'm drinking wine and eating cheese, and catching some rays, you know."

Exegesis: Sacred Rest and Strategic Inaction.

This is the parable of sacred rest and strategic inaction. It teaches that there are times when the most powerful, productive, and strategic thing you can do is to stop. It is a rebellion against the cult of busyness, the pervasive modern belief that productivity is measured by frantic activity.

Oddball affirms that rest is not laziness, and that simple, sensual pleasure—wine, cheese, sun—is a form of spiritual and intellectual nourishment. It is also a profound lesson in trust: trust in your crew to do their jobs without your interference, and trust in the universe to handle the details.

By stepping back, you gain perspective, and your subconscious mind, unburdened by the noise of constant action, is free to find the solution. The picnic is not an escape; it is a tactical manoeuvre.

Deeper Exploration: The Default Mode Network.

This parable is a prescription for engaging the brain's Default Mode Network (DMN).

The DMN is a set of interconnected brain regions that become active when we are not focused on the outside world—when we daydream, mind-wander, or rest.

Neuroscientists have found that the DMN is crucial for creative problem-solving, self-reflection, and consolidating memories. Oddball's "wine and cheese" moment is a deliberate activation of the DMN. By stepping away from the immediate problem, he allows his brain to process information in a non-linear, holistic way, often leading to the "Aha!" moment that brute-force effort could never achieve.

The ancient Chinese concept of Wu Wei, or "effortless action," perfectly captures this idea: the most effective action is often no action at all, but a state of being that allows things to unfold naturally.

Case Study: The Coder and the Bug.

Elena, a software engineer, was stuck on a complex, frustrating bug for three days.

She was "powering through," fuelled by caffeine and sheer will, but the more she stared at the code, the opaquer the solution became. She was generating negative waves and getting nowhere. Her partner, a student of Oddballism, simply said, "Time for a picnic of power, baby."

Elena reluctantly closed her laptop, went to a nearby park, and spent an hour reading a novel and catching some rays. She wasn't thinking about the bug at all. As she was packing up to leave, the solution—a simple, elegant refactoring of a function—popped into her head, fully formed.

The strategic inaction of the picnic had allowed her DMN to connect the necessary dots. She returned to her desk and fixed the bug in ten minutes. She learned that sometimes, the fastest way to the finish line is a detour to the nearest patch of sun.

Application: The Non-Negotiable Picnic.

Schedule "wine and cheese" moments into your life. These are non-negotiable appointments with rest and pleasure.

1. Identify Overwhelm: When you feel the urge to "power through" a problem, recognise this as a sign of diminishing returns.

2. Declare the Picnic: Announce a 30–60-minute period of strategic inaction. This must be a complete break from the problem.

3. Engage the Senses: Do something sensual and straightforward: listen to music, eat a good meal, sit in the sun, or take a walk.

4. Trust the Process: Let your subconscious mind work. The solution will not come from staring harder; it will come from looking away.

Parable 6: The Creative Arsenal

"We got our own ammunition; it's filled with paint... We have a loudspeaker here, and when we go into battle, we play music, very loud. It kind of... calms us down."

Exegesis: Asymmetric Advantage.

This is the parable of asymmetric advantage. It teaches that creativity, humour, and psychological insight are more powerful weapons than brute force. Oddball instructs us to re-purpose the tools of conflict for the ends of art and psychology. The goal is not to destroy the enemy, but to confuse them, to scare them, and, most importantly, to keep ourselves calm and centred.

The paint shell is a symbol of non-lethal disruption, a way to mark the target without committing to total war. The loud music is a form of emotional regulation, a way to control the crew's internal weather while simultaneously disrupting the opposition's emotional weather. It is a lesson in fighting smarter, not harder, by changing the very nature of the conflict.

Deeper Exploration: The Power of Play and Reframing.

This approach is deeply rooted in the psychology of play and the strategic use of reframing. By using paint and music, Oddball transforms a deadly military operation into a kind of performance art. This reframing reduces the internal stress of his team—the music "calms us down"—and introduces an element of the absurd that is deeply unsettling to a conventional enemy.

The enemy is forced to fight a ghost, a clown, a force that doesn't play by the rules. This psychological warfare is often more effective than confrontation. The concept aligns with Sun Tzu's teaching that the supreme art of war is to subdue the enemy without fighting. Oddball simply adds a killer soundtrack and a splash of colour.

Case Study: The Negotiator and the Loudspeaker.

Julian, a corporate negotiator, was facing a hostile takeover attempt.

The opposing team was aggressive, formal, and relied on intimidation. Julian decided to deploy his own creative arsenal. Instead of meeting in a sterile boardroom, he insisted on meeting in a casual, brightly lit art gallery space. He started the meeting not with financials, but by playing a short, upbeat jazz track on a small portable speaker, explaining, "Just setting the vibe, gentlemen. Helps me think." He also brought a small, brightly coloured stress ball for everyone, which he called his "paint shell."

The opposing team was entirely thrown off balance. Their formal, aggressive strategy was incompatible with the playful, relaxed atmosphere Julian had created. By changing the emotional weather of the room, Julian gained a psychological edge, forcing the opposition to negotiate on his terms, which ultimately led to a favourable resolution.

Application: The Arsenal Audit.

In any conflict or challenge, ask yourself: "What is my paint shell? What is my loudspeaker?"

1. Identify the Brute Force: What is the conventional, hard-power approach to this problem?

2. Find the Paint Shell: What is the non-lethal, creative way to disrupt the situation? (e.g., humour, a surprising gesture, a reframed proposal).

3. Choose the Loudspeaker: What is the tool you can use to control your own internal state and change the emotional weather of the environment? (e.g., a specific playlist, a mantra, a change of venue).

Look for the unconventional solution that relies on creativity, humour, and psychological insight rather than direct confrontation.

Parable 7: The Price of Glory

"But for 1.6 million dollars, we could become heroes for three days."

Exegesis: The Personal Mission.

This is the parable of the personal mission and the flexible principle. It teaches that our independence and principles need not be rigid or absolute. They can be flexible, but only for a price that aligns with our ultimate goal. Oddball is not a zealot; he is a pragmatist. He is willing to play the hero game, but only if it serves his larger purpose of getting the gold.

This gives him immense power and flexibility. He has a clear, non-negotiable goal (the gold), and he is willing to temporarily adopt a high-risk, high-status role (the hero) to achieve it. The key is that the price—$1.6 million—is a clear, quantifiable metric that justifies the temporary compromise of his usual low-profile, high-pleasure lifestyle.

DEEPER EXPLORATION: STRATEGIC PRAGMATISM AND VALUE ALIGNMENT.

This parable is a masterclass in strategic pragmatism.

It is about knowing your core values (your "gold") and assigning a clear, non-emotional price to any action that deviates from your default path. Most people compromise their principles for vague reasons—fear of missing out, a desire to please, or a lack of clarity.

Oddball's price is specific and tied directly to his ultimate goal. This concept is vital in modern decision-making, particularly in business and career choices. It's not about selling out; it's about making a clear-eyed, strategic trade. It is the difference between being a victim of circumstance and being a master of negotiation with the universe.

Case Study: The Freelancer and the Compromise.

Maria, a freelance graphic designer, had a strict rule: she only took on projects that were creatively fulfilling and allowed her to maintain a 30-hour work week. Her "gold" was creative freedom and work-life balance. A massive, high-paying corporate client offered her a project that was creatively dull and would require a brutal 60-hour week for two months. It was a classic weird sandwich, but the money was enormous, enough to pay off her student loans and take a six-month sabbatical. Maria applied the Parable of the Price. She calculated that the price—the complete elimination of her debt and the guarantee of a long, restorative break—was worth the temporary sacrifice.

She took the job, worked the 60 hours, and used the money to buy back six months of her life. She didn't compromise her principles; she invested her principles, trading a short-term loss of freedom for a massive long-term gain. She knew her price, and she got it.

Application: The Price Tag Exercise.

Know your "gold." What is the ultimate, non-negotiable goal you are working toward?

1. Define Your Gold: Write down your core, long-term goal (e.g., financial independence, creative mastery, deep relationships).

2. Set the Price: What is the specific, quantifiable price at which you would be willing to compromise your usual practices (e.g., a particular amount of dollars, a guaranteed outcome, a unique opportunity)?

3. Hold the Line: Do not compromise for anything less than that price. Knowing your price doesn't make you a sellout; it makes you a strategist. It allows you to make clear-headed decisions about when to hold 'em and when to fold 'em.

Additional Section: The Eighth Parable - The Philosophy of the Ride

The seven parables are the core texts, but the entire philosophy is encapsulated in the spirit of the man himself—the way he moves, the way he talks, the way he rides.

"Man, I just ride 'em."

Exegesis: Surrender to the Flow.

This is the unstated, ultimate teaching. When asked how he handles the chaos, the danger, the absurdity of his life, Oddball says, "I just ride 'em."

This is the philosophy of radical acceptance and non-resistance. It is the understanding that life is a series of waves—some smooth, some choppy, some terrifying—and your job is not to stop the waves, but to ride them with skill, grace, and a righteous vibe.

It is the ultimate antidote to anxiety, which is fundamentally the desire to control what cannot be controlled. To "just ride 'em" is to trust your own ability to adapt, to pivot, and to find the fun in the turbulence. It is the final, most advanced lesson in Oddballism.

Application: The Wave Rider's Stance.

When you feel overwhelmed by the sheer momentum of events, when the negative waves are crashing down, adopt the Wave Rider's Stance:

1. Drop the Anchor of Control: Acknowledge that you cannot stop the wave. Trying to stop it will only make you drown.

2. Find the Board: Focus on your immediate point of control—your breath, your attitude, your next small action.

3. Just Ride 'Em: Lean into the momentum. Use the energy of the chaos to propel you forward. Trust your instincts. The ride is the point.

This is the Book of Oddball.

Read it, live it, and keep those positive waves flowing, baby.

Chapter Twenty-Seven:

The Apocrypha

The Prophet did not speak in a vacuum. He was surrounded by a crew whose own words, while less enlightened, often serve to illuminate his wisdom through contrast or confirmation. These are the Apocrypha—the non-canonical but still instructive words of the disciples.

They are the echoes in the garage, the static on the radio, the human element that proves the theory of the wave. Oddball's philosophy is a solo act, but it is best understood in the context of the ensemble. To truly ride the wave, you must understand the currents and the undertows created by the people around you—and the different voices within yourself.

The Gospel of Moriarty: The Voice of Pragmatic Fear

"The motor's a piece of crap! The gearbox is junk! The clutch is slipping! And we're losing oil!"

Exegesis: The Necessity of the Negative Wave

Moriarty's constant litany of problems is not just negativity for its own sake; it is the voice of the engineer, the mechanic, the one who has to deal with physical reality. While Oddball manages the spiritual reality, Moriarty manages the material. His fear is born from his expertise. He knows all the ways the tank can fail because he knows the tank inside and out.

His role is to be the early warning system, the canary in the coal mine. He is the embodiment of risk assessment, a necessary counterpoint to Oddball's pure faith. Without Moriarty, Oddball's tank would break down before it ever reached the front line. The Moriarty in your life, or in your head, is not trying to stop you; he is trying to ensure you are prepared. He is the shadow of the wave, the trough that precedes the crest.

Connecting the Wave: Stoicism and the Premeditation of Evils

This concept is not new. The ancient Stoics called it *premeditatio malorum*, the premeditation of evils.

Seneca, the Roman Stoic, advised his followers to mentally rehearse potential misfortunes—poverty, illness, exile—not to invite them, but to strip them of their power. Moriarty is your internal Seneca. He forces you to confront the worst-case scenario so that when the worst-case scenario arrives, it is not a surprise, but a known variable.

Modern neuroscience supports this, suggesting that mentally simulating a negative outcome can prime the prefrontal cortex for better problem-solving and emotional regulation when the event actually occurs. The key is to listen to the critique without internalising the panic. You must hear the facts about the slipping clutch without adopting the emotional state of the man who is yelling about it.

Case Study: The Architect and the Code Review

Consider Elara, a brilliant but overly optimistic software architect leading a project to build a new financial trading platform.

Her internal Oddball is strong: she sees the vision, the elegance, the potential. But her team includes Ben, a senior security engineer— her Moriarty.

Every time Elara presents a new feature, Ben responds with a barrage of worst-case scenarios: "What if the API is hit with a DDoS attack?

What if the encryption key is compromised? What if a single point of failure in the database is exploited?"

Elara initially found Ben exhausting and demoralising. She saw him as a drag on the positive wave. However, after a near-catastrophic security breach on a competitor's platform, she realised Ben wasn't a pessimist; he was a realist with a specific domain of knowledge.

She learned to schedule a "Moriarty Hour" where Ben was given the floor to tear apart the design. By institutionalising the negative wave, she channelled its energy into resilience. The platform they built was slower to launch, but it was virtually unhackable, a testament to the balance between vision and vigilance.

Practical Application: The Moriarty Audit

You must have a Moriarty in your life, or at least a Moriarty in your own head. This is the voice of due diligence, of risk assessment. Before you embark on any mission, you must listen to Moriarty and ask, "What could go wrong here?" The key is to listen to this voice, thank it for its input, and then let the Oddball in you make the final decision with faith.

- **Step 1: The Brain Dump of Failure:** Before starting a new venture (a business, a relationship, a major purchase), dedicate 30 minutes to writing down every single way it could fail. Be specific. Don't write "I could run out of money." Write "I could run out of money in month six because I underestimated the cost of marketing by 40% and a key supplier raised their prices."

- **Step 2: The Moriarty-Oddball Dialogue:** For each point of failure, write a two-part response. The Moriarty part is the problem. The Oddball part is the solution, the contingency plan, the "positive wave" countermeasure. Moriarty: "The motor's a piece of crap!" Oddball: "We'll carry two spare motors and a full field repair kit. And we'll drive slower."

- **Step 3: The Gratitude and Release:** Once the audit is complete, thank your internal Moriarty for doing his job. Acknowledge that the risks are now known, and you have a plan. Then, consciously release the fear associated with the list. The fear has served its purpose. Now, the wave must take over.

The Gospel of Kelly: The Power of Belief

"No, because you're gonna be up there, baby, and I'll be right outside showing you which way to go."

Exegesis: The Pure Transmission of Faith

This is the most powerful positive wave in the entire film. It is a pure transmission of belief from one person to another. Kelly doesn't offer technical advice or more money. He offers presence, guidance, and faith. He shows that the most valuable thing you can give another person is your unwavering belief in them. It is this wave that gives Oddball the courage to take on the Tigers.

Kelly's words are not a prediction; they are a declaration of potential. He is not saying, "You might succeed." He is saying, "You will succeed, and I will be your anchor."

This is the essence of true leadership: the ability to see the best version of a person and hold that vision for them until they can see it for themselves.

Connecting the Wave: The Pygmalion Effect and Self-Efficacy

In modern psychology, this phenomenon is known as the Pygmalion Effect, or the self-fulfilling prophecy. Studies have shown that when a leader or mentor holds high expectations for an individual, that individual's performance tends to improve to meet those expectations.

Kelly is triggering Oddball's self-efficacy, the belief in one's ability to succeed in specific situations. Oddball, for all his confidence, is still a human being facing a near-impossible task. Kelly's belief acts as a psychological fuel, a temporary external locus of control that allows Oddball to tap into his own internal power.

It is the ultimate act of trust, a non-verbal contract that says, "My faith in you is greater than your current doubt."

Case Study: The Startup Founder and the Investor

Meet Javier, a brilliant engineer who has developed a revolutionary, open-source educational platform.

He was technically sound but suffered from crippling imposter syndrome when pitching investors. He was about to give up after a string of rejections. His mentor, Ms Chen, an experienced venture capitalist, saw his potential. She didn't just give him money; she gave him the Kelly.

In their final meeting before the successful funding round, Javier was sweating, stumbling over his words. Ms Chen leaned forward and said, "Javier, you're not selling a product. You're sharing a solution that the world desperately needs. I'm not investing in your pitch deck; I'm investing in the man who built this thing from nothing. You're gonna be up there, baby, and I'll be right outside showing you which way to go."

Her words weren't a business strategy; they were a transfer of confidence. Javier straightened up, finished his pitch with clarity and passion, and secured the funding. He later said that in that moment, he stopped trying to convince the room and started simply being the founder Ms Chen already believed him to be.

Practical Application: Being a Kelly for Your Crew

Your most important role as a crew member is to be a Kelly for someone else. When a friend is facing their own Tiger tanks, your job is to hit them with a positive wave of pure belief.

Don't offer advice unless asked. Just provide your presence and your faith. "You've got this. And I'll be right here with you."

- **Technique 1: The Declaration of Potential:** When someone you care about is struggling, avoid phrases like "You should try..." or "Have you thought about..." Instead, use declarative statements that affirm their inherent capability. Example: "I have seen you handle tougher situations than this. You already have the tools to solve this problem."

- **Technique 2: The Physical Presence:** Kelly didn't just speak; he was right outside. True belief requires presence. Put down your phone. Make eye contact. Give your full, undivided attention. Your physical presence is a non-verbal affirmation that their struggle is necessary and that you are a stable anchor in their storm.

- **Technique 3: The Past-Tense Reminder:** Remind them of a specific, past success where they overcame a similar challenge. This grounds your belief in their history, making it undeniable. Example: "Remember when you launched that project with half the budget and a week less time? This is nothing compared to that. You've already proven you can do this."

The Gospel of Crapgame: The Cynic's Hope

"What are you trying to do, scare the pants off of me? I'm scared enough already!"

Exegesis: The Ordinary Man's Journey

Crapgame represents the ordinary person, caught between the cynical realism of Moriarty and the enlightened calm of Oddball.

He is us. He is anxious, greedy, opportunistic, but also loyal and, deep down, hopeful. He is a follower, looking for a leader to believe in. His journey from a cynical hustler to a committed member of the crew is the journey that many of us will take.

Crapgame is the human condition distilled: a mixture of self-interest and a yearning for something greater. He is the one who needs the wave the most, because he is constantly fighting the undertow of his own anxiety. His cynicism is a defence mechanism, a way to manage a world that he finds overwhelming and unpredictable.

Connecting the Wave: Existentialism and the Search for Meaning

Crapgame's anxiety is the existential dread that philosophers like Jean-Paul Sartre and Albert Camus wrote about. He is acutely aware of the absurdity of his situation—a soldier in a war he doesn't fully believe in, risking his life for gold he may never get to spend.

His hustling is his attempt to impose meaning and control on a chaotic universe. Oddball's philosophy, with its emphasis on "positive waves" and living in the moment, offers Crapgame a temporary, experiential antidote to his dread. He doesn't intellectually grasp Oddballism, but he feels its effect. He is drawn to the vibe because it offers a brief respite from the burden of his own freedom and anxiety. His hope is not a grand philosophical conviction, but a simple, human desire for a better, less terrifying day.

Case Study: The Mid-Career Manager and the Side Hustle

Consider Marcus, a mid-level marketing manager.

He is Crapgame personified. He is good at his job, but he constantly complains about the company, the pay, and the lack of opportunity. He has a dozen "side hustles" he's always trying to get off the ground—selling vintage sneakers, trading crypto, writing a screenplay—all driven by a Crapgame-like greed and anxiety to escape his current reality.

He meets Sarah, a colleague who embodies the Oddball spirit: calm, effective, and genuinely happy with her work, not because of the money, but because she finds meaning in the process.

Marcus is initially cynical, constantly mocking Sarah's "zen" attitude. But he keeps coming back to her desk, drawn by the calm. Sarah doesn't preach; she just keeps sharing her "bread and cheese"—her genuine enthusiasm and simple, effective methods.

One day, Marcus admits, "I'm scared I'm going to wake up at 60 and realise I wasted my life chasing the wrong things." Sarah simply smiles and says, "Then stop chasing, Marcus. Start building. You don't need a new hustle; you need a new wave."

By not judging his anxiety, Sarah allowed Marcus to drop his cynical shield and finally articulate his underlying fear. He didn't become an Oddball overnight, but he started to dig the vibe, channelling his energy into one meaningful project instead of a dozen anxious hustles.

Practical Application: Being Patient with the Crapgames

Be patient with the Crapgames in your life. They may not understand your philosophy, but they are drawn to your vibe. They are looking for something to believe in. Don't judge their cynicism or their anxiety. Just keep blasting your righteous tunes and sharing your bread and cheese. Sooner or later, they'll start to dig it.

- **Technique 1: Non-Judgmental Presence:** When a Crapgame starts complaining, do not try to fix them or argue them out of their cynicism. Simply listen and validate the feeling, not the complaint. Example: "That sounds incredibly frustrating. I get why you'd feel anxious about that." This disarms their defence mechanism.

- **Technique 2: The Shared Bread and Cheese:** The "bread and cheese" is your genuine, simple, and unpretentious joy. Share your enthusiasm for your work, hobbies, or philosophy without trying to convert others. Let them see the positive results of your wave-riding firsthand.

- **Technique 3: The Invitation, Not the Demand:** Never demand that a Crapgame change. Simply invite them to join the wave. Example: "We're going to try this new approach on the project. It's a bit unconventional, but it's working for us. Want to see how we set it up?" The invitation respects their freedom and allows them to choose the wave on their own terms.

The Gospel of Big Joe: The Way of the World

"Look, you guys are soldiers, right? So start acting like soldiers!"

Exegesis: The System and the Free Individual

Big Joe is the voice of the system. He represents the traditional, hierarchical, rule-following world that Oddballism rejects. He believes in orders, in discipline, in doing things by the book.

He is not a villain; he is simply a man who has fully bought into the dominant paradigm. His frustration with Oddball is the system's frustration when it encounters a truly free individual.

Big Joe is necessary for the world to function—he manages logistics, maintains order, and ensures the basic machinery of society keeps turning. But his rigidity is the antithesis of the wave. He sees the world as a set of fixed rules, while Oddball sees it as a fluid, ever-changing opportunity.

Big Joe's greatest fear is chaos; Oddball's greatest tool is controlled chaos.

Connecting the Wave: Taoism and the Concept of Wu Wei

The conflict between Oddball and Big Joe is a classic philosophical tension, perhaps best articulated in Taoism. Big Joe embodies the rigid, effortful, rule-bound approach, while Oddball embodies Wu Wei, or "effortless action."

Wu Wei is not laziness; it is action that is so perfectly aligned with the flow of the universe (the "wave") that it appears effortless. Oddball doesn't fight the system; he flows around it. He doesn't follow the rules; he follows the spirit of the mission.

When Big Joe demands "act like soldiers," he is demanding conformity. When Oddball responds with calm, humour, and unshakeable commitment to his own way of being, he demonstrates the power of Wu Wei. He lets the system exhaust itself trying to contain him, while he simply keeps moving toward the objective.

Case Study: The Corporate Bureaucracy and the Maverick Team

Imagine Brenda, the new Chief Operating Officer of a massive, established tech company.

She is Big Joe in a power suit. Her goal is to streamline, standardise, and enforce strict protocols—"Look, you guys are employees, right? So start acting like employees!"

Her frustration is focused on the "Skunkworks" team, led by Devon, a brilliant but unconventional product developer. Devon's team operates on Oddball principles: they work odd hours, they use non-standard tools, and they refuse to fill out the required 10-page quarterly compliance reports.

Brenda sees them as a liability, a source of chaos. Devon, however, consistently delivers the company's most innovative and profitable products. When Brenda finally confronts Devon, demanding conformity, Devon doesn't argue. He simply presents the latest quarterly revenue report, showing his team's product line has generated 60% of the company's new income. He says, "We're not breaking the rules, Brenda. We're just using a different set of tools to get the gold."

Brenda, the ultimate pragmatist, realises that while she needs the system (Big Joe) to manage the 90% of the company that runs on routine, she needs the wave (Oddball) to generate the future. She doesn't convert to Oddballism, but she creates a special, protected "Wave Rider" designation for Devon's team, allowing them to operate outside the system as long as they keep delivering the gold.

Practical Application: Navigating the Big Joes

You will encounter Big Joes every day. They are your bosses, your parents, your well-meaning friends who just don't get it.

Do not argue with them.

Do not try to convert them.

You cannot win a debate with the system. Your response should be that of Oddball: a calm, humorous, and unshakeable commitment to your own way of being. Let your results be your argument. When you show up with the gold, even Big Joe will have to admit that your weird methods work.

- **Technique 1: The Humorous De-escalation:** When Big Joe demands conformity, a calm, humorous response is the most effective tool. It acknowledges the demand without accepting the premise. Example: When asked why you're wearing a non-standard uniform, you might reply, "The positive wave requires maximum comfort, sir. It's a tactical advantage."

Humour short-circuits the system's need for a serious, rule-based conflict.

- **Technique 2: The Results-Based Argument:** Never argue about how you do something; only argue with what you produce. Big Joe respects results above all else. Focus your energy on delivering the "gold"—the undeniable, measurable success—that makes your unconventional methods irrelevant to the final outcome.

- **Technique 3: Strategic Conformity:** Oddball is not an anarchist. He is a pragmatist. Know which rules are essential for safety and function (Moriarty's domain) and which are merely bureaucratic noise (Big Joe's domain). Conform to the essential rules to avoid unnecessary conflict, and reserve your wave-riding energy for the areas that truly matter.

The Synthesis: The Crew as a Complete Mind

The Apocrypha, when taken together, form a complete psychological model for the Wave Rider. Oddball is the Self, the enlightened centre of calm and purpose. But the Self is not alone.

- Moriarty is the Critical Function (the internal risk assessor, the shadow).

- Kelly is the Affirming Function (the internal cheerleader, the source of self-efficacy).

• Crapgame is the Anxious Ego (the part that worries about money, status, and survival).

• Big Joe is the Superego (the internalised voice of authority, rules, and society).

A true Wave Rider doesn't eliminate these voices; they orchestrate them.

You need Moriarty to check the engine before the journey. You need Kelly to give you the final push of belief. You need to be patient with your own internal Crapgame when anxiety flares up.

And you need to calmly navigate the external Big Joes without letting them derail your mission.

The wisdom of the Apocrypha is that the wave is not just about you; it is about how you interact with the entire crew, both inside your head and out in the world. The greatest act of Oddballism is not just riding your own wave, but understanding and harmonising the waves of everyone around you.

Part Nine:

The Practical Guide

(Expanded Introduction)

Welcome to the garage. This is where we put on our coveralls, get out the tools, and start working on the tank. The first eight parts of this book have been the owner's manual. This part is the hands-on workshop. Here, we will provide you with a structured program, practical exercises, and a toolkit to help you integrate Oddballism into your life, one day at a time. This is your 30-day journey to becoming a Wave Rider.

The Apocrypha teaches us that the first tool in the garage is self-awareness.

You must be able to identify which voice is speaking in your head at any given moment. Is that anxiety about your bank account the voice of Crapgame? Is that meticulous checking of your work the voice of Moriarty? Is that feeling of unshakeable confidence the voice of Kelly?

The practical guide begins with the simple, yet profound, act of listening to your internal crew. Only when you know who is driving the tank can you gently guide the wheel back to the path of the positive wave. The following sections will provide step-by-step techniques for managing this internal crew, transforming your inner critic into a consultant, your anxiety into action, and your external conflicts into opportunities for effortless flow. The wave is waiting.

Chapter Twenty-Eight:

The 30-Day Wave Rider Challenge:

Mastering the Art of the Oddball Life

This challenge is not a self-help fad; it is a boot camp for the soul, designed to build the core, non-negotiable habits of Oddballism. For the next 30 days, you will commit to a series of daily and weekly practices that will fundamentally rewire your response to the world. Oddball never asked for perfection, and neither do we.

The goal is not to be flawless; the goal is consistency. Show up, do your best, and when you inevitably slip, get back on the tank and keep rolling. This is about building muscle memory for the good life. Your most critical tool in this journey will be your Tank Journal, a dedicated space—physical or digital—to log your experiences, your victories, and, most importantly, the negative waves you successfully deflected.

The Philosophical Underpinnings of the 30-Day Challenge

Before we dive into the weeks, understand the deeper currents at play.

This challenge is a practical application of Stoicism, Cognitive Behavioural Therapy (CBT), and modern neuroscience. The Stoics, like Epictetus, taught that we are disturbed not by things, but by the views we take of them.

Oddball's philosophy is the same: the negative wave only has power if you let it crash over you. The challenge is designed to create a cognitive distance between the stimulus (the negative wave) and your response (your action).

It's about creating a pause, a moment of Oddball-esque detachment, where you can choose your wave.

Week 1: Building the Shield (Focus: The Doctrine of Positive Waves)

The first week is dedicated to defence. You cannot ride a wave until you can recognise and deflect the ones that will drag you under. This is about establishing a sanctuary of the mind—a mental tank that is impervious to the daily barrage of cynicism, anxiety, and manufactured urgency.

Extended Narrative Example: The Case of Eleanor and the Digital Drag

Eleanor, a 42-year-old marketing executive, started the challenge feeling constantly drained.

Her first hour of the day was a frantic sprint: phone in hand before her feet hit the floor, scrolling through news headlines, work emails, and social media feeds. By 8:00 AM, she was already anxious, feeling behind, and carrying the weight of the world's problems and her colleagues' demands. She was, in Oddball's terms, getting hit with a tsunami of negative waves before she'd even had her first cup of coffee.

Her Week 1 commitment was brutal but straightforward: First Hour Screen-Free. For the first three days, she felt phantom vibrations and a deep, physical urge to check her phone.

She replaced the scroll with a simple, quiet routine: a glass of water, a five-minute stretch, and writing her Morning Declaration in her Tank Journal.

The declaration, "Don't hit me with them negative waves so early in the morning," became her mantra. By Day 5, the anxiety had lessened. She was no longer starting her day in a state of reaction.

She was starting it in a state of intention. She realised the negative waves weren't just external; they were the anticipation of external demands, a neurological feedback loop she had trained herself into.

Daily Practices: The Foundation of Defence

1. Morning Declaration: Every morning upon waking: "Don't hit me with them negative waves so early in the morning." This is your Verbal Shield, a simple, immediate act of boundary-setting. It's a neurological reset, a declaration of sovereignty over your own mind.

2. First Hour Screen-Free: This is a non-negotiable act of self-respect. It allows your prefrontal cortex—the part of your brain responsible for planning and decision-making—to wake up before your amygdala—the part responsible for fear and anxiety—is hijacked by the digital world.

3. Wave Spotting (The CBT Connection): In your journal, log every significant negative wave you encounter. Note the source (person, media, inner critic) and how it made you feel. This practice is directly aligned with Cognitive Behavioural Therapy (CBT), specifically the thought record technique. By externalising the negative wave, you stop identifying with it and start observing it. You realise the wave is not you; it is merely a phenomenon passing through your environment.

4. Evening Gratitude: Before bed, write down one positive wave you experienced today. This is the final, crucial act of the day. It shifts your brain's focus from a threat-detection system to a resource-finding system. It ensures your last conscious thought is one of abundance, not lack.

Weekly Mission: The Gentle Redirection

Have one conversation where you consciously practice a Verbal Shield.

When someone hits you with a negative wave—a complaint, a piece of gossip, a doomsday prediction—try a gentle redirection. Oddball's wisdom here is never to engage the wave head-on.

You don't argue; you simply change the channel.

- **Example:** A colleague says, "This project is a disaster, we're all going to miss the deadline."

- **Your Redirection:** "That's a heavy thought. Before we get into the disaster, what's the one small thing we can do right now to make the next hour better?"

Note how it feels and how they respond. Often, the negative wave is simply a cry for help or a communication habit. Your gentle redirection is an act of leadership, showing them a better wave to ride.

Week 2: Digging the Beauty (Focus: The Doctrine of Presence and Beauty)

Once the shield is up, you can stop defending and start seeing. Week 2 is about moving from defence to appreciation. Oddball knew that the world is full of beautiful things, but you have to dig for them. This is the practice of radical presence, pulling your mind out of the past and the future and anchoring it firmly in the now.

Deeper Exploration: Neuroscience and the Default Mode Network

The constant stream of internal chatter—the planning, the worrying, the rehashing—is managed by the brain's Default Mode Network (DMN). While essential, an overactive DMN is a primary source of anxiety and disconnection.

The practices in Week 2 are designed to temporarily quiet the DMN and activate the Task Positive Network (TPN), the part of the brain engaged in focused, external tasks. When you are truly digging for beauty, your DMN quiets down. This is the neurological mechanism behind mindfulness and meditation, but with an Oddball twist: it's active, sensory, and fun.

Daily Practices: The Art of Seeing

1. The Five-Sense Dig: Once a day, perform the Five-Sense Dig exercise. Stop what you are doing and consciously log:

• 5 things you can see (the texture of the wood grain, the way the light hits a dust mote).

• 4 things you can feel (the weight of your shirt, the cool air on your skin).

• 3 things you can hear (distant traffic, the hum of the refrigerator).

• 2 things you can smell (the faint scent of coffee, the fresh air).

• 1 thing you can taste (the lingering flavour of your last drink). This is a hard reset for your nervous system, a moment of pure, unadulterated presence.

2. The Beauty Log: In your journal, write down three beautiful things you "dug" today. Be specific. Don't write "The sunset was nice." Write, "The way the low-hanging clouds caught the last orange light, turning the underside a deep, bruised purple." Specificity is the key to presence.

3. Sacred Pleasure (The "Wine and Cheese" Ritual): Engage in one of your chosen "wine and cheese" rituals, giving it your full, undivided attention. This is not about indulgence; it is about sanctifying the small joys. If you are drinking coffee, don't scroll your phone. Smell it, taste it, feel the warmth of the mug. This practice teaches your brain that pleasure is available now, not just at the end of a long, stressful task.

Weekly Mission: The Beauty Hunt

Go on a Beauty Hunt. Take a 30-minute walk with the sole purpose of finding and appreciating beautiful things. This is not an exercise; it is a sensory pilgrimage. Leave the headphones at home. The main goal is to see. This mission is a direct challenge to the modern tendency to consume the world through a screen. You are reclaiming your primary senses as the true interface to reality.

Week 3: Declaring Independence (Focus: The Doctrine of Anti-Heroism and Independence)

Week 3 is where you learn to say "No, baby, I ain't." This is the week of boundary-setting, of recognising the "weird sandwiches" the world tries to feed you, and refusing to take a bite.

Oddball was the ultimate anti-hero: he did his job, but he did it on his own terms, for his own reasons. This week is about defining your terms.

Case Study: Marcus and the Hero Complex

Marcus, a 30-year-old software developer, was the office "fixer."

He was constantly praised for his willingness to work late, take on impossible deadlines, and rescue failing projects. He was, in his own mind, a hero.

In reality, he was a burnt-out martyr, constantly resentful of the colleagues who took advantage of his "heroism." He was eating a steady diet of weird sandwiches—the expectation that his value was tied to his self-sacrifice.

His Week 3 breakthrough came when he identified a "weird sandwich": his boss asked him to cancel his vacation to fix a non-critical bug. In the past, he would have said yes, fuelled by the need for external validation.

This time, he logged it in his journal: Weird Sandwich: Cancelling my rest for a non-emergency that is not my responsibility. He then practised his Weekly Mission and said "no" politely but firmly, offering a solution for when he returned. The world did not end. The bug was fixed by someone else. Marcus realised that his "heroism" was actually a form of co-dependence on external praise. His true independence was in choosing his own battles.

Daily Practices: Identifying the Traps

1. Weird Sandwich Watch: Identify at least one "weird sandwich" offered to you by the world—a demand for pointless heroism, self-sacrifice, or conformity. A weird sandwich is anything that asks you to compromise your peace or your values for a reward that is ultimately empty. Log it. Just notice it. The act of noticing is the first step to freedom.

2. "I Ain't" Affirmation (The Ancient Philosophy Connection): When you feel boxed in by a label, an expectation, or a self-limiting belief, internally recite the mantra: "No, baby, I ain't." This is the modern echo of Socratic self-inquiry. Socrates believed the unexamined life was not worth living. Oddball's version is simpler: the unexamined expectation is not worth fulfilling. You are not your job title, your past mistakes, or someone else's projection. You are an independent entity, a Wave Rider.

Weekly Mission: The Art of the Polite "No"

Say "no" to one thing. It could be a small request, an invitation you don't want to accept, or a piece of work that isn't your responsibility. The key is to do it politely but firmly. This is the practice of setting boundaries. A boundary is not a wall; it is a filter. It allows the positive waves in and deflects the negative ones. Practice the phrase: "I appreciate you asking, but I can't take that on right now."

No further explanation is required. Your time and energy are the fuel for your tank; you are the only one who gets to decide where to spend them.

Week 4: Mastering the Tank (Focus: The Doctrine of Competence and the Crew)

The final week is about action and connection. Oddball's tank was his competence, and his crew was his strength. You have built your shield and found your independence; now it is time to focus your energy on what truly matters: becoming excellent at your chosen craft and nurturing the relationships that sustain you.

Practical Application: The Competence Loop

The Doctrine of Competence is not about being the best in the world; it is about being the best you can be at the things that matter to you. This creates an internal locus of control. When you know you are competent, external negative waves—like criticism or failure—become less threatening. You have a solid foundation to stand on.

- **Step-by-Step Guidance for Competence Practice:**

1. Identify Your Tank: What is the core skill that gives you the most satisfaction and provides the most value to your crew (family, work, community)? (e.g., coding, writing, gardening, parenting).

2. The 30-Minute Deliberate Practice: Spend 30 minutes deliberately working on that core skill. This is not passive consumption (watching a full documentary); it is active engagement (practising a specific technique, writing a difficult paragraph, debugging a small piece of code).

3. Log the Learning: In your journal, log what you learned and one specific way you improved. This reinforces the neural pathways associated with growth and competence.

Case Study: Sofia and the Power of the Crew

Sofia, a small-business owner, was a classic solo hero.

She believed she had to do everything herself. By Week 4, she was competent but isolated. Her Crew Connection practice forced her to reach out. She started with a simple text to a former mentor, sharing a small victory. The mentor responded with a joke and a piece of advice that saved Sofia three hours of work.

Her Shared Loaf ritual was a simple Tuesday night dinner with her husband, where they agreed to put their phones away and talk only about their "wins" for the day. This small, intentional connection—the "Shared Loaf"—transformed their relationship.

It wasn't a grand gesture; it was the consistency of presence. Sofia realised that the strength of her tank wasn't just the armour (her competence) but the engine (her crew).

Daily Practices: Fuelling the Engine

1. Competence Practice: Spend 30 minutes deliberately working on a core skill related to your "tank." This is your investment in your future self, a daily dose of self-efficacy.

2. Crew Connection: Make one positive connection with a member of your crew—a text, a call, a shared joke, a genuine compliment. Oddball knew that a tank is useless without a crew. Your crew is the network of people who support your positive waves and deflect your negative ones.

Weekly Mission: The Shared Loaf Ritual

Schedule and hold a "Shared Loaf" ritual with at least one member of your crew. It could be a coffee, a meal, or a drink. The only agenda is to connect. The "loaf" is the shared experience, the simple act of breaking bread and being present. This ritual is the antidote to the modern, transactional relationship. It is a reminder that the greatest wealth is the quality of your connections.

The Nuance: What Happens After Day 30?

The 30-Day Challenge is not a finish line; it is the launch sequence. By the end of these 30 days, you will have laid the foundation. You will have built the core habits. You will have experienced the profound shift that comes from actively choosing your waves.

The Edge Case: The Unavoidable Negative Wave. What about the truly catastrophic events—the job loss, the illness, the betrayal? Oddballism does not promise a life free of pain. It promises a life free of unnecessary suffering. When the unavoidable negative wave hits, your 30 days of practice will kick in. Your Shield will be stronger, allowing you a moment of pause before reaction. Your ability to Dig the Beauty will allow you to find the one small thing to be grateful for, even in the rubble. Your Independence will remind you that your value is not tied to the external loss. And your Crew will be there to help you tow the tank back to the garage.

You will be a Wave Rider in training, and the journey will have just begun.

The only thing left to do is to keep rolling.

Chapter Twenty-Nine:

The Wave Riders Toolkit:

Advanced Maintenance for the Soul-Tank

Every tanker needs a good toolkit, and not just a wrench and a roll of duct tape. We're talking about the specialised, psychological instruments you use to keep your internal engine humming, your treads gripping, and your cannon aimed true.

These are the practical resources, templates, and frameworks you can use to diagnose problems and repair your vibe. Revisit these whenever your tank breaks down, or better yet, use them for preventative maintenance. Remember, the best repair is the one you never have to make.

Section 1: The Negative Wave Diagnostic—Advanced Troubleshooting

The original Negative Wave Diagnostic is a quick-and-dirty checklist for immediate triage.

When you feel anxious, angry, or drained—when the engine starts sputtering and the smoke is thick—you need to identify the source fast. But sometimes the source isn't a single, obvious leak; it's a slow, insidious seep from multiple places.

That's when you need the advanced diagnostic, a deeper dive into the four core areas of influence.

Tool 1.1: The Negative Wave Diagnostic (Refined)

1. Who am I with? (The Social Contagion)

The basic question is: Is there a Moriarty in the room? The advanced question is: Am I allowing a Moriarty to rent space in my head, even when they're not in the room? This isn't just about the people physically present. It's about the people you are mentally engaging with. The demanding boss whose email you keep re-reading. The critical parent whose voice echoes in your self-talk. The ex-friend whose social media feed you compulsively check.

Case Study: The Ghost of the Boardroom

Meet Elias, a 35-year-old software architect.

Elias was a high-performer, but for the last six months, he'd been plagued by a low-grade, persistent anxiety. His initial diagnosis pointed to his boss, Mr Sterling, a notoriously demanding and emotionally volatile executive. Elias would leave meetings with Sterling feeling physically ill. The problem was that the anxiety didn't stop when he left the office. He'd be at home, playing with his kids, and suddenly his stomach would clench.

The refined diagnosis revealed the issue: Elias was constantly rehearsing future confrontations with Sterling in his mind. He was letting the ghost of Sterling into his living room. The solution wasn't just to avoid Sterling (impossible), but to build a mental firewall.

Elias started a practice he called "The 5 PM Lockout." At 5 PM, he would physically write down three things he could control about his work, and three things he couldn't. He would then visualise a large, steel door slamming shut on the list of uncontrollables, explicitly telling his mind, "Sterling is locked out until 9 AM tomorrow."

This simple, deliberate act of mental boundary-setting cut his evening anxiety by 70% within a month. The wave was external, but the damage was internal, caused by his own mental engagement.

2. What am I consuming? (The Information Diet)

The basic question is: Am I doom-scrolling? Watching stressful news? The advanced question is: Is my information diet nourishing my mission or feeding my fear? This extends beyond news and social media to the books you read, the podcasts you listen to, and the background noise in your life. Are you constantly consuming content that reinforces scarcity, cynicism, or outrage?

<u>Connection to Neuroscience: The brain is a prediction machine.</u>

When you feed it a steady diet of negative, high-arousal content (fear, anger, threat), you are training your amygdala—the brain's alarm centre—to be hyper-vigilant. This is a survival mechanism, but in the modern world, it leads to chronic stress.

Oddball's wisdom is a pre-scientific understanding of Neuroplasticity. You are literally rewiring your brain with every piece of content you consume. To change the output (your mood), you must change the input (your diet).

Practical Application: The 10-Minute Wave Wash

If you catch yourself in a consumption spiral, immediately implement the "10-Minute Wave Wash."

• **Step 1:** Stop the Input. Turn off the screen, close the book, mute the podcast. Total silence.

- **Step 2:** Change the Channel. For 10 minutes, engage in a sensory activity that requires full presence: wash dishes, walk outside and name five things you see, or listen to a piece of music you love without doing anything else.

- **Step 3:** Reset the Feed. Before returning to any screen, deliberately choose one piece of content that is positive, educational, or inspiring. A short documentary, a chapter from a good book, or a five-minute video of a puppy. This acts as a palate cleanser for your mind.

3. What am I saying to myself? (The Inner Moriarty)

The basic question is: Is my Inner Moriarty broadcasting? The advanced question is: What is the specific, core belief that Moriarty is trying to sell me? The Inner Moriarty is a master salesman, and his product is always the same: The belief that you are fundamentally inadequate or unsafe.

This connects directly to Cognitive Behavioural Therapy (CBT). Oddball's approach is a street-smart way to challenge Automatic Negative Thoughts (ANTs).

Technique: The Oddball Interrogation

When you hear the Inner Moriarty, don't just dismiss him. Interrogate him like a captured spy.

- **Moriarty's Claim:** "You're going to fail this presentation, and everyone will know you're a fraud."

- **Oddball's Interrogation:**

- "Says who?" (Challenge the authority.)

- "What's the evidence?" (Demand proof. Usually, there is none.)

- "What's the worst-case scenario, and can I survive it?" (Pre-empt the fear. Yes, you can survive a bad presentation.)

- "What's the most likely scenario?" (Introduce realism.)

- "If my best friend said this to me, what would I tell them?" (Apply compassion.)

The goal is not to silence Moriarty, but to make him a minority shareholder in your mental corporation. He can have his say, but he doesn't get the final vote.

4. What are my physical needs? (The Tank's Fuel and Maintenance)

The basic question is: Am I hungry, tired, or dehydrated? The advanced question is: Am I treating my body like a high-performance tank or a rusty jalopy? This is the ancient philosophical concept of Soma (the body) as the foundation for Psyche (the mind).

Connection to Ancient Philosophy: The Stoics believed that a clear mind was essential for virtue. It's hard to be virtuous—or even just patient—when your blood sugar is crashing.

Oddball's toolkit recognises that the mind is not separate from the body; it is the body. Your brain is a physical organ that requires fuel, rest, and movement. Neglect the tank, and the commander (your conscious mind) will be operating on faulty equipment.

Practical Guidance: The 20/20/20 Rule

To combat the modern sedentary life, implement the 20/20/20 rule:

- Every 20 minutes of focused work, look 20 feet away for 20 seconds (to rest your eyes).

- Every 2 hours, take a 20-minute break to move your body (walk, stretch, do a few push-ups).

- Every day, dedicate 20 minutes to deep, restorative rest (meditation, nap, or just lying down in silence).

Section 2: The "Another Bridge" Framework—The Art of the Pivot

The world is full of bridges that get bombed. A job loss, a failed relationship, a business venture that collapses. The "Another Bridge" framework is your psychological blueprint for navigating catastrophic failure, moving you from the shock of the explosion to the excitement of the next mission.

Tool 2.1: The "Another Bridge" Framework (Expanded)

1. Acknowledge the Bombing: The 10-Minute Mourning
State the brutal fact. "The bridge is gone." The expansion here is the crucial concept of The Defined Mourning Period. You must allow the disappointment, grief, or anger to be felt, but you must put a fence around it. Oddball knows that suppressed emotion is like a ticking time bomb. You can't ignore the explosion; you have to deal with the debris.

Case Study: The Architect's Blueprint

Dr Anya Sharma, a brilliant medical researcher, had spent 5 years developing a novel drug-delivery system.

She secured a massive grant, built a team, and was weeks away from the final, critical trial.

Then, a competitor published a paper demonstrating a fatal flaw in the core mechanism—a flaw that Anya's team had missed. The bridge was not just bombed; it was vaporised.

Anya initially spiralled into self-recrimination. Her team leader, a Wave Rider himself, reminded her of the framework. She set a timer for 10 minutes. She allowed herself to cry, to rage, to feel the crushing weight of five years of work being invalidated. When the timer went off, she stood up, washed her face, and said, "The bridge is gone. Now, what's left?" This deliberate, time-boxed emotional release prevented the failure from becoming a permanent identity crisis.

2. Assess the Resources: The Inventory of the Unbombed

What do you still have? This step shifts your focus from the loss (the bombed bridge) to the assets (the Unbombed resources).

Most people, after a failure, only see the hole. Wave Riders see the tools, the crew, and the fuel still in the tank.

The Inventory Checklist:

• **Intangible Assets:** Experience gained, lessons learned, network built, resilience proven, reputation (if you handled the failure with grace).

• **Tangible Assets:** Money, equipment, physical health, time, and the support of your crew.

• **Core Skills:** What did you do well, even in failure? Anya still had her brilliant mind, her team-building skills, and her deep knowledge of the biological pathway.

These were the real assets, not the failed drug system.

3. Brainstorm New Crossings: The Paint Shell Phase

List at least five unconventional ideas, no matter how crazy they seem. This is the divergent thinking phase. The key is to suspend judgment. The old bridge was straight. The new crossing might be a tunnel, a helicopter, or a giant rubber duck. The point is to break the mental pattern that led to the first bridge.

Connection to Modern Psychology: This step is a powerful technique for overcoming Functional Fixedness, the cognitive bias that limits a person to using an object only in its traditional way. In this context, the "object" is your career, your relationship, or your life path. You are functionally fixed on the old solution. By forcing yourself to list five "crazy" ideas, you bypass the inner critic and unlock creative problem-solving.

4. Choose a Direction and Move: The Smallest Step

Pick the most promising option and take one small step in that direction. The goal is to restore a sense of agency and forward momentum. The first step doesn't have to be the biggest or the best; it just has to be forward.

For Anya, the most promising "new crossing" was to pivot her research. Her failed system had revealed a new, unexpected biological interaction. Her first small step was to schedule a 30-minute meeting with her team to discuss the "accidental discovery" and nothing else.

That single, small step—a conversation—was the first tread mark of the new tank, moving away from the debris of the old bridge.

Section 3: The Crew Vibe Check—The Ecology of Relationships

A tank is only as good as its crew. Your personal ecosystem—your relationships—determines the quality of the waves you ride. The Crew Vibe Check is not a tool for cutting people out; it's a tool for investing your most precious resource: your time and energy.

Tool 3.1: The Crew Vibe Check (Deep Dive)

1. Energy Balance: The Emotional Ledger

When I leave a conversation with this person, do I generally feel more energised or more drained? This is the most critical metric. Energy is the currency of the Wave Rider.

Connection to Psychology: This relates to the concept of Emotional Labour and Social Support Theory. Some relationships are high-maintenance, requiring constant emotional output from you (draining). Others are reciprocal, providing genuine support and uplift (energising). A healthy life is not about having zero draining relationships (some family or work relationships are unavoidable), but about ensuring the ratio is heavily weighted toward the energising ones.

Practical Application: The 80/20 Rule of Vibe

Apply the Pareto Principle to your social life. Identify the 20% of your relationships that provide 80% of your positive energy. Invest more time, attention, and vulnerability in those 20%.

Simultaneously, identify the 20% that drain 80% of your energy. You don't have to cut them off, but you must consciously limit your exposure and lower your emotional investment in them. Treat them like necessary administrative tasks, not like a weekend joyride.

2. Wave Ratio: The Signal-to-Noise Ratio

What is the ratio of positive waves to negative waves they send my way? This is about the quality of communication. Are they primarily focused on problems, gossip, and complaints (negative waves), or on solutions, opportunities, and gratitude (positive waves)?

<u>Narrative Example: The Perpetual Critic</u>

Marcus had been friends with David since childhood. David was a good man, but a perpetual critic. Every time Marcus shared a success—a promotion, a new hobby, a great vacation—David would find the flaw. "That promotion means more stress, right?" "That hobby is expensive, isn't it?" David's wave ratio was 1:5 (one positive comment for every five negative ones).

Marcus realised that David wasn't malicious; he was riding a negative wave himself. Marcus didn't end the friendship, but he changed the context. He stopped sharing his dreams and successes with David. Instead, their interactions focused on shared, low-stakes activities—watching a game or working on a simple project. He kept David in his life, but he removed him from his "Mission Alignment" crew. He protected his own wave by adjusting the nature of the interaction.

3. Mission Alignment: The Shared Heading

Are we generally trying to get to the same place in life? This is the most overlooked aspect of relationship health. Your crew doesn't have to have the same job or the same hobbies, but you must share a fundamental direction: growth, integrity, contribution, and purpose.

If your mission is to build a life of quiet contribution, and your friend's mission is to chase fleeting fame and drama, you are on fundamentally different headings. Every time you interact, you are pulling each other off course. It's like two tanks tethered together, trying to drive in opposite directions. It creates friction, not momentum.

4. Trust Level: The Authenticity Test

Do I feel safe being my authentic self with them? This is the bedrock of a strong crew. If you have to wear a mask, censor your thoughts, or constantly manage their perception of you, the relationship is a performance, not a partnership.

Connection to Ancient Philosophy: This is the core of Aristotelian Friendship of Virtue. These are the friends who love you for who you are, not for what you can do for them. They are the ones who will tell you the truth, even when it's hard, because their primary mission is your well-being. A Wave Rider needs at least one or two of these friends—the ones who can look inside your tank and tell you honestly if the engine is smoking.

SECTION 4: THE ODDBALL'S EDGE: CONNECTING THE TOOLKIT TO MODERN WISDOM

The Wave Rider's Toolkit is simple, but its power lies in its deep resonance with both ancient wisdom and modern science. Oddball didn't read the journals, but he understood the principles.

The Stoic Tanker

The "Another Bridge" framework is pure Stoicism. The Stoics, like Marcus Aurelius, taught the absolute necessity of distinguishing between what you can control (your actions, your response, your effort) and what you cannot control (external events, other people's opinions, the past).

The bombing of the bridge is an external event—uncontrollable. Your response—assessing resources, brainstorming new crossings, and taking the first step—is entirely within your control. Oddball's philosophy is a practical manual for applying the Dichotomy of Control in a crisis.

The Psychology of Flow

The entire toolkit is designed to help you get into a state of Flow, a psychological state of complete absorption in an activity. Negative waves—anxiety, self-criticism, physical discomfort—are the primary barriers to flow.

Using the Negative Wave Diagnostic clears the mental and physical clutter that prevents deep engagement. When the Inner Moriarty is quieted, the body is fuelled, and the social environment is supportive, your mind is free to focus entirely on the mission, which is the definition of flow.

The Wisdom of the Tao

The ultimate goal of the Wave Rider is to move with the current, not against it. This is the Taoist concept of Wu Wei—effortless action. The toolkit is not about forcing a good life; it's about removing the obstacles to the good life that is already trying to happen.

The "Another Bridge" framework is the ultimate expression of Wu Wei in the face of disaster: don't fight the fact that the old path is gone (that's resistance); find the new path of least resistance (that's flow).

The Wave Rider's Toolkit is your comprehensive maintenance manual. Use it daily, not just in emergencies. Keep your tank clean, your crew aligned, and your focus on the next crossing. Because in the end, life isn't about avoiding the bombs; it's about always having another bridge ready to build.

Chapter Thirty:

A Final Word from the Prophet

"Crazy... I mean like, so many positive waves... maybe we can't lose, you're on!"

This is the final destination. This is enlightenment, Oddball-style. It is the moment when you have so thoroughly practised the doctrines, so diligently built your shield and mastered your tank, that you reach a tipping point.

It is the moment when the force of your own positive wave, combined with the waves of your crew, becomes so powerful that it feels like an objective force of nature. It is the moment when faith transcends itself and becomes a kind of certainty.

You may not feel it today. You may not feel it next week. But if you stay on the path, if you keep practising, if you keep digging the beauty and rejecting the negativity, there will come a day when you face your own three Tiger tanks.

You will look at the impossible odds, you will feel the belief of your crew, you will feel the strength of your own spirit, and you will smile. And you will say, with a calm and joyful heart, "Crazy... maybe we can't lose." You're on.

THE TIPPING POINT: WHEN THE WAVE BECOMES A TSUNAMI

The initial chapters of this book were about building a seaworthy vessel—your mind, your habits, your immediate environment.

We focused on the mechanics of the tank: the engine of discipline, the armour of self-awareness, the turret of humour.

But the final word, the true culmination of the Wave Rider's journey, is the realisation that the tank is merely a conduit for a far greater force: the Positive Wave.

This wave is not just a feeling; it is a measurable, palpable energy that you project into the world. Modern neuroscience, in its clumsy, lab-coat way, calls this "affective presence" or "emotional contagion." Ancient Stoics called it Eudaimonia, a flourishing state of being that naturally influences one's surroundings.

Oddball, with his characteristic economy of language, calls it "so many positive waves."

The tipping point is the moment when your internal state of positive certainty—your belief in the mission, your trust in your crew, your acceptance of the chaos—becomes so robust that it begins to organise the external world around it.

It's not magic; it's the profound power of a mind operating without friction. When you are truly "on," your decisions are clearer, your communication is sharper, and your resilience is unbreakable. People are drawn to this energy. Opportunities seem to materialise. The universe, as it were, starts saying, "You're on."

Case Study 1: The Architect and the Impossible Deadline

Meet Anya, a brilliant but perpetually stressed architect in Seattle.

Her firm had landed a career-defining project: a sustainable, high-rise residential tower. The problem was the timeline. The client, a notoriously demanding tech mogul, had moved the deadline up by six months.

Anya's team was in a state of collective panic. They were working 18-hour days, fuelled by caffeine and fear. The negativity was a thick, suffocating fog in the office. Every minor setback—a software crash, a delayed material sample—was treated as a catastrophe.

Anya, a long-time, though inconsistent, student of the Wave, recognised the pattern. Her crew was losing the war not against the deadline, but against their own internal chaos. She called an emergency meeting, not to discuss blueprints, but to discuss waves.

She didn't preach. She implemented a few Oddball-isms:

1. The "Why Bother?" Protocol: She mandated a 15-minute "Why Bother?" session every morning. Instead of a status update, the team had to share one thing they were genuinely excited about in the design, one thing they were grateful for (even if it was just the good coffee), and one thing they were going to let go of that day intentionally. This was a deliberate act of rejecting the negativity.

2. The "Tank Maintenance" Hour: She enforced a mandatory one-hour, no-work, no-email lunch break. The team had to leave the office, walk, or simply sit in silence. This was the building of the shield—protecting their mental energy.

3. The "Crazy... Maybe We Can't Lose" Mantra: She put up a small, hand-drawn sign with the quote above the main drafting table. It wasn't about blind optimism; it was about reframing the impossible. The impossibility of the deadline was so extreme that it became absurd, almost humorous. The pressure was so high that it circled back to zero. Crazy... maybe we can't lose.

The shift was subtle at first, then dramatic. The team didn't work more hours; they worked better hours. The positive wave Anya projected—calm, focused, and utterly certain of the team's talent—began to wash over the fear.

When a major structural issue was discovered three weeks before the final submission, instead of collapsing into despair, the team leader, a young engineer named Ben, looked at the sign, smiled, and said, "Well, that's a Tiger tank. Let's get the tow cable." They solved the problem in 48 hours, not because they were smarter, but because their minds were not cluttered with panic. They hit the deadline. Anya's positive wave had become a self-fulfilling prophecy of success.

The Neurobiology of the Positive Wave

Oddball's philosophy is not just folk wisdom; it is a practical application of advanced neurobiology. When you are in a state of high anxiety and fear, your prefrontal cortex—the part of the brain responsible for planning, decision-making, and impulse control—is effectively hijacked by the amygdala, the brain's fear centre. This is the "tank breaking down" scenario. You become reactive, short-sighted, and prone to error.

The Wave Rider's practice—the humour, the calm acceptance, the focus on the immediate task—is a systematic way to down-regulate the amygdala and restore executive function. When Oddball says, "Why don't you knock it off with them negative waves?" he is giving a direct command to the nervous system to switch from a sympathetic (fight-or-flight) state to a parasympathetic (rest-and-digest) state.

The "tipping point" is achieved when this parasympathetic state becomes your default setting, even under extreme duress. This is what psychologists call cognitive flexibility and emotional regulation. You are not suppressing the fear; you are simply choosing a more effective operating system. The "positive wave" is the external manifestation of a perfectly regulated internal system. It is the sound of a well-oiled machine.

Part Ten:

Advanced Wave Riding

Welcome to the graduate-level course.

You have mastered the Five Pillars, studied the Sacred Texts, and completed your initial 30-day training. You are no longer a novice. You are a Wave Rider. But the journey is not over. Life will inevitably present you with challenges that go beyond the scope of the foundational doctrines. This section is for those advanced challenges. It's for the moments when the tank doesn't just break down, but is set on fire. It's for navigating the complexities of money, loss, and legacy. This is where we learn to ride the biggest and most dangerous waves of all.

SUB-SECTION 1: THE WAVE AND THE WALLET (NAVIGATING FINANCIAL CHAOS)

Money is the modern Tiger tank, often appearing in threes: debt, market volatility, and the fear of scarcity. The foundational doctrines teach us to dig the beauty and reject the negativity, but how does that apply when the rent is due, and the bank account is empty?

The advanced Wave Rider understands that financial stress is not a monetary problem; it is a wave problem. The negativity wave of fear, shame, and panic is what causes the worst financial decisions: the impulsive investment, the desperate loan, the paralysis that prevents action.

The Advanced Technique: The "Gold Bar" Reframing.

Oddball's crew was after gold bars. They weren't after a paycheck; they were after a tangible, absurdly valuable, and concrete goal. When facing financial chaos, you must reframe your problem from "I need to pay bills" (a negative, fear-based frame) to "I am executing a plan to acquire the gold bar" (a positive, mission-based frame).

Case Study 2: The Entrepreneur & the Failed Series A

Julian ran a promising tech startup, but his Series A funding round collapsed after a key investor pulled out. He was left with three months of runway, a team of 15 employees, and a crushing sense of personal failure. The negativity wave was a monster. He felt shame, anger, and a deep sense of betrayal.

Julian's initial reaction was to panic-cut salaries and fire half his team—a classic reactive move.

But he paused. He remembered the core lesson: The mission is the mission, the tank is the tank.

His mission was to build his product. His tank was his team and his remaining capital.

He gathered his crew and was brutally honest, but he reframed the crisis. "We just hit a minefield," he told them. "The mission hasn't changed, but the route has. We were aiming for the gold bar via the paved highway. Now we're taking the dirt road. The good news? We're a better crew for it. We're going to treat the next 90 days as a guerrilla operation."

He didn't fire anyone. Instead, he proposed a temporary, voluntary 30% pay cut for everyone, including himself, with a promise of a 2x bonus upon securing new funding. He created a new, lean "Tiger Team" focused only on revenue generation. By reframing the failure as a strategic pivot and a test of crew loyalty, he turned the negative wave of fear into a positive wave of shared purpose.

His certainty—his "Crazy... maybe we can't lose" attitude—became their certainty. They secured a smaller, strategic investment 60 days later, not because the product was suddenly better, but because the investors saw a team that was unbreakable under pressure. Julian had learned to ride the financial wave by focusing on the mission, not the money.

Sub-Section 2: The Ultimate Loss (Riding the Wave of Grief)

The most dangerous wave is the one that threatens to sink the entire vessel: the loss of a loved one, the end of a long career, the destruction of a dream. Here, the Oddball philosophy meets ancient wisdom head-on.

The Stoics taught us to accept what we cannot control (Amor Fati—love your fate). Oddball teaches us to accept the chaos while keeping the engine running. When the tank is set on fire, the immediate human reaction is to stop, to mourn, to surrender.

The Advanced Wave Rider does not deny the fire; they refuse to let it consume the mission.

The Practical Application: The "Salvage Operation" Technique.

When faced with profound loss, the technique is to treat your life as a salvage operation. The tank is damaged, but the mission—to live a life of purpose and positive waves—is still active.

1. Acknowledge the Damage (The Fire): Allow the grief. Oddball is not a robot. He is deeply human. The loss is real. But set a boundary. You will mourn, but you will not wallow. You will feel the fire, but you will not become the ash.

2. Identify the Salvageable (The Crew and the Mission): What remains? Your health, your other relationships, your core values, your skills. These are the gold bars you still possess. Focus your energy on protecting and utilising these assets.

3. Execute the Immediate Task (The Tow Cable): Grief often paralyses. The antidote is action. What is the smallest, most immediate, most positive thing you can do right now? Make a phone call. Clean a room. Go for a walk.

This is the equivalent of getting the tow cable out. It is a small, physical act of defiance against the paralysis of the negative wave.

This is the deep connection to modern psychology's Acceptance and Commitment Therapy (ACT). ACT teaches that suffering comes not from pain itself, but from the struggle to avoid pain. Oddball's acceptance of the chaos—"Always with the negative waves, man. Always with the negative waves"—is the ultimate acceptance of the human condition. The loss is a negative wave, but you are the Rider. You do not fight the wave; you ride it.

Sub-Section 3: The Legacy Wave (The Prophet's Long Game)

The final word is about legacy. Oddball is not just concerned with the immediate mission; he is also worried about the wave's propagation. His final words are an invitation: You're on.

This is the concept of Positive Contagion—the idea that your state of being is not isolated but is constantly being transmitted to those around you. The final stage of Wave Riding is to become a source, a generator, a prophet of the positive wave.

Step-by-Step Guidance: Becoming a Wave Generator

1. Master the Inner Frequency: Your internal dialogue must be impeccable. You must have eliminated the internal critic and replaced it with the calm, humorous voice of the Wave Rider.

This is the silent, constant practice of digging the beauty in your own mind.

2. Amplify the Outer Signal: Your actions, your words, and your non-verbal communication must be a clear, strong signal of positive certainty.

This means:

• **Praise in Public, Critique in Private:** Always amplify the positive waves of your crew.

• **Lead with Humour:** Humour is the ultimate tool for diffusing negativity and creating cognitive flexibility. It is the oil that keeps the tank running smoothly.

• **Be the Calm Centre:** In any crisis, be the person who is the least reactive. Your calm is the anchor for everyone else's sanity.

3. Recruit the Next Generation: The true legacy is not the gold bar; it is the creation of more Wave Riders. Look for the novices, the stressed, the panicked, and quietly, humorously, show them the way. Give them a tow cable. Tell them to knock off the negative waves.

The final enlightenment is the realisation that the mission is not yours alone. It is a collective effort.

When you say, "Crazy... maybe we can't lose," the "we" is not just your immediate crew; it is the entire community of Wave Riders, past, present, and future.

Your positive wave, once a small ripple, has joined the ocean. You are no longer just riding the wave; you are the wave.

You're on.

Chapter Thirty-One:

The Dark Night of the Tank

"The only way I got to keep them Tigers busy is to LET THEM SHOOT HOLES IN ME!"

There will come a time in your life when the negative waves are not just a passing storm, but a tsunami. A time when the bridge is not just bombed, but every possible crossing point for a hundred miles has been obliterated. A time of profound loss, grief, or despair. A time when the simple act of raising your shield feels impossible, and the idea of a positive wave feels like a cruel joke.

This is the Dark Night of the Tank. This is not just a bad day; this is a season in hell.

It could be the death of a loved one, a devastating illness, a crushing betrayal, or a period of deep, clinical depression. In these moments, the cheerful, laid-back vibe of Oddballism can feel inadequate, even insulting. This is the ultimate test of the philosophy. Can it hold up when the sun has truly disappeared from the sky?

The answer is yes. But it requires a different application of the doctrines. This is Oddballism in winter, and it is perhaps the most important lesson in the entire book. It is the wisdom of the tank commander who knows that sometimes, the only winning move is not to play, but to endure.

The Doctrine of Hibernation: Shrinking the Perimeter

When a tank is catastrophically damaged, it does not try to go on the offensive. It finds a safe place, powers down all non-essential systems, and waits for repair. When you are in the Dark Night, your first job is not to "think positive" or "fight back." Your first job is to survive.

This is the Doctrine of Hibernation. It is a radical act of self-preservation, a strategic retreat from the impossible demands of the world. The world will keep spinning, but for a time, you must stop spinning with it.

Shrink Your World: Your world must become very, very small. Your mission is no longer to get the gold. Your mission is to get through the next hour. Sometimes, the next five minutes.

Your only goal is to breathe. That's it. Just breathe. This is the psychological equivalent of reducing your cognitive load to zero. The grand plans, the career goals, the social obligations—all of it is jettisoned.

You are operating on emergency power only. The ancient Stoics spoke of apatheia, not as apathy, but as a state of mind free from emotional disturbance. In the Dark Night, Oddball's Hibernation is a modern, practical path to a temporary, necessary apatheia. You are not trying to be happy; you are trying to be still.

Conserve All Energy: You have no energy for Wave Rejection. You must retreat. This means radical disengagement from all sources of negativity, and even from neutral demands.

Turn off the news. Log off social media. Politely but firmly tell well-meaning friends that you cannot talk right now. Your energy is a precious, dwindling resource.

Use it only for the absolute essentials: eating, sleeping, breathing, and the occasional, minimal self-care ritual. Think of it as a tank's engine running on fumes—you wouldn't waste that fuel on a joyride. You use it to crawl to the nearest safe harbour.

Find Your Hull: A tank crew will shelter in the burnt-out hull when their vehicle is destroyed.
It's not comfortable, it's not safe, but it's better than being out in the open.

What is your hull? It could be your bed. It could be a specific chair. It could be one, single, trusted member of your crew. Find the one place or person where you feel even 1% safer, and stay there. This is your temporary sanctuary, your psychological foxhole. It is a place where the expectation of performance is suspended, where you are allowed to simply be a damaged machine waiting for the repair crew.

Case Study: The Architect and the Avalanche

Consider the case of Elias, a brilliant, high-achieving architect in his late forties.

Elias had built his life on the principle of the Positive Wave: relentless optimism, constant forward motion, and the belief that any problem could be solved with enough ingenuity.

Then, an avalanche hit his life: his wife, Maria, was diagnosed with a rare, aggressive form of cancer. The medical bills, the emotional toll, the sheer, crushing weight of watching his partner suffer—it was a Dark Night of the Tank that lasted eighteen months and culminated in her passing.

In the immediate aftermath, Elias tried to apply his old philosophy. He tried to "find the positive" in the situation, to "reject the negative waves" of grief. He tried to keep his architecture firm running at full speed. He was, in Oddball's terms, trying to go on the offensive with a catastrophically damaged tank.

The result was a total breakdown. He couldn't sleep, he couldn't eat, and he began to experience panic attacks in the middle of design meetings.

His turning point came when a friend, a fellow Oddballist, didn't offer him a pep talk, but a single, profound piece of advice: "Elias, your tank is totalled. Find the hull."

Elias took this literally. He cancelled all his projects, put his firm on a temporary hiatus, and retreated to a small, dark room in his house that he had once used as a reading nook. For three months, his world was that room. His only mission was to get out of bed, eat a single meal, and then return to the quiet darkness. He conserved all energy. He didn't answer emails. He didn't look at blueprints. He didn't try to be happy. He simply hibernated.

This radical acceptance of his broken state, this willingness to shrink his world to the size of a single room, was the only thing that allowed his mind and body to begin the slow, agonising process of repair. He wasn't healing; he was surviving. And in the Dark Night, survival is the highest form of victory.

The Parable of the Holes: Surrender as Strategy

In the final battle, Oddball's strategy is to let the Tigers shoot holes in his tank. This is a terrifying, counterintuitive, and deeply profound teaching for the Dark Night. He is not trying to avoid the damage. He has accepted that the damage is inevitable. He is using the damage as part of a larger strategy.

The quote is not, "I will try to avoid the holes." It is, "I will let them shoot holes in me."

When you are in the Dark Night, you cannot avoid the holes. The pain is going to come. The grief is going to hit you. The despair will feel overwhelming. Do not fight it. To fight it is to waste precious energy. Your job is to let the pain shoot holes in you, but to do so with a purpose.

This concept finds a fascinating echo in modern neuroscience, particularly in research on emotional regulation. Trying to suppress a strong emotion, like grief or anxiety, is a bit like holding a beach ball underwater—it takes immense energy, and the moment you let go, it explodes to the surface.

Oddball's strategy is to let the ball float, to allow the emotion to pass through you.

What is the purpose? To keep the Tigers busy. The "Tigers" in this case are the ultimate negative forces: self-destruction, giving up completely, the final, fatal blow of hopelessness.

By consciously engaging with your pain, by allowing yourself to feel the grief, you are keeping those ultimate Tigers busy. You are saying, "I am in so much pain right now, I have no energy left to consider giving up." You are letting the feeling of sadness shoot holes in you, so that the feeling of hopelessness cannot land a fatal blow. You are using the immediate, sharp pain as a shield against the deeper, existential threat.

This is a high-level, dangerous technique. It requires a small, deep part of you to remain the observer, the commander who is choosing this strategy. It is the act of surrendering to the pain without surrendering to the despair.

The ancient Greek philosopher Heraclitus noted that "The way up is the way down."

In the Dark Night, the way out is the way through. You must descend into the experience, not fight it from the surface. This is the paradoxical strength of vulnerability: by allowing yourself to be completely broken, you become too heavy to be swept away.

The Faintest Positive Wave: The Micro-Observation

In the depths of the Dark Night, you cannot generate a mighty positive wave. You must search for the faintest, most microscopic flicker of light. It will not be joy. It will not be hope. It might be… less bad.

This is the practice of Micro-Observation, a technique that bypasses the broken emotional centres of the brain and appeals directly to the raw, sensory experience of the present moment.

Your old Positive Waves were tidal forces—a promotion, a new relationship, a successful venture. Your new waves are ripples in a puddle. They are tiny. They are fragile. Your job is to notice them and to hold onto them as if they are the last embers of a dying fire.

Do not demand more of them. Just notice them. "Ah," you can whisper to yourself. "A wave. Not a negative one."

• The coffee this morning tastes slightly less like ash than it did yesterday.

• The physical pain has subsided for three minutes.

• A member of your crew sent a text that said, "No need to reply. Just thinking of you."

• The sun, for a brief moment, hit the dust motes in the air just right, and it was beautiful.

• The cat decided to sleep on your chest, and its weight was a grounding presence.

This is where Oddballism meets the core principles of mindfulness and modern cognitive therapy. When the brain is overwhelmed by negative rumination, the only way to break the cycle is to introduce a neutral or positive sensory anchor.

You are not trying to feel happy about the cat; you are simply registering the fact of the cat's weight, the fact of the sun's light. These faintest positive waves are enough to keep the tank's minimal life support systems running.

The Nuance of Grief: The Oddballist's Mourning

A common edge case in the Dark Night is the feeling that one is "failing" at grief. Society often imposes a timeline or a set of stages on mourning, suggesting that one must "move on" or "find closure."

The Oddballist rejects this notion entirely. Grief is not a problem to be solved; it is a landscape to be traversed.

Case Study: Sarah and the Unfinished Symphony

Sarah, a talented musician, lost her younger brother, Leo, in a sudden accident.

Leo was her greatest fan and her primary source of creative inspiration. Her Dark Night was characterised by a profound inability to touch her cello. The instrument, once a source of joy, became a monument to her loss. Her friends, trying to be helpful, kept urging her to "play for Leo," to "honour his memory" by performing. This only made her feel worse, a failure at both grief and music.

The Oddballist approach, guided by the Doctrine of Hibernation, gave her permission to fail. She didn't have to play for Leo. She didn't have to honour his memory in a way that felt false. Her hull became a worn armchair in her apartment, and her only mission was to listen to one piece of music a day—not her own, not Leo's favourite, but something completely neutral, like a Bach fugue. She allowed the pain of her loss to shoot holes in her, to be a constant, raw presence, but she refused to let the despair of creative failure land a fatal blow.

After six months, she didn't suddenly pick up her cello and compose a masterpiece.

Instead, she noticed a Faintest Positive Wave: the sound of the rosin scraping against the bow of a street performer outside her window. It wasn't a call to action; it was just a sound that was "less bad" than the silence.

Slowly, she began to clean her cello, not to play it, but just to feel the wood. Her healing was not a sudden burst of light, but a gradual, almost imperceptible increase in the size of her world, moving from the armchair to the cleaning rag, and eventually, to a single, quiet note.

The Oddballist's mourning is not about closure; it is about carrying the weight of the loss without letting it crush you.

Practical Application: The Three-Step Protocol for the Dark Night

When the Dark Night descends, the mind is incapable of complex planning. You need a simple, three-step protocol that can be executed even when operating at 1% power.

This is the Oddballist's emergency procedure:

Step 1: The Hull Check (Daily)

• **Action:** Identify your Hull (your safe space/person) and physically move to it. If you are already there, acknowledge it.

• **Mantra:** "I am in the Hull. I am safe for now."

• **Purpose:** To establish a physical and psychological boundary against the overwhelming world. This is the non-negotiable first move.

Step 2: The Minimal Fuel Burn (Hourly)

• **Action:** Choose one, and only one, essential task: Drink a glass of water, eat a handful of nuts, or take five deep breaths.

• **Mantra:** "This is my fuel. I am conserving."

• **Purpose:** To maintain the absolute minimum biological and psychological functions. This is the conservation of energy, the single-digit percentage of effort that keeps the lights on.

Step 3: The Hole Observation (Whenever Pain Hits)

• **Action:** When a wave of pain, grief, or despair hits, do not fight it. Name it, and then allow it to pass. Do not analyse it; simply observe its presence.

• **Mantra:** "A hole has been shot. I feel the pain. The Tigers are busy."
• **Purpose:** To consciously engage the Parable of the Holes. You are using the immediate pain as a strategic distraction for the ultimate despair. You are surrendering to the feeling without surrendering your will to survive.

THE BRIDGE WILL BE REBUILT. NOT TODAY.

Faith, in the Dark Night, is not the belief that another bridge is just around the corner. It is the quiet, stubborn, almost imperceptible trust that, someday, far in the future, someone will eventually get around to rebuilding a bridge.

You don't have to see it. You don't have to believe it will be soon. You just have to hold open the possibility that your current reality is not the final reality.

This is the Oddballist's ultimate, long-term positive wave: the belief in the inevitability of change, even if that change is currently invisible.

The Dark Night of the Tank is the most difficult part of the Oddballist journey. It is the part where you earn your command. It is the part where you learn that this philosophy is not about being happy all the time.

It is about being alive. It is about surviving the winter so that you can be there to feel the sun on your face when the spring finally, eventually, comes. You are not a failure for being broken. You are a commander for choosing to survive the breaking. And when the spring comes, you will be the one who knows the true, unshakeable meaning of a Positive Wave.

You will have earned it in the dark.

Chapter Thirty-Two:

Oddball & Money:

The Real Gold

Kelly: "Sixteen million dollars. That's the pot."

Oddball: "Oh, wow."

Let's talk about the gold. For a philosophy that seems so anti-materialistic, Oddballism begins with a very material goal: stealing $16 million in Nazi gold. This is no contradiction; it is a key to understanding the Oddballist relationship with money. Money itself is not evil. It is not the root of all problems, nor is it inherently corrupting.

In the world of Oddballism, money is a tool—a powerful, flexible, and often necessary tool that can open the gates to the ultimate prize: **freedom.**

Oddball's gold is not about greed or excess; it's about escape. It's about carving out a space to live on your terms, free from the tyrannies of circumstance, obligation, and fear.

It's about building a "F-You" Fund that grants you the power to say no without trembling, the power to walk away from a broken system or a toxic relationship. It's about armour against the relentless barrage of life's uncertainties.

Money as a Defensive Weapon

Imagine Oddball and his crew, not as gold-hoarding pirates, but as freedom fighters. They don't lust after the gold to fill vaults or flaunt wealth; they want it as a ticket out of the war. Their fortune is their shield and their parachute. This is Oddballism's first and most important lesson about money: it is a defensive weapon first.

Take the concept of the "F-You" Fund.

This is not just a savings account; it is a financial fortress. Picture it as the fastest engine in the European Theatre that can rocket you away from any miserable situation. It's your escape route, your peace of mind. The size of this fund varies from person to person, but a common yardstick is having six to twelve months of living expenses stashed away. This fund is a quiet revolution in your psyche—it transforms anxiety into calm, desperation into confidence.

Consider the story of Rachel, a graphic designer in her early thirties living in a bustling city. For years, she stayed in a job that drained her creative spirit and stifled her voice because she feared the financial fallout of quitting. She was shackled by rent, credit card debt, and the invisible handcuffs of a paycheck-to-paycheck life.

When Rachel finally scraped together a "F-You" Fund worth eight months of her expenses, something remarkable happened.

The very next time her boss dumped an impossible deadline on her desk, she smiled and said, "No." She left the job soon after and started her own freelance studio, not because she was reckless, but because she was free.

On the flip side, debt acts like a negative wave that crashes relentlessly against your mental shores. High-interest consumer debt is a storm that erodes your options, drags you down into stress, and hands power over to creditors. Oddballism insists on purging this debt as a form of spiritual cleansing. It is a form of liberation, a shedding of chains.

The psychological weight of debt is well-documented in modern psychology. Studies show that debt activates the brain's threat response, flooding the system with cortisol and diminishing decision-making capacity. By systematically paying down debt, you quiet the storm inside your head and clear the path to freedom.

Money as a Tool for Joy and Beauty

Once your defences are secure, money can become an offensive weapon in the service of joy, connection, and beauty. Oddballism is not about conspicuous consumption or accumulating things. It's about using money intentionally to enrich your life, to deepen presence, and to savour the world's finer textures.

Oddball's famous advice to "buy the good cheese" is a metaphor for this idea. Don't waste your money on ten cheap, plastic-wrapped blocks of flavourless cheese that bring no pleasure.

Instead, invest in one small piece of artisanal cheese that melts on your tongue and fills you with delight.

This philosophy extends beyond cheese to everything you consume: your tools, your food, your clothes, and your experiences.

The pursuit of quality over quantity aligns with the ancient philosophy of Epicureanism, which teaches us to seek pleasure not in excess, but in moderation and refinement. The pleasure derived from a well-chosen experience or object is deeper, more lasting, and more meaningful.

Take the story of Marcus, a mid-level manager who used to buy cheap gadgets and fast food in a desperate attempt to fill an emotional void. He found himself trapped in a cycle of fleeting pleasures and deeper dissatisfaction.

When Marcus embraced Oddballism and started prioritising quality, he bought a handcrafted leather wallet that lasted years, joined a local cheese-tasting club, and invested in a well-made bicycle for weekend rides—he discovered that his happiness was less about acquiring more and more about savouring what he had. His life became richer, not because he had more, but because he valued better.

Oddballism also teaches us to "fund the shared loaf."

Use your resources to bring your crew together. Host a dinner party, buy concert tickets, or chip in for gas on a road trip. There is immense value in investing in shared experiences because human connection is the currency of a meaningful life.

Neuroscience supports this: social bonding releases oxytocin, reduces stress, and enhances well-being. Money spent on experiences that weave you closer to your tribe yields returns that material goods rarely can match.

Finally, the ultimate luxury in Oddball's eyes is not a fancy car or a sprawling mansion; it is control over your own time. Time is the one resource you can't replenish. As you accumulate resources, look for ways to buy back your time. Pay for a cleaning service so you can spend your Saturday writing your novel, or order takeout so you can enjoy a relaxed dinner with your family. This is not laziness; it is an investment in presence and quality of life. The freedom to choose how you spend your time is the real gold.

Consider Sophia, a high-powered lawyer who worked sixty-hour weeks and rarely saw her children. When she decided to redirect her resources, she hired a housekeeper and started using meal delivery services. These choices cost money, but Sophia gained hours she could spend reading bedtime stories and attending school plays. The peace and joy she found were priceless dividends.

The Trap of the Second War

Yet, there is a great danger lurking beneath the surface of money: the mission to get the gold can become a new war, just as stressful and soul-crushing as the one you were trying to escape. Many people achieve financial freedom only to find themselves still trapped, drowning in a mindset of scarcity, anxiety, and constant striving.

Oddballism warns us to know when we have enough.

There must be a point where you say, "The pot is big enough." This is not a number pulled from thin air, but a deeply personal definition of victory. For some, it might be a specific amount in the bank. For others, it might be the freedom to work only twenty hours a week or the ability to live in a cabin in the woods off the grid. Without this definition, the fight never ends; the war becomes endless.

This concept echoes the Stoic philosopher Epictetus's teaching that desire should be measured and moderated. The Stoics believed that the root of suffering is not external hardship but the endless craving for more. Oddballism channels this ancient wisdom into modern life: define your gold, then stop chasing and start living.

Another caution is not to become a "Big Joe of Finance"—that obsessive, anxiety-ridden investor who is forever checking the stock market, panicking at every dip, and being dragged down by the negative waves of financial news. Big Joe is trapped in the system he tried to master. Oddballism advocates for a simple, robust, "good enough" financial plan. This might mean investing in broad, low-cost index funds, automating your contributions, and sticking to your strategy through market ups and downs. Let the system work for you; don't become a slave to it.

Practical Applications: Building Your Own Freedom

How do you build your own Oddball-style relationship with money? It begins with defining your personal "gold." Sit down and ask yourself what financial freedom looks like for you. Is it enough to quit your job tomorrow? Is it having a small business that covers your expenses? Is it buying a home outright? Write it down clearly.

Next, start building your "F-You" Fund. Calculate your monthly expenses—including rent, utilities, food, transportation, insurance—and aim to save six to twelve months' worth. Set this as your primary goal before investing or splurging. Automate your savings by setting up a direct deposit to a separate account. This makes the process painless and resistant to your own impulses.

Simultaneously, tackle your debts with relentless clarity. List them all with interest rates and minimum payments. Use the "debt avalanche" method by paying off the highest-interest debt first while maintaining minimum payments on others. Celebrate each payoff as a victory, each step bringing you closer to freedom.

Once your defences are secure, shift your focus to quality of life. Practice buying the good cheese in all areas. When shopping for clothes, tools, or gadgets, choose items that are durable, functional, and bring you joy. Don't be afraid to pay more for something that improves your experience and lasts longer.

This is an investment in your joy and presence.

Prioritise experiences that connect you with your community. Organise potlucks, buy tickets to a play, or start a book club. The emotional returns from shared moments far exceed what money can buy alone.

Finally, think about ways to buy back your time. Identify tasks that drain your energy but don't require your unique talents. Can you outsource cleaning, lawn care, or grocery shopping? Use the money you save from cutting wasteful spending to reclaim your hours. Time is the rarest currency, and spending it wisely is the ultimate form of wealth.

The Ethics and Nuances of Wealth

Oddballism is not blind to the ethical questions around money. Wealth can be a source of power, and power can be used for good or ill.

The question arises: how much wealth is ethical? What responsibilities come with abundance?

While Oddballism promotes freedom, it also emphasises connection and responsibility.

Building generational wealth is not inherently greedy; it can be a means to uplift your family and community. But it should not become a fortress that isolates or a weapon that oppresses. The philosophy encourages transparency, generosity, and humility.

Consider Jamal, who inherited a small fortune from his grandparents. Instead of hoarding it, Jamal started a community garden project in his neighbourhood, creating jobs and green space.

His wealth became a tool for connection and upliftment. Oddball would salute that.
Conversely, Oddballism warns against wealth hoarding that disconnects you from your crew or your values. If money becomes an idol, it warps your freedom into slavery. The goal is to be the master of money, not its servant.

THE MODERN MIND AND MONEY: PSYCHOLOGY AND NEUROSCIENCE

Understanding the Oddballist relationship with money also benefits from modern science. The brain's reward system responds to money, but often in ways that lead to hedonic adaptation—the phenomenon in which increased wealth or consumption yields diminishing returns in happiness. This is why constantly chasing more gold can feel like a treadmill with no end.

Oddballism sidesteps this trap by focusing on freedom, presence, and connection rather than accumulation. This aligns with psychological research showing that spending money on experiences and time-saving services yields more lasting happiness than material goods.

The scarcity mindset—the feeling of never having enough—triggers the amygdala, the brain's fear centre, which hijacks reasoning and decision-making. Building your "F-You" Fund is a direct antidote, calming this primal alarm and freeing your prefrontal cortex to make wise choices.

Edge Cases and Grey Areas

Life is messy. What about those who cannot build a large "F-You" Fund due to systemic barriers or low income?

Oddballism recognises that freedom is relative and encourages focusing on what you can control. Even small steps toward financial stability—like opening a savings account, seeking community support, or developing skills to increase earning power—are victories.

For the wealthy, Oddballism challenges the endless pursuit of more. The philosophy invites you to define what freedom means beyond money and to invest in joy, time, and connection.

Money is not the goal. Freedom is the goal. Joy is the goal. Connection is the goal. Money is just the mother, beautiful tank that can help you get there.

Get the gold, but don't forget to dig the beauty along the way.

The Book of Oddball

www.ingramcontent.com/pod-product-compliance
Lightning Source LLC
Chambersburg PA
CBHW020922090426
42736CB00010B/1003